Microsoft®
Office 365™

for
dummies®
A Wiley Brand

2nd Edition

by Rosemarie Withee, Ken Withee, and Jennifer Reed

for
dummies®
A Wiley Brand

Microsoft® Office 365™ For Dummies®, 2nd Edition

Published by: **John Wiley & Sons, Inc.,** 111 River Street, Hoboken, NJ 07030-5774, www.wiley.com

Copyright © 2016 by John Wiley & Sons, Inc., Hoboken, New Jersey

Media and software compilation copyright © 2016 by John Wiley & Sons, Inc. All rights reserved.

Published simultaneously in Canada

For general information on our other products and services, please contact our Customer Care Department within the U.S. at 877-762-2974, outside the U.S. at 317-572-3993, or fax 317-572-4002. For technical support, please visit www.wiley.com/techsupport.

Wiley publishes in a variety of print and electronic formats and by print-on-demand. Some material included with standard print versions of this book may not be included in e-books or in print-on-demand. If this book refers to media such as a CD or DVD that is not included in the version you purchased, you may download this material at http://booksupport.wiley.com. For more information about Wiley products, visit www.wiley.com.

Library of Congress Control Number: 2016938719

ISBN 978-1-119-26531-3 (pbk); 978-1-119-26353-1 (epub); 978-1-119-26533-7 (epdf)

Manufactured in the United States of America

10 9 8 7 6 5 4 3 2 1

Contents at a Glance

Table of Contents

Introduction

In the last decade, the cloud has taken the information technology community by storm. As companies have struggled with the learning curve and cost of adopting Enterprise class software on their own the cloud has created a simplified and streamlined alternative. The complexity of keeping software running has been taken out of the equation. The result is that organizations can focus on using software to drive business and competitive advantage instead of using critical resources to keep the lights blinking green.

Office 365 is the cloud offering by Microsoft and bundles popular server software such as SharePoint, Exchange, and Skype for Business, along with such consumer software as Office Word, Excel, PowerPoint, OneNote, and Outlook into a single product that is accessed over the Internet and paid for on a monthly basis per user. The consumer products are downloadable to many different devices, including iPhones, iPads, Macs, and Android-based phones and tablets, in addition to the familiar Windows-based devices. Microsoft runs the server products in their data centers with their engineers, you can be assured that they know what they are doing. After all, who better to manage these products than the same people who actually built them in the first place? To ease the mind of the risk averse, Microsoft puts their company name and piles of cash behind Office 365 in a very attractive service level agreement.

For those who are still not convinced the cloud is the place to be, Microsoft has taken the unique step of designing Office 365 in a way that lets you use the Office 365 for your enterprise in a hybrid environment. Should you want to keep some of your data and management in house you can still use Office 365. If you feel more comfortable moving to Office 365 in waves, then it is designed to accommodate you. You can start with a pilot group in order to prove the benefits that the cloud provides before turning your trust over to Microsoft engineers. Microsoft is convinced that after you try Office 365, it will change your perspective on Enterprise software forever, and you will never look back.

About This Book

This book is about understanding Microsoft Office 365. This book looks at the cloud in general to give you the fundamentals and then dives into the specifics of the Microsoft cloud. The Office 365 product consists of a number of sub-products and applications and the book walks you through most of them. Microsoft is constantly adding new features and products to Office 365 so this book should be used as a base to get started and then you can explore further on your own.

If you are considering moving to Office 365 or have already moved, then this book is the first book you should read in order to get up to speed on the concepts and terms as quickly as possible.

How to Use This Book

This book is designed to be read as you want to find out about the specific components of Office 365. You do not need to read the parts of the book in any order. It is recommended that you read the first part first to gain foundational knowledge of the cloud and, in particular Office 365, but then feel free to jump around as you see fit.

The familiar *For Dummies* icons offer visual clues about the material contained within this book. Look for the following icons throughout the chapters:

TIP

Whenever you see a Tip icon take note. We use the tip icon whenever we want you to pay particular attention. Throughout the process of writing the book, we worked closely with Microsoft on any bugs or issues that have come up. When we found something worth a special note, we use this icon for emphasis.

REMEMBER

Whenever you see a Remember icon get out your notebook. The Remember icon is used to point out key concepts that you should remember as you walk through the Office 365 product. Of course, there is a cheat sheet at the front of the book, so you can always just use that, too.

WARNING

Throughout our careers we've come across many roadblocks. It often takes hours to figure something out the first time and then only minutes the next time you encounter it. Often the root cause of your problems is a bug or some quirky behavior. We have tried to call out whenever you should take note of something and beware of how it will affect your Office 365 environment.

TECHNICAL STUFF

Office 365 is designed to be simple and intuitive; however, nothing is ever as easy as it appears. When we talk about something that is fairly technical in depth, we use the Technical Stuff icon. You definitely don't need to understand every technical detail, but it is there if you decide you want to dig further.

Beyond the Book

The Internet is huge! Search www.dummies.com for the Cheat Sheet for *Office 365 For Dummies.*

Let's Get Started!

Office 365 is one of the fastest growing products in Microsoft's history.

People are using Office 365 as they upgrade from traditional the traditional Microsoft Office that you would buy in a store and install. Now you sign up for an Office 365 subscription and download and install Office products to your devices. Oh, and you don't have to worry about upgrading because as a subscription-based product you are always guaranteed to have the latest apps and updates as Microsoft releases them.

Organizations large and small have been moving their infrastructure over to the Microsoft cloud in order to reap the cost savings, predictability, and peace of mind that comes with the cloud. Because Microsoft has included many of their most popular Enterprise products in the Office 365 offering, it becomes a game changer from the very beginning. As with any technology, however, there is a learning curve. Microsoft has done everything they could to make Office 365 as user-friendly and intuitive as possible but you will still require guidance. This book is the first step in your Office 365 journey and is designed to get you up to speed as quickly as possible. If you're ready to take your first step, then you can get started!

1
Recognizing the Cloud Momentum

Chapter 1

Getting to Know the Cloud

f you own an Android device, you most likely contributed to the estimated 15 *exabytes* of data stored in the Google "cloud." And just what exactly is an exabyte? You can think of it in three ways:

>> An exabyte is equivalent to one quintillion bytes, or one billion gigabytes.

>> If the entire population of Thailand each owned a 16 GB smartphone, their data storage would be equivalent to one exabyte.

>> Supposedly, if you type 1,000,000,000,000,000,000 characters and print those characters on paper, you would have to cut down about 50,000 trees.

Simply put, there is a lot of data in the cloud, and it grows every day. This is why it isn't unusual nowadays to hear the buzz phrase *big data* when talking about cloud computing.

Big data is simply a huge volume of data that cannot be stored or processed in the traditional way. Imagine processing the data from 400 million tweets a day from Twitter, or analyzing the patterns and behaviors of the 1 billion YouTube viewers who watch 4 billion videos per day. There are valuable insights from such data, but there's no way you can gather those insights without cloud computing. For this specific reason, analysts are predicting that the growth of the IT industry will be driven by big data and cloud computing. And why not? The combination of big data and cloud computing will give rise to very smart computers that can learn through artificial intelligence without being programmed. This is called *machine learning.* Don't be alarmed by yet another new term here. Machine learning already is so pervasive that you probably don't even know you've used it.

The way we introduced cloud computing in this book when it first came out four years ago is no longer coming from the same lens we are looking through now. According to www.cloudcomputing-news.net, the cloud computing industry grew from $46 billion to more than $150 billion from 2008-2014. In the very near future, the question will no longer be about what cloud computing is, but more about what cloud computing can do for you and/or your business.

If you're still confused about cloud computing, don't despair. Unless you've been living under a rock in the last five years, you most likely have used cloud computing in one shape or form, so it isn't as mystical as you might think.

This chapter is for those of you who have a keen interest in understanding the basic principles of cloud computing with the intent of leveraging that knowledge to help your business, your organization, or your professional career. You'll see the interconnections between cloud computing, big data, and machine learning, and how they all feed into the overall Office 365 services. You'll read about the various services within Office 365, what they cost, and gain insight into Microsoft's strategy for helping individuals and organizations become more productive in keeping with their mission. It's the information you need to chart your cloud journey.

Defining Cloud Computing

The cloud is a metaphor for the Internet. In very simplistic terms, *cloud computing* means that your applications or software, data, and computing needs are accessed, stored, and occur over the Internet "in the cloud."

If you've had a Facebook account, played online games, shared files with Dropbox, or sync'd your photos from your mobile devices, then you've been computing in the cloud. You're using the services of an entity to store your data, which you can then access and transform over the Internet. Imagine what life would be like if you wanted to share photos of your lunch to all of your 500 friends if cloud computing didn't exist.

For businesses and other organizations, cloud computing is about outsourcing typical IT department tasks to a cloud service provider who has the experience, capability, and scalability to meet business demands at a cost that makes sense.

Let's take for example a small business owned by a friend of mine. It's a boutique accounting firm that services over 200 businesses locally. Email is a critical communication platform for them. To be productive, the firm decided to hire an independent IT consultant to install an email server in their office. The deal was that the IT consultant would train a couple of people from the firm to do basic server administration. Beyond the basics, the consultant would be available to remotely access the server to troubleshoot or show up in person if something breaks.

Like most horror stories I've heard from people who try to manage their own servers without a highly trained IT staff, the situation turned out to be a nightmare for this firm. Their email server went down during tax season at a time when the IT consultant wasn't immediately available. In an industry where highly sensitive data is exchanged and customer trust is paramount, you can imagine the stress the company owner experienced dealing with emails containing sensitive attachments ending up in a black hole, irate customers who didn't get a response to their time-sensitive requests, and lost opportunities impossible to even quantify.

Cloud computing for this firm meant migrating their emails to Office 365. So instead of running their own email server, fixing it, patching it, hounding their IT consultant, and dreading another doomsday, they simply paid a monthly subscription to Microsoft. If anything breaks, Microsoft's highly trained engineers will fix it. They also know that emails will not be lost, because they don't rely on one piece of equipment getting dusty in one corner of their office break room. Instead, they're taking advantage of Microsoft's huge and sophisticated data centers, which replicate and back up data on a regular basis.

Understanding the cloud deployment models

The type of deployment model the firm used in this story is referred to as the *public cloud* where the cloud computing service is owned by a provider (Microsoft) offering the highest level of efficiency in a shared but secure environment. My friend did not own or maintain any hardware. The company accessed and used the email and other services from the public cloud on a subscription model. In cloud computing-speak, this firm is referred to as a *tenant* in a public cloud.

For organizations where a one-size-fits-all approach doesn't work, two other deployment models for cloud computing are available: private clouds and hybrid clouds (see Figure 1-1).

Cloud Computing Deployment Models

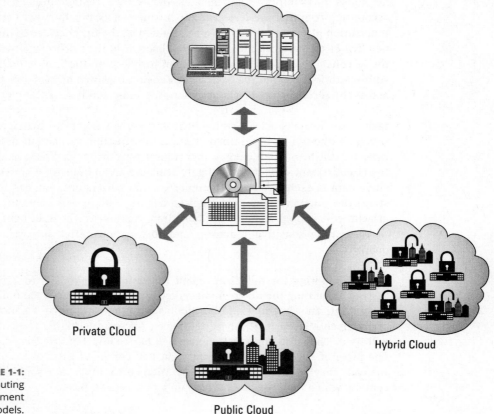

Private Cloud

Public Cloud

Hybrid Cloud

FIGURE 1-1:
Cloud computing
deployment
models.

A *private cloud* typically is dedicated to one organization on its own highly secure, private network over a company intranet or hosted datacenter. Unlike the public cloud, a private cloud doesn't share resources with other tenants. Industries with privacy concerns such as financial institutions and healthcare organizations typically opt for a private cloud.

A *hybrid cloud* is simply a combination of the public and private clouds. As an example, an organization may run their email applications in a public cloud but store customer information in a database in a private cloud.

Regardless of the deployment model used, cloud computing means that your business applications are outsourced somewhere on the Internet where you don't have to worry about paying for capacity you don't need or needing—in a hurry—capacity you don't have. It also means that the version of the software you're using is always the latest version; it's accessible anytime, anywhere, on most devices.

The advantages of cloud computing aren't limited to just big companies. Cloud computing is also beneficial for small- and medium-size organizations, and even solo-preneurs like consultants. We've all heard people say that in American society, education is the greatest equalizer. In my opinion, cloud computing is the greatest equalizer for businesses not just in America, but throughout the world. It breaks down the barriers for small and even one-man-show businesses from competing in the global market. For a small monthly fee, any business can have the appearance of a large enterprise with a full staff of highly trained IT personnel.

Knowing the cloud service models

Contrary to general belief, cloud computing isn't a new concept. The idea of an "intergalactic computer network" was first introduced in the 1960s by J. C. R. Licklider, one of the most influential men in the history of computer science. Other people attribute the emergence of cloud computing to John McCarthy, another computer scientist who in the 1960s proposed that computing be delivered as a public utility similar to service bureaus that provided services to businesses for a fee.

Back then, massive computing was conducted with supercomputers, and mainframes occupying whole buildings. Thousands of central processing units (CPUs) were connected to divide the computing tasks of supercomputers in order to get results faster. The very high cost for creating and maintaining these supercomputers precipitated the discovery of more economical computing means, which brings us to where we are today.

With cloud computing today, not only can businesses use the services of specialized providers for massive computing, they also benefit from the lower cost of these services stemming from the efficiencies of shared infrastructure. Generally, there are three types of cloud computing service models (see Figure 1-2):

>> Software-as-a-Service (SaaS)

>> Platform-as-a-Service (PaaS)

>> Infrastructure-as-a-Service (IaaS)

Software-as-a-service (SaaS)

A SaaS service model is where software application is paid for on a subscription basis and installed from the cloud provider's datacenter. Office 365 is an example of a SaaS model where all your collaboration and productivity applications are bundled together as part of your subscription. You don't have to run your own email servers, for example, nor do you need to maintain and update the servers.

For desktop applications like Office Pro Plus, you can install the software from a web-based portal instead of buying the packaged software from a store. After you've installed the software, updates and bug fixes automatically are installed in the background.

Platform-as-a-service (PaaS)

In a platform-as-a-service (PaaS) service model, developers can create online applications (apps in short) in platforms provided by the PaaS provider. The developers develop their own code for the apps, store it in the PaaS provider's datacenter, then publish the apps. They don't have to worry about planning for capacity, security, or managing the hardware—the PaaS provider does that. For example, if you've played Angry Birds on your Android phone, it may interest you to know that the publishers used Google App Engine as a PaaS solution to make their addicting games available to millions of fans without worrying about scaling the app automatically to match the amount of traffic at any given time.

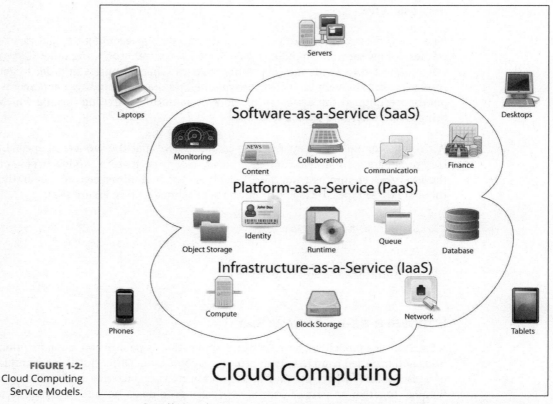

FIGURE 1-2:
Cloud Computing Service Models.

Created by Sam Johnston using OmniGroup's OmniGraffle and Inkscape (includes Computer.svg by Sasa Stefanovic)

Infrastructure-as-a-service (IaaS)

In an infrastructure-as-a-service (IaaS) service model, organizations have access to computing power and storage capacity, using a cloud provider's hardware. This enables them to have control over the infrastructure and run applications in the cloud at a reduced cost. The organization, however, is responsible for managing and updating the operating system running the applications. While capacity planning, security, and hardware management is the responsibility of the IaaS provider (similar to PaaS), it is the organization's job to monitor the performance of their apps and/or add more resources to meet the demand. Amazon Web Services offer several IaaS cloud hosting products that can be purchased by the hour. Rackspace is another player in the IaaS market offering managed and cloud hosting services. Microsoft Azure (formerly known as Windows Azure) started out as a PaaS solution, but extended its services to include IaaS capabilities.

Getting a grasp on Big Data and Machine Learning

According to a report from Gartner in September 2014, strong investments and planned investments in big data adoption continue across all industries—communications and media lead the pack. This isn't surprising, because big data offers opportunities for businesses to increase sales, target marketing, and enhance customer care.

If you have ever given a Yelp review, liked a Facebook post, tweeted, posted images on Instagram, or bought anything online, then you have contributed to big data. Even if you do nothing but sit in an airplane, you are still contributing big data because aircrafts continually send data to air traffic control during the flight for real-time tracking and monitoring.

The benefits of big data aren't limited to companies. Big data can help build smart cities to benefit its citizens and environment. The city of Oslo in Norway, for example, reduced their street lighting energy consumption by 62 percent by analyzing big data and acting on the insights from the analysis. Portland, OR eliminated more than 157,000 metric tons of CO_2 emissions in just six years by optimizing the timing of its traffic signals by intelligence gathered from big data. That's about 30,000 cars off the streets for a whole year!

Machine learning, on the other hand, has taken a giant leap from when the idea started floating around 50 years ago with the advent of big data. A computer with artificial intelligence consumes big data to pick up on patterns, predict the future, and train itself to respond to a user under certain conditions. If you've used speech recognition on your mobile device, that's machine learning in action. The other day, I was using my smartphone to look for a restaurant; to my delight, the top listings had vegetarian options. I can only guess that machine learning has picked up from my Facebook likes and posts that I'm vegetarian.

The combination of big data and machine learning can help not just to prevent malware, it can also proactively address the changing security landscape where threats and attacks are getting more sophisticated every day. 2015 was a banner year for data breaches, from the U.S. Government's Office of Personnel Management, to health insurers Anthem and Premera, to the IRS, to extramarital affairs site www.ashleymadison.com. This issue is top of mind for many organizations. Consequently, cloud providers are taking steps to alleviate concerns around privacy and security.

Microsoft's latest addition to the Office 365 plans (E5) includes the Advanced Threat Protection capability. Among other capabilities, it scans email attachments and links in basically a "detonation" chamber to do behavior analysis and look for signals by using machine learning and big data to protect users from both known and unknown threats.

Recognizing why you should care

In the early 20th century, people were skeptical about cars and viewed the new invention as horseless carriages, based on a centuries-old dominant paradigm: the horse and carriage.

Gottlieb Daimler, the inventor of the automobile, estimated long-term auto popularity to be no more than a million cars. A Michigan Savings Bank president once advised Henry Ford's lawyer not to invest in Ford Motor Company in 1903 because "the horse is here to stay but the automobile is only a novelty, a fad."

Today, over 600 million cars are on the road . . . and not many horses. The important role cars play in our daily lives has proven both Daimler and the Michigan Savings Bank president wrong. Prior constraints to the production of cars have been overcome to bring the cars to the masses.

Today, our society faces a similar change. Just as in the early days of the automobile industry, it's still unknown where this paradigm shift will take us. What we do know is that cloud computing, big data, and machine learning promise not just cheaper but also faster, easier, more flexible, and more effective solutions to problems for our business or our society.

THE "HORSELESS CARRIAGE" SYNDROME

When the first cars came out, they looked very similar to the horse and carriage but without the horse (see the figure below). The problem with the design was that the engineers back then didn't understand the opportunities of the new paradigm (faster and safer cars). The engineers insisted on putting a whip holder into the early car models before realizing that without a horse, there was no need for a whip holder! We may not fully grasp the true potential of cloud computing, but it's a good idea not to fall prey to the horseless carriage syndrome.

Introducing the Microsoft Cloud Solutions

As of this writing, Microsoft has invested $15 billion to build its massive cloud infrastructure. Its comprised of more than 100 datacenters around the globe hosting over 1 million servers managed by a team of experts working 24/7/365 to support more than 1 billion customers. Their fiber optic network is so huge, it could stretch to the moon and back—three times over. This staggering set up provides the backbone for the company's 200-plus online services, including Office 365, Bing, Xbox Live, Skype, OneDrive, and Microsoft Azure.

While a lot of focus has been in the "cloud," Microsoft newest frontier is way down on the ocean floor. Their recent investment in a research (codename: Project

Natick) to submerge servers below the surface of the ocean as a way to speed up cloud computing proved to be a success. So who knows: soon, slow and expensive internet connection during a Disney or Royal Caribbean cruise may be a thing of the past.

These investments are surely paying off for Microsoft. Every day of the week, 3 billion minutes of calls are made by Skype users. As of January 2015, Microsoft claims that 80 percent of Fortune 500 companies are in the Microsoft cloud. The Texas state government alone has 100,000 employees using Office 365 to collaborate in full compliance of privacy and security requirements.

In this section, we cover the top three Microsoft cloud products that empower businesses: Microsoft Azure, Microsoft Dynamics CRM, and Office 365.

TIP

Microsoft's Skype Translator can translate your voice conversations in real time in seven languages: English, Spanish, French, German, Italian, Mandarin, and Portuguese. It can also translate your instant messages in over 50 languages, from Arabic to Yucatec Maya.

What can you do with Microsoft Azure?

Microsoft Azure (formerly known as Windows Azure) is an open platform comprised of a growing collection of integrated cloud services: computing, database, mobile, networking, storage, analytics, web, and more. The flexibility of this platform makes it easy to scale up or down to meet business needs under a pay-for-use, per-minute billing business model.

If you're a developer, you can take advantage of the integrated tools and built-in templates in Microsoft Azure to build your web and mobile apps. It supports the same technologies millions of developers and IT professionals already use and trust. After your apps are published, you can run them from any of the worldwide network of Microsoft datacenters. Having a global footprint means that you have a lot of options for running your applications and ensuring great customer experience.

The big data and machine learning scenarios covered earlier in this chapter are run in Azure. This new era of business intelligence enables organizations to make smarter decisions, improve customer service, and uncover more opportunities for growth.

To address data security and privacy concerns, Microsoft has made an industry-leading commitment to the protection and privacy of data. They've been recognized by leading data protection authorities and were the first major cloud provider to adopt the new international cloud privacy standards. They have also launched

Azure Government, a stand-alone version of Azure designed for U.S. public agencies with rigorous compliance requirements.

Better customer engagements with Dynamics CRM Online

If your organization is looking for a better way to store and manage customer information, increase sales, and provide great customer experience, then you need a customer relationship management (CRM) solution.

Microsoft Dynamics CRM is a customer relationship management (CRM) solution that easily integrates with Microsoft tools and technologies such as Outlook and SharePoint. The user-friendly interface allows sales professionals to manage prospects and clients from their desktop computers or on most popular mobile devices. Marketing professionals can create and monitor marketing campaigns and measure their effectiveness using built-in analytics tools.

Understanding that customer service is key to business success, Dynamics CRM's core functionality includes a ticketing system to log, respond to, and manage requests, complaints, and other types of feedback. It can create cases automatically from email as well as posts on social networks like Twitter and Facebook.

Beyond just making the sale and providing great support, you can also proactively manage your brand by using the Microsoft Social Engagement tool with Dynamics CRM. The tool has powerful social intelligence functionalities that enable you to gain insights about your brand based on what people are saying about you on social media. Those insights can then help you engage with your existing and potential customers more effectively. You can even drill down from the topics you're monitoring to quickly analyze the conversations, locations, and even sources of the feedback or sentiment!

The explosion of Office 365 and why

More than 1.2 billion people use Microsoft Office. Outlook.com has more than 400 million active users. Office 365 is now available in 140 markets in 40 languages. These are the latest official stats from Microsoft as of this writing.

A much more interesting statistic, however, comes from Okta, a cloud service provider established in 2012, which offers passwords and employee accounts management for other cloud services. According to Okta, Office 365 has skyrocketed in a short span of 6 to 9 months, surpassing Salesforce as the most popular app used by their clients.

As a consultant and a Microsoft Partner focused on helping small businesses with their cloud journey, it's easy for me to see why Office 365 is so popular. The latest iteration of Office 365 is the most secure cloud productivity and communications solution I've seen so far. It now includes such capabilities as

>> Broadcasting web conferences to up to 10,000 people

>> Using Skype for Business like a traditional phone to make and receive phone calls to people outside your organization

>> Understanding work time and interactions

>> Ensuring that email attachments and links first pass through a "detonation" chamber for extra protection

When this book first came out, much of the productivity focus in Office 365 was on these services:

>> Email and calendar (Exchange Online)

>> Document collaboration (SharePoint Online)

>> Web conferencing (Lync Online—now called Skype for Business)

>> Office applications

Today, the Office 365 productivity story includes

>> Social networking (Yammer)

>> Professional digital storytelling (Sway)

>> Corporate YouTube portal (Office 365 Videos)

>> Personally relevant content for you (Office Delve)

Microsoft continues to add more services in Office 365 as evidenced in their roadmap. Clearly, they aren't letting up on their strategy to build the best-in-class platforms and productivity services for a mobile-first, cloud-first world.

Knowing the Different Microsoft Office 365 Plans

Office 365 is the answer to a modern workplace where people no longer have to work in the same location to get things done. As a cloud productivity and communication solution in one place, Microsoft Office 365 offers service plans for practically all types of businesses and organizations.

Analyzing the Office 365 Small Business Plans

For the price of one venti Caramel Macchiato (plus tax) from Starbucks, a small business can use

>> 50 gigabyte mailbox

>> 1 terabyte of online file storage (which is about $80 if you buy the same storage in a hard drive)

>> High-definition video conferencing

>> Online version of Microsoft Office

>> Social communication with colleagues

In other words, if you're a small business just starting out or a professional services provider working from home, there is no excuse for not impressing your customers or clients by exuding the perception of a large organization. All you have to do is give up one cup of coffee a month to be able to afford to subscribe to the *Office 365 Business Essentials* at $5 per user per month with an annual commitment.

If you already have a cloud-based email, subscribing to the *Office 365 for Business* plan gives you the newest version of Office for Mac and PC, Office apps you can run on your tablets and phones, online versions of Office including Word, Excel, and PowerPoint, 1 terabyte of online storage, and professional digital storytelling tools. This will cost you $8.25 per user per month with an annual commitment.

The *Office 365 Business Premium* plan, on the other hand, combines all the features of the two plans above into one integrated subscription for $12.50 per user month with an annual commitment.

All of the preceding plans have a 300-user limit, but they include

>> Guaranteed 99.9 percent uptime, financially backed service level agreement

>> IT-level web support and 24/7 phone support for critical issues

>> Active Directory integration to easily manage user credentials and permissions

>> World-class data security

Breaking down the Office 365 enterprise plans

There are four enterprise Office 365 plans ranging from $8 per user per month to $35 per user per month. You can have a variety of enterprise subscriptions plans based on the needs of your users. There is no limit to the number of users on the enterprise plans.

Table 1-1 lists the cost (per user, per month) for the subscription and the key features associated with each of these plans.

TABLE 1-1   **Enterprise Plans Pricing Model**

Office 365 Enterprise (per user, per month)	E1 ($8)	Pro Plus ($12)	E3 ($20)	E5 ($35)
Fully installed Office applications on up to 5 PCs or Macs per user (Office Pro Plus)		✓	✓	✓
Office on tablets and phones for the fully installed Office experience on up to 5 tablets and 5 phones per user		✓	✓	✓
Online versions of Office, including Word, Excel, and PowerPoint	✓	✓	✓	✓
File storage and sharing with 1 TB storage per user (OneDrive for Business)	✓	✓	✓	✓
Business class email, calendar, and contacts (Exchange Online)	✓ *50 GB inbox per user*		✓ *unlimited inbox*	✓ *unlimited inbox*
Unlimited online meetings, IM, and audio, HD video, and web conferencing (Skype for Business)	✓		✓	✓
Intranet site with customizable security settings (SharePoint Online)	✓		✓	✓
Corporate social network (Yammer)	✓		✓	✓
Professional digital, interactive storytelling tool (Sway)	✓	✓	✓	✓

Office 365 Enterprise (per user, per month)	E1 ($8)	Pro Plus ($12)	E3 ($20)	E5 ($35)
Personalized search and discovery across Office 365 (Delve)	✓		✓	✓
Corporate video portal (Videos)	✓		✓	✓
Meeting broadcast on the Internet to up to 10,000 people (Skype for Business)	✓		✓	✓
Discover, analyze, and visualize data in Excel		✓	✓	✓
IT management of your apps, reports of usage, and shared computer activation		✓	✓	✓
Compliance Center tools to support eDiscovery (important for your lawyers in case of litigation)	✓	✓	✓	✓
Compliance and information protection (archiving and legal hold, rights management, data loss prevention, and encryption for email and files)			✓	✓
Advanced security for your data				✓
Analytics tools to illustrate your own and your team's productivity (Power BI and Delve Analytics)				✓
PSTN conferencing to allow invitees to join Skype for Business meetings by dialing in from a telephone				✓
Cloud PBX for cloud-based call management to make, receive, and transfer calls across a wide range of devices				✓

Taking care of the Kiosk or Deskless workers

If you own a retail chain or run a business with "deskless" workers, you don't have to leave these workers out from the benefits of using Office 365. Deskless workers, shift workers, retail store employees, truck drivers, and similar employees who use shared PCs, have minimal collaboration requirements, and limited communication needs can be signed up with either of these plans:

>> The *Exchange Online Kiosk* plan for $2 per user per month provides access to

- Web email (2 gigabyte storage)
- Premium anti-malware protection and anti-spam filtering
- Support for sync'ing emails to smartphones
- Support for POP email clients like Comcast and Yahoo.

>> The *Office 365 Enterprise K1* plan for $4 per user month includes all the features from the Exchange Online Kiosk plan, plus

- Corporate social network with Yammer
- SharePoint Online for document collaboration and access to intranets
- Office Online (Word, Excel, PowerPoint, and OneNote)

Addressing the needs of other types of organizations

Not all organizations are created equal. Therefore, Microsoft has created the following plans to meet the requirements of non-business organizations.

Office 365 Education

This plan offers free collaboration tools for students and teachers to enable them to work and learn together using best-in-class cloud technologies.

TIP

This is a great way to expose students to technologies they will be using in the workplace.

To take advantage of the free subscription for students and teachers, you must be verified as an academic institution, which usually takes 3-7 days. The best thing about this is that Exchange Online for email and calendar for alumni is provided as a free service even after the student graduates. Learn more about this plan at

https://products.office.com/en-us/academic/office-365-education-plan

Office 365 U.S. Government

The U.S. government has unique needs and requirements when it comes to cloud technologies. Therefore, Microsoft has created a segmented cloud community specifically designed to ensure these types of organizations meet U.S. compliance and security standards. This plan still provides all the features and capabilities of Office 365 for business, but it's only available to qualified U.S. government organizations, including federal, state, local, and tribal governments. Learn more about this plan at

```
https://products.office.com/en-us/government/compare-office-
365-government-plans
```

Office 365 Nonprofit

Qualified nonprofit organizations are eligible to receive basic Office 365 services as a donation. The Office 365 Nonprofit Business Essentials is a free plan for up to 300 users, while the Office 365 Nonprofit E1 is free with unlimited users.

If your organization needs the advanced features, you can subscribe to the Office 365 Nonprofit Business Premium for $2 per user per month or the Office 365 Nonprofit E3 for $4.50 per user per month.

Learn more about the different plans for nonprofits and the plan requirements at

```
https://products.office.com/en-us/nonprofit/office-365-nonprofit-
plans-and-pricing
```

Chapter 2

Moving to the Office 365 Cloud

A s we mention in Chapter 1, cloud computing is simply using a software application over the Internet. Microsoft Office 365 is a grouping of Microsoft products that are hosted and managed by Microsoft. You sub-scribe to the service on a monthly basis. This model of using software is often called Software as a Service (SaaS).

With the Office 365 offering, Microsoft takes care of all the installation and man-agement of the complicated server products, such as SharePoint, Exchange, and Skype for Business. Your organization simply signs up, starts paying the monthly fee, and uses the software over the Internet (meaning in the cloud). The burden of the installation, patches, upgrades, backups, and maintenance (among other stuff) is all taken care of by smart Microsoft employees. To make you feel more comfortable, Microsoft has a 99.9 percent uptime guarantee that is backed by a legal contract called a Service Level Agreement (SLA).

In this chapter, you get a high-level view of the software products that Microsoft includes in the grouping of software products known as Office 365 and which are delivered over the Internet. These products include SharePoint, Exchange, Skype for Business, and Office. You also get some of the basics under your belt including why the cloud and Office 365 in particular are generating such buzz. After all, when Microsoft invests billions of dollars, it must be something worthwhile.

Discovering Office 365 Features and Benefits

Moving to the Office 365 cloud comes with some key features and benefits. Namely, your organization gets to continue to use the software you have been using for years, but you now get to shift the burden onto Microsoft. In addition to shifting the burden to Microsoft, we cover some other key benefits that we describe in the following sections.

Generating greater productivity

Productivity is a great word that management-consultant types love to use. In the real world though, productivity can be summed up in a simple question: Can I do my job easier or not? Microsoft has invested heavily and spent a tremendous amount of time trying to make the user and administrator experiences of Office 365 as easy and simple as possible.

The idea is that increasing simplicity yields greater productivity. Whether it is an administrator setting up a new employee or a business analyst working with big data and writing game-changing reports in Word. When the technology gets out of the way and you can focus on your job, you become more productive. Don't believe me? Try using a typewriter instead of a word processor. Whoever thought copy and paste would be such a game changer?

Accessing from anywhere

Accessing your enterprise software over the Internet has some big advantages. For one, all you need is your computer—desktop, laptop, tablet, or phone—and an Internet connection or phone coverage. Because the software is running in a Microsoft data center, you simply connect to the Internet to access the software, as shown in Figure 2-1.

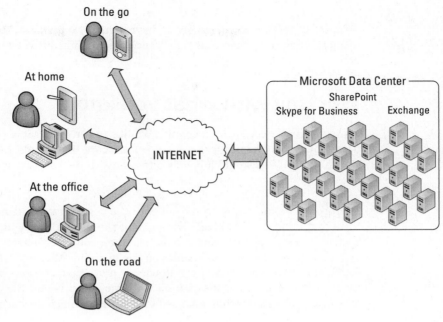

FIGURE 2-1:
Accessing Office
365 software over
the Internet
(cloud).

Another benefit of accessing centrally located data is that you always have a single source of the truth. If you make a change to a document from your tablet at home and then your colleague views the file from her phone, she will see the most up-to-date document. Gone are the days of emailing Excel documents between machines with long file names, such as Forecast_Q1_2011_KW-Reviewed_Jenn-Edited-2-1-11_Revised_2-14-11_KW_final_More_edits_now-really-FINAL.xlsx.

With SharePoint Online and OneDrive (part of the Office 365 package), a single file, say Forecast_Q1_2011.xlsx, lives out in the cloud (meaning in Microsoft's globally distributed billion dollar data centers). Because the document lives in the cloud, the security permissions can be set up to allow anyone in the organization, regardless of geographic location, to view the document. Security can be as strict or as lenient as desired. For example, you may want everyone in the organization to be able to see a company policy document but only want a select group of individuals to edit the document. In addition, SharePoint takes care of all of the versioning and even lets you check out a document to edit so that nobody else can edit it at the same time.

TIP

OneDrive for Business has taken on a life of its own, but it is still powered by SharePoint. Think of OneDrive for Business the same way you think of Dropbox or Box. It is personal cloud storage for your files. And remember that OneDrive is powered by SharePoint. In essence, OneDrive for Business is your personal file store, while a SharePoint library is shared across your organization.

TIP

Need to collaborate on the document in real time? No problem. You can do that by using nothing more than your web browser as you find out in later chapters of the book.

Working with what you know

Humans aren't very keen on change. We like to drive the same route to work for years before we figure out there is a better route that avoids all of those snarly traffic snafus. Why would it be any different with the software you use on a daily basis?

Microsoft does not always come out with the best software. Remember Windows Vista and Windows 8? Shiver! Rather than running far away and never looking back at Windows again, users simply held their collective breath until Windows 7 and then Windows 10. And thank you for hurrying Microsoft! Microsoft Word, Excel, and PowerPoint have been in use for more than 20 years and even though new analysis software comes out all the time, Excel is still the one to best. You know that you can do what you need to do without much headache.

One thing Microsoft did incredibly right is recognize that users don't want to give up the things that make them comfortable. "Don't take away our Word, Excel, and PowerPoint," we shouted! And Microsoft listened. Office 365 hasn't changed our favorites one bit. The only difference is that now they are seamlessly connected to the enterprise software living out in the cloud. In other words, our favorite applications are cloudified.

TIP

One of the coolest features about SharePoint and Office is that you can work with SharePoint and OneDrive without ever having to leave the Office applications. For example, you can fire up Word, check out a document stored in SharePoint or OneDrive, make some changes, check it back in, review versions, and even leave some notes for your colleagues. All without even having to know SharePoint is handling the content management functionality behind the scenes.

Robust security and reliability

With Microsoft taking on all of the responsibility for security and reliability, your IT team can rest on their laurels. After all, they spent their entire careers keeping the systems up and running. Shouldn't they get a break? All kidding aside, letting Microsoft do the heavy lifting frees up the IT team to do more important things. No, not playing computer games, but helping users get the most out of enterprise software. Ever wonder why nobody could ever find time to implement a company-wide blog and discussion board? Now they can finally be a reality.

TIP

Microsoft understands if you aren't fully comfortable about letting them do the heavy lifting. In my opinion, it is the best scenario. After all, who better to handle managing software products than the same people who built them? To address some of the questions, however, Microsoft has extensive service level agreements to help put your mind at ease.

IT control and efficiency

If you have ever met an IT person, you might have generalized one thing about them. They are control freaks. They like to know exactly what everyone is doing with their systems at all times. If something goes wrong, then it is probably due to user error. Our systems do what they are supposed to do. Microsoft has gone out of its way to create an unprecedented level of control for administrators. But that is not all. Not only do administrators have control over the environment, but it is actually designed to be simple in nature and, get this, intuitive.

Getting Familiar with Office 365 Products

The Office 365 product is actually a package of products rented on a monthly basis. In particular, these include Office, SharePoint Online, OneDrive for Business, Exchange Online, and Skype for Business Online.

TIP

The online part just means that you access these server products over the Internet. If your IT team were to buy these products and install them for your use in the company data center, then they would be called on premise.

Microsoft Office

Finding someone who doesn't use some aspect of Microsoft Office on a daily basis is difficult. Whether it is Outlook for email, Word for creating and editing documents, Excel for manipulating data, and PowerPoint for creating and making presentations, these old standbys seem to dominate the life of the modern-day information worker.

TIP

The newest version of Office came out in 2016. When you have Office 365, you pay on a monthly basis and can always be assured you have the latest version of Office installed on your device.

Microsoft Office includes much more than these old stalwarts, though. In particular, Office includes the following applications:

>> **Word:** Microsoft Office Word is used for word processing, such as creating and editing documents.

>> **Excel:** Excel is used for data analysis and numeric manipulation.

>> **PowerPoint:** PowerPoint is used to create and deliver presentations.

>> **Outlook:** An application that is used for email, contacts, and calendaring including scheduling meetings, meeting rooms, and other resources.

>> **OneNote:** An application that is used for capturing and organizing notes.

>> **Publisher:** An application that is used to create and share publications and marketing materials, such as brochures, newsletters, post cards, and greeting cards.

>> **Access:** A database application that is used to collect, store, manipulate, and report on data.

>> **SharePoint:** SharePoint is a web-based platform that lets you easily create an Intranet for your organization. An Intranet is just an internal-only website where you find content, see company policies, and find other such internal tasks.

>> **OneDrive for Business:** OneDrive for Business is a cloud-based, file storage service that is part of Office 365.

TIP

> If you're tech savvy, you will quickly recognize that OneDrive for Business is powered by SharePoint.

>> **Delve:** Delve is a newcomer to Office 365. Think of it as an extension to SharePoint and OneDrive. Delve helps you handle the deluge of digital content. Delve shows you content it thinks you want to see, and learns from your behaviors as you work. For example, you might see the latest content your immediate coworkers have updated or updates to content you have had interest in previously.

>> **Power BI:** Power BI is not necessarily a part of the traditional Microsoft Office, but it falls squarely within the Office 365 suite of critical applications. Power BI was born in the cloud, and has only ever lived in the cloud. Power BI is designed to take the mountains of data from all over the place and help you make sense of it through reports, dashboards, and other analysis tools.

>> **Skype for Business:** When you need to connect with other people, Skype is the tool for you. Skype for Business allows you to connect with others using features such as instant messaging and conferencing including screen sharing, polling, and shared presentations. Using Skype for Business, you can also add regular old Skype users to your business communications.

Pay-As-You-Go flexibility

With pay-as-you-go licensing your organization is able to turn on or off licensing, depending on the number of users that require Office 365. In addition, Microsoft has added flexibility for you as a user by allowing you to activate the licensing on up to five different computers at a single time, depending on your plan. For example, when your organization adds you as an Office 365 subscriber, you can activate the software on your workstation at work, your laptop, your home computer, and your home laptop. When you buy a new computer, you will find a simple user screen where you can update the computers that Office is activated on. This flexibility makes managing your Office applications and licensing as easy and straightforward as possible.

Native apps experience integrated into web apps

In addition to running Office applications, such as Word, Excel, PowerPoint, and Outlook on your local computer, Office 365 also includes a web version of these applications called Office Online Apps and mobile versions called Office Mobile. When working with the Office Online Apps, you simply open your web browser and browse to your SharePoint portal that contains your document. You can then open or edit your document right in the web browser. Likewise, when using the Mobile Apps you open up the mobile version of the Office app, such as Word, on your mobile device and edit it, just like you would on your laptop or desktop computer.

Microsoft has gone to great pains to make the Office Online Apps and Mobile Apps experience very similar to the traditional Office experience. For example, when you are checking email in Outlook, writing a Word document, or reviewing or editing an Excel document or PowerPoint presentation you expect certain behavior. Microsoft has tried very hard to retain the familiar feel of the Office you love. We cover Office Online Apps in great detail in Part IV and touch on the Office Mobile Apps throughout the book.

Latest versions of the office apps—always

Because Office 365 uses a SaaS model, you are always instantly up to date. When Microsoft releases a new version of Office, your licensing is instantly upgraded. You don't need to wait for the IT team to finally get the new product purchased and rolled out. When Microsoft flips the switch, everyone has the latest and greatest instantly available.

Severing Ties to Your Desk

If you are used to using Outlook for your email, then you won't experience any changes when your organization moves to Office 365. The only difference will be that Microsoft is now hosting your email instead of your local IT department. Should you decide to look a bit further, however, you can find a great deal of extra functionality just waiting to make your life easier. For example, the new Outlook Mobile apps are integrated with Exchange in order to push email directly to your phone whether you use iPhone, Android, or a Windows phone. Prefer a different email app? No problem. Almost every email app on the market can be setup to receive Office 365 email.

Using Outlook Online

Office 365 provides the ability for you to check your enterprise Exchange email using nothing more than a web browser. Instead of using Outlook on your local computer you simply browse to a web address, such as `http://mail.myorganization.com` and then login and check your email. The experience is very similar to other web email services, such as Google's Gmail or Microsoft's Hotmail. What's exciting about Outlook Online, however, is that you finally get access to your enterprise email, calendar and contacts from any computer with an Internet connection and a web browser.

REMEMBER

Outlook and Exchange are both email related products, but one is for users and the other is server software. Exchange is a server product that sits on a server in a data center and manages all of your email. Outlook is an application that you install on your local desktop and then use to connect to the Exchange server to check and manage your email, contacts, and calendaring. With Office 365, you still use Outlook (installed on your local computer or phone) but instead of connecting to an Exchange server managed by your IT team, you connect to an Exchange server managed by Microsoft.

Grouping conversations in your inbox

Like it or not, email has become a primary means of communication for the modern information worker. It is not uncommon for many people to send and receive a truck load of emails on a daily, if not hourly, basis. Keeping track of different emails on different topics with different people can be a daunting task. Outlook 2016 has a feature geared towards helping you keep track of all of those conversations. The feature automatically groups conversations by subject, as shown in Figure 2-2. Notice that Proposal is the subject of the emails and the entire conversation is grouped for easy reading. You can even see your response emails and any meetings associated with this conversation. No more digging through your Sent box looking for how you responded to a particular email.

TIP

You can turn on the Conversations feature by clicking on the View tab in Outlook and then checking the Show as Conversations checkbox, as shown in Figure 2-2.

Show as Conversations checkbox

Proposal conversation

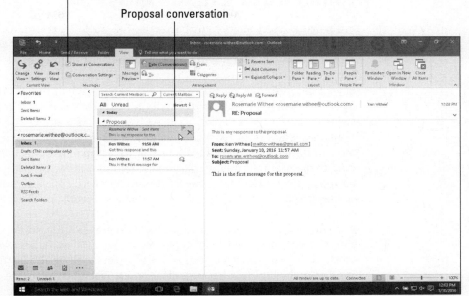

FIGURE 2-2:
Grouping
conversations in
Microsoft Outlook
2016.

Getting organized with Office 365 Groups

Office 365 is constantly adding features, and a relatively new one is called Office 365 Groups. The Groups feature is aptly named, because it allows you to create public and private groups.

Outlook 2016 is one component of Office that takes advantage of Office 365 Groups. Other apps that work with Office 365 Groups include OneDrive for Business, Skype for Business, and OneNote. Microsoft has plans to integrate most of the Office 365 apps with Groups, so if you have a favorite, check whether Groups is already available.

When a new member joins a group, they can see the history of the group and quickly get up to speed. Everyone in the group can chat with each other, share files, schedule meetings, share notes, and use Skype for Business for real-time communication.

Archiving just got personal

Exchange Online gives you access to your own personal email archiving system. Your personal archive shows up as another mailbox right next to your regular mailbox. You access your archive just like you access your regular mailbox. On top of that, when you need to search for an old email, you can choose to search your archive in addition to your regular mailbox.

Collaborating made easy

In the last decade, SharePoint has taken the world by storm. As consultants, we had a large property management client ask us about SharePoint the other day. We were curious what was driving their decision because they knew very little about SharePoint. Our client told me that when he talks with his peers in the industry, they all tell him they use SharePoint extensively. When he asks them about their experience using SharePoint they tell him that they can't imagine running their business without SharePoint. That was enough of a driver for him to find out about SharePoint right away. After all, when the competition moves toward something that increases their advantage, other companies have to move quickly in order to maintain the ability to compete. And thus is the case with the adoption of the technology wave consisting of communication, collaboration, content management, and consolidation, which is all made possible by SharePoint.

With Office 365, your organization gets SharePoint without the hassle of having to work through a complicated deployment. Your IT staff has an administrative interface and can provision sites and setup users with minimal effort. With SharePoint up and running, your organization can spend its resources on solving real business problems with SharePoint, instead of working through the technical details of an implementation. Using SharePoint is covered in detail in Part 3.

Creating communities for the corporate world

An online community is nothing more than a group of people coming together by using their computers regardless of geographic location. If you have used Facebook or LinkedIn or even AOL or Yahoo Groups, then you have been involved in an online community. SharePoint brings online communities to the corporate world in a secure corporate environment. You can imagine the scenario where you are in the accounting department and the team is working on company financials. The team needs to collaborate with each other, but you wouldn't want to be posting to each other's Facebook walls or Twitter accounts. Some of the online community features that SharePoint provides include Wiki's, blogs, content tagging, document sharing, discussion boards, people search, alerts, and notifications.

In addition to the online community features already discussed, every person who has a SharePoint account also has his or her own personal online file store that is powered by SharePoint. This feature is called OneDrive for Business; it allows you to store your files and share them with others. If you are familiar with Dropbox, Box, or Google Drive, then you already understand the concept of cloud-based file storage. OneDrive for Business comes with most Office 365 subscriptions, so you don't have to go searching for it. You access it on the Office 365 waffle, along with the rest of your Office 365 apps. The Office 365 waffle is shown in Figure 2-3.

Waffle icon   OneDrive app

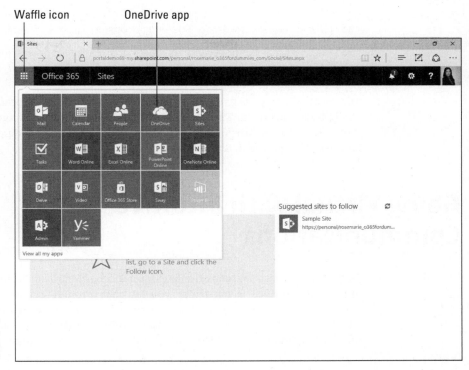

FIGURE 2-3:
Accessing Office
365 apps using
the "waffle."

TIP

Depending on the resolution of your screen, the waffle will show up in the upper left or the upper right of your browser screen.

Sharing information with customers and partners with extranet sites

Because SharePoint Online (one of the components of Office 365) is online, you have the ability to share information with partners that are not part of your local network. These sites that you can make available to people outside your organization are called extranet sites. An example of an extranet site might be a partner network made up of complementary companies. The people in these other companies won't have access to your company network, but you still need to be able to share information and collaborate with them. SharePoint Online offers extranet sites for just such a purpose. SharePoint and extranet sites are covered in Chapter 5.

Microsoft has gone to great lengths to create a secure, safe, and stable SharePoint environment. In particular, Microsoft guarantees the following:

>> The environment is available 99.9 percent of the time

>> All content and configuration details are backed up regularly

>> Virus scanning software for SharePoint constantly scans content for threats

>> File types that can pose a risk to your SharePoint environment are blocked from upload

TIP

Microsoft Office 365 is truly a global product with data center locations distributed throughout the world. The product supports more than 40 languages including Chinese, Arabic, Spanish, and Portuguese. Need your site to support the Catalan language? No problem, SharePoint Online has you covered.

Going Virtual with Intuitive Communications

Skype for Business Online is the latest iteration of Microsoft's cloud-based communications service. In particular, you can chat through text, talk to people using voice, and even have face-to-face meetings by using your webcam. In addition, Skype for Business allows you to conduct online meetings by using screen sharing, virtual white boards, electronic file sharing, and even online polling.

Text/Voice/Video in a single app and service

You can think of the Skype for Business application as a one-stop shop for instant communication. Because Microsoft has tightly integrated the Office 365 applications, you can move seamlessly between them. For example, you might be reading a post on SharePoint and want to instantly communicate with the poster. You can view the presence icon and if it is green that means the user is available. Or maybe you are reading your email and want to see whether the person that sent you the email is available for a chat. From within the Outlook Online App, you can see the Skype for Business status of the user. If it is green, then the person is available and you can instantly open Skype for Business and communicate. The Skype for Business status shown in Outlook Online App is shown in Figure 2-4.

As you are chatting with the person that posted, you might decide that you want to share screens and invite others to join the meeting. By using Skype for Business, it is as simple as a couple of button clicks. We cover using Skype for Business for online meetings in Chapter 15 and 16.

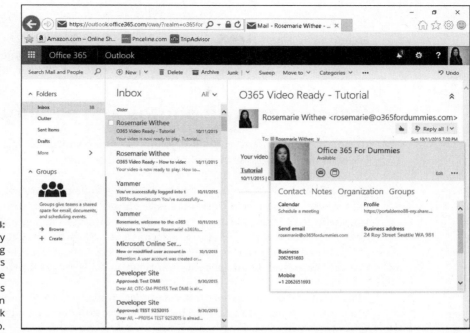

FIGURE 2-4:
Instantly
communicating
with users
using Skype
for Business
from within
the Outlook
Online App.

From conversations to ad hoc meetings— yes, it's possible

By using Skype for Business, you can instantly connect with others from multiple locations. As previously mentioned, you might be reading a SharePoint post but you also might receive an email and want to meet with that person right away if he is available. You can see his status on the presence icon next to his name in your Outlook email message. If you want to communicate with this person, you can hover over his Skype for Business presence icon to access the Skype for Business menu. You may want to send a chat message to the user, so you click the Chat button. A chat session instantly opens, and Skype for Business takes care of pulling in the subject of the email as the subject of the chat so that the person knows what the chat is about. It's almost as good as walking across the hall to talk to someone, only now that someone can be anywhere in the world.

Online meetings unleashed

An online meeting is nothing new. There are many services that offer the ability to share your screen or co-author documents. What has finally come together with Office 365 is the tight integration between all of the different products. You can now see if someone is available for a meeting right from within the applications you use day in and day out, such as Outlook, Office, and SharePoint. Using

Skype for Business it is also possible to setup meetings with those outside your organization. Skype for Business meetings enable you to conduct meetings using chat rooms, audio, video, shared white boards, and even polling. Conducting meetings with Skype for Business is covered in detail in Chapter 15.

Interacting with photos and activity feeds

In addition to instant communication, Skype for Business can also contain personal information, such as photos and activity feeds.

Being able to put a face with a name is nice. Just about anywhere you might connect with another person, be it Outlook, SharePoint, or the author information property from within an Office document, you can view information about the person. The name of a person will have a presence icon next to it. Hover over the presence icon or photo and then click the details screen. Figure 2-5 illustrates viewing the details of a colleague from within the Author property of a Word document.

The activity feed is a current status sentence similar to Twitter but on a corporate level. For example, you might be heads down working on a document and update your status with "Working heads down on a document but here if you need me in a pinch!" Other users will see this status message and know that even though you are online at the moment, you are busy working on a document. Of course, another use for the status message could be something along the lines of, "Left over cake in the break room! Get it while it lasts!"

FIGURE 2-5: Viewing information about a colleague who authored a specific Word document.

Author's name

2

Getting Connected and Getting Social

IN THIS PART . . .

Understand the flexibility of Exchange Online.

Dive into how Exchange Online works with both the Outlook client that installs locally on your computer and a web version that provides email from any computer that has a web browser and Internet connection.

See how to manage your mailbox and some of the fringe benefits that come with using Microsoft's most famous email server in the cloud.

Chapter 3

Unleashing the Power of Exchange Online

I f you are like most people, you couldn't care less about how your email gets into your inbox as long as it does. If your company uses Microsoft products, then chances are that you use an application called Outlook to send and receive email. Outlook also has some other nifty features, including a calendar, the ability to reserve conference rooms, invite people to meetings, store contacts, and even create your to-do lists and tasks. Although you are probably familiar with the Outlook application, you may not know that it has a behind-the-scenes partner. That partner is Exchange, a server application that handles all the heavy lifting. The Outlook application on your desktop is constantly connecting to the Exchange server to find out what information it should present to you.

Because Outlook and Exchange communicate with each other over a computer network, the physical locations of these two hand-in-hand applications are irrelevant. All that matters is that they can communicate with each other. The Outlook software can be installed on your workstation on your desk, and the Exchange software may be installed on a server under your desk or in a data center somewhere out there.

Because Exchange can be located anywhere, a whole bunch of possibilities open up around who is responsible for managing the fairly complicated server software. If Exchange is running on a server under your desk, then it is highly likely that you are the lucky person responsible for it. If it is in your company data center, then you probably have a person, or team of people, responsible for administering Exchange. When you sign up for Office 365, you are letting Microsoft take on all the responsibilities of managing Exchange. Microsoft has Exchange running in their data center, and you simply connect to it with Outlook and use all the nice functionality.

In this chapter, you find out why letting Microsoft take responsibility for Exchange creates a flexible and reliable option for your email, calendaring, contacts, and task needs. You discover that you can access your corporate Exchange system from almost anywhere at any time and on any device. You also find out about some of the protection and compliance features that take some of the risk out of letting Microsoft take the lead by managing its Exchange product.

Gaining Flexibility and Reliability

Key traits in any good relationship are reliability and flexibility. You look for these same qualities in computer software. When you deploy software, you want the process to be flexible and predictable. After the software is deployed, you want it to be reliable and dependable. Exchange Online falls into the category of service-based software. With service-based software, you don't have to develop, install, or manage the software. You simply sign up and start using it.

Deployment flexibility

When it comes time to roll out software, you have a number of options. You can pay someone to develop software from scratch, which is known as custom development. You can buy software, install it, and manage it yourself. Or, you can sign up to use software that is installed and managed by someone else. This third option is called Software as a Service (SaaS). You sign up to use the software and pay for it as a service on a monthly basis. Microsoft Office 365 is a SaaS offering by none other than Microsoft. Microsoft has invested billions of dollars building state-of-the-art data centers all over the world. These data centers are staffed by Microsoft employees whose entire responsibility is managing the Microsoft products offered in the Office 365 product.

Because Microsoft is making the service available on a monthly basis, you have the greatest flexibility of all. You sign up for the service and begin using it. No need to go through a deployment phase. Exchange Online is already deployed and ready to go.

The Office 365 product is actually a bundle of products, and Microsoft is continually adding more. There are Office 365 plans for home users, and there are Office 365 plans for work. The products that your bundle contains depend on the plan you choose. If you sign up for an Office 365 For Work subscription, some of the products you might have in your bundle are the Office productivity suite, SharePoint, Exchange, and Skype for Business. For more about the different plans available, see Part 6.

Deployment predictability

Most decision makers cringe when they hear the words custom development. You will hear horror story after horror story when it comes to a custom software development project. If you get really good developers who have been working together as a team and use a solid process (such as Scrum), then you might have extraordinary results and the best software available. On the other hand, you may end up with something that doesn't do what you want it to do and costs 12 times what you thought it was going to cost in the beginning. In short, you can end up with a disaster. For this reason, many decision makers want to remove the risk and go with packaged software. Because packaged software is already developed and only needs to be installed and managed, the risk associated with adopting the software is greatly reduced.

You will still hear horror stories, however, about the implementation process for packaged software. It generally falls along the lines that someone thought someone else had configured the backups and the person that the other person thought had configured them had already left the company. Oh yeah, and the system was designed to be redundant so that if one key server went down everything would keep working. The only problem is that you only find out if everything works properly when something goes wrong. If the proper procedures were not followed during the implementation, then your organization may find itself in a very bad position.

Those with experience will say that it is often not the fault of any particular person. IT teams are overworked and stretched beyond their capacity to handle everything effectively. For this reason, using a SaaS is becoming increasingly popular. With service-based software, another company specializes in managing the software and keeping it available, reliable, and backed up. You pay on a monthly basis and connect to and use the software over the Internet. This last realm removes the risk for chief technology officer-type decision makers (CTOs). Not only do they not have to pay someone to develop the software, they don't even have to worry about stretching their valuable IT resources beyond the breaking point. And, should the worst-case event happen, another company is liable for the problem based on the service contract signed.

Because the hosting company is liable for anything that goes wrong with hosted software, making sure that the company is reputable and capable of dealing with a major issue is important. Microsoft is one of the biggest names in the software industry with an established business record and lots of money in the bank. Your cousin's friend who started hosting software in his basement probably doesn't have the same resources that Microsoft has in case something goes wrong.

Flexible provisioning

In addition to the predictability of the deployment costs in both time and resources, Exchange Online offers the ability to easily adjust the number of licenses for people using the software. A hiring manager might plan to hire 45 people but find out later in the year that they need to hire another 30 as the company grows more rapidly than expected. It is easy to provision new users for Office 365 through the simple administrative interface.

Another benefit of SaaS software is that chief financial officer-types can find out exactly what the costs will be now and in the future. The CTO doesn't need to explain why the project was eight times over budget or why four more people were required for the IT team to support the new software. The price in resources, people, and time is very transparent and obvious from the beginning. In other words, the costs are very predictable, which is what accounting people and executives like to see.

Continuous availability

Although it may seem blatantly obvious that software should be available all the time, you may be surprised by how many enterprise systems are only available during certain business hours. Exchange Online is available all day, every day, without interruption. In fact, Microsoft guarantees a 99.9 percent uptime.

Simplified administration

If you have ever spent time talking with someone who is responsible for configuring Exchange Server, you know that it is not for the faint of heart. In fact, many people are so specialized that their entire careers are spent doing nothing but administering the Exchange Server software. If your organization is lucky enough to employ a full-time team of these rock-star administrators, then you have probably not experienced any major email issues. Everything works as expected and nobody really cares why. The problem, however, is that if one critical person leaves the organization, you might not be as lucky with the replacement.

Exchange Online offers a simplified and intuitive administrative interface. You no longer need extraordinary expertise to get the very most out of the Exchange

Product. Microsoft handles all the heavy lifting and provides an interface that allows even people with minimal technology skills to administer the company email system by using nothing more than their web browser. The Exchange Online control panel, also known as the Exchange admin center, is shown in Figure 3-1.

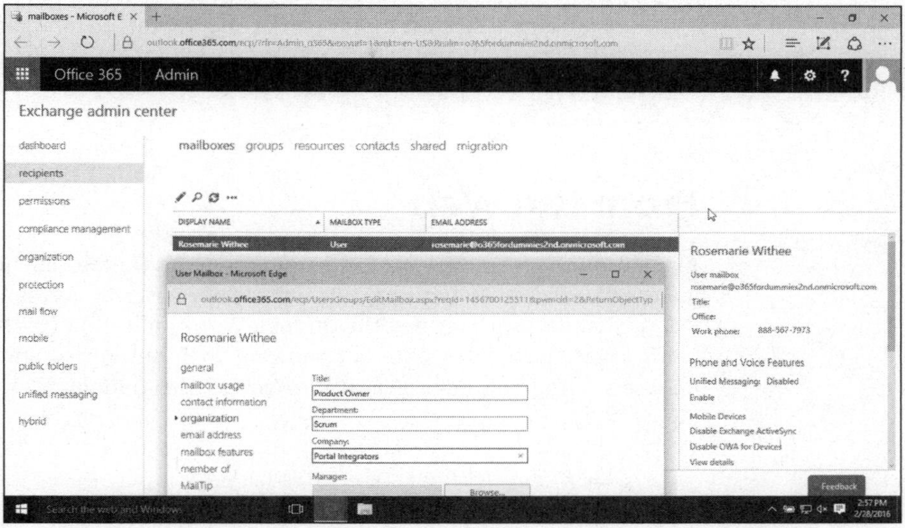

FIGURE 3-1:
The Exchange Online admin center is used for administration. Note that the recipients tab is selected and the mailbox for Rosemarie is being edited.

Accessing from Anywhere

Not all that long ago, email was a relatively new thing. We checked our email like we would check the regular mail, and often we could only email people within the organization. Email has come a long way since then. Now you will be hard pressed to find someone who doesn't use email, especially in a work environment. Email is tremendously important for the modern workforce.

Exchange Online provides a continuously available service that can be accessed from just about anywhere at any time. All you need is an Internet connection and a web browser. We recently spent time at a firm that didn't have regular email access for those people not in the office. A couple of years ago, this would have been no big deal. In today's connected world, however, we found it almost impossible to cope with my lack of connectivity when not in the office. With modern smartphones, you can carry around instant email access right in your pocket. There are a number of email apps for every device. Exchange works with almost all of them. Microsoft even has the popular Outlook email client for your iPhone, iPad, and Android devices. And although Microsoft was late to the party, the new Windows 10 phones provide complete integration with all of Office 365.

From your Outlook email client

The Outlook application that so many people use day in and day out for email, meetings, tasks, and contacts continues to work the same way with Exchange Online but with some added bonuses. In particular, you get an even tighter integration with the other products that are part of the Office 365 offering. For example, you may have a task list that is part of SharePoint. To integrate your SharePoint tasks with Outlook, you navigate to the SharePoint Online list and click a button that says Connect To Outlook. Bingo. Your SharePoint tasks now show up in your Outlook Tasks folder.

From the Web

In addition to accessing your Exchange from your Outlook client, you can also use your web browser. When you use your web browser to access Exchange, you are using what has been termed the Outlook Web Application (OWA). Office 365 provides a very rich experience for working with enterprise email right from the browser. Using the Edge browser to access the Outlook Web App is shown in Figure 3-2.

From multiple devices

Microsoft has released versions of Outlook for all types of devices, including iPhones, iPads, and Android phones and tablets. You don't have to use a Windows PC in order to be productive with Outlook wherever and whenever you want.

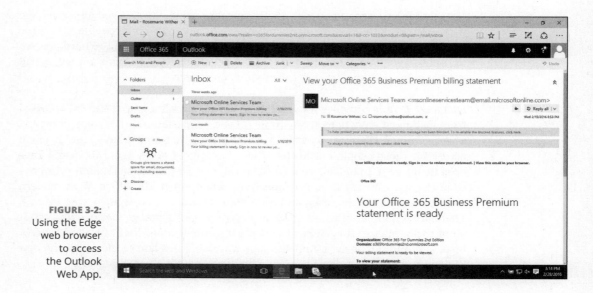

FIGURE 3-2: Using the Edge web browser to access the Outlook Web App.

In the past, Mac users have faced a difficult decision. Use a Mac and struggle with compatibility with the corporate email system or use a PC and use Outlook for full integration. Exchange Online supports the popular Outlook, which is part of Office 2016 for Mac. Outlook on a Mac provides similar integration to Outlook for the PC. By using Outlook on your Mac, you can access your Exchange Online email, calendars, tasks, and contacts.

From any email client

Exchange Online supports all the standard email protocols, including IMAP, POP, and SMTP. As a result, you can use any email client you like to send and receive email.

WARNING

If you want advanced functionality, such as calendaring and meetings, contacts, tasks, and advanced email features, such as presence information for contacts, then you need Microsoft Outlook as your email client.

Manage inbox overload

The number of emails most people send and receive in a given day is amazing! If you are like many office workers, your inbox can quickly become overloaded. Exchange Online attempts to help you manage your email by using a number of different features.

One of the most important features is that you can access your email any time and from any location that has either cell reception for your smartphone or a computer with a web browser and Internet connection. This feature allows you to stay current with your email on your own time and not just when you are sitting in front of your work computer staring at hundreds of unread emails. Have some downtime while waiting for the bus? Twiddling your thumbs at the doctor's office? Get caught up on your email and find out whether that important proposal has arrived.

Some other features that Microsoft has recently rolled out in Outlook also help you manage email overload. One particularly useful feature is called Clutter. The Clutter feature learns which emails are important to you and which emails are, well, just clutter. It then moves the annoying emails to a folder called Clutter and lets you focus on the emails you find important.

TIP

A cool feature when using Outlook on your iPhone, Android phone, or Windows phone is the *swipe* feature. When you look at your email on your phone, you can just swipe an email message left or right. You can configure what swiping a message off to the right or swiping a message off to the left does. For example, you may want to move an email out of your Inbox and into another folder when you swipe left, and delete an email when you swipe right. When you get the hang of it, swiping messages left or right lets you empty your Inbox in no time!

In addition to anywhere access, some powerful productivity features come along with Outlook. For example, you can view all those messages about the same topic in a single email thread known as a conversation. You can also quickly set up a meeting with those involved in the topic of the email with a few clicks of the mouse.

TIP

Skype for Business is closely integrated with Exchange Online and provides even more communication and productivity saving options, such as instant chats, voice and video calls, and screen sharing.

Efficient collaboration

Anyone who works with email on a daily basis has experienced the scenario where an email thread goes on and on, and on some more. People are added to the thread, and those people add more people to the thread. At some point, it would be much easier to just set up a meeting and discuss everything in person. With Outlook and Exchange Online, you can do this with a single click of a button, as shown in Figure 3-3.

A meeting is instantly created, and all the email participants are included in the meeting. The subject of the email thread instantly becomes the subject of the new meeting. This major timesaver increases efficiency on a number of fronts.

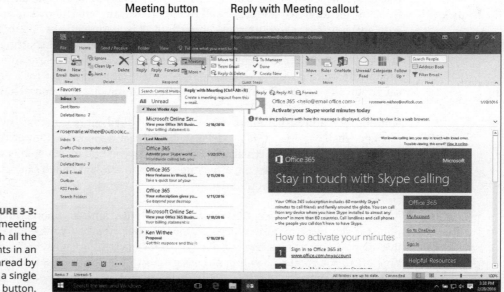

FIGURE 3-3:
Set up a meeting with all the participants in an email thread by using a single button.

Enhanced voicemail

A nifty aspect of Exchange Online is that it includes a unified messaging component. Unified messaging means that different types of messaging are tied together. In this case, we are talking about a physical phone. You remember when you used to have to actually wait for a dial tone, right? Yep, that is the type of voice phone we are talking about.

Exchange Online can be used as your voicemail system and automatically transcribe a message that is then sent to your email or texted to your phone. Need to check your email but don't have Internet access? Exchange Online has a dial-in interface for callers. All you need to access your email is a phone. Listening to your email may take longer than glancing at your smartphone but at least it is a possibility. This functionality extends email access to anywhere with a phone.

Protecting Information

One of the most important aspects of any system is the protection of information and compliance with company and government rules. Exchange Online is simple to use and administer, but don't let that fool you. Under the covers, Microsoft has spent a tremendous amount of effort on protecting you from digital threats and making sure that you are in compliance without hindrance.

Archiving and retention

Each person has an email box as well as her own archiving system. An archive shows up in Outlook as another mailbox, as shown in Figure 3-4.

The intended purpose of the additional archiving folder is to store older email in a permanent storage location. You can think of your archiving folder as your electronic attic or basement. You can go in there to retrieve stuff if you need to, but it is really a long-term storage location.

TIP

The size of a user mailbox and archive are dependent on the SaaS plan. Some plans have a maximum mailbox capacity and others have unlimited archiving capacity. For more information about the plans that are available and the resources allocated for each plan, check out Chapter 18.

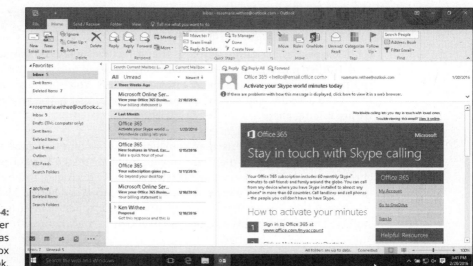

FIGURE 3-4:
The archive folder
shows up as
another mailbox
in Outlook.

Archive folder

Information protection and control

The Exchange Online offering includes antivirus and antispam control without needing to install any third-party or external software. When a new message comes into Exchange Online, it is scanned for risks before being delivered to the intended email box.

TIP

The technology that makes all this protection possible works behind the scenes to make the environment safe and secure. Don't worry though—you don't have to pay extra or even know how it works. As an end user, you just know that someone is looking out for you so that you don't inadvertently receive spam or virus-infested files.

The government has added many rules and regulations around corporate email. Exchange Online provides the ability to meet these rules with features, such as eDiscovery and legal holds.

TIP

eDiscovery refers to Electronic Discovery, which simply means that electronic messages can be searched for relevant communications in the event of a legal process. This might not be a big deal but if you are in a heavily regulated industry or government organization, then these features are often required by Uncle Sam.

Chapter 4

Giving Your Productivity a Boost

We live in a world where the line between personal and professional lives is becoming more blurred every day. When our mobile devices synchronize both personal and work emails, it's hard not to send a quick response to a co-worker after office hours. When our colleagues are also our Facebook friends, we sometimes end up talking about work in our personal spaces.

What tools can we use to help us maintain a work/life balance? How do we measure productivity these days?

Office 365 not only provides tools that help get things done faster, it also comes with a dashboard that displays data to help you manage how much time to spend where, which colleague to stay in touch with, gain insight into basic email etiquettes, and more.

Last week, my dashboard showed I spent 3.7 hours writing and 4.3 hours reading emails while working on a project for a key client. Based on a typical work week in the United States, that means a fifth of my time last week was spent managing my mailbox. That wouldn't have seemed so bad until I realized only 20 percent of the emails I sent to individuals were actually read! For the emails I sent to a group of people, only 2 percent were read. When I checked my Sent Items folder, I found out I had an email thread of 30 messages just to set up one meeting, several threads forwarding documents to people who were not copied in on the original email, and a few threads trying to get input from groups of people resulting in only one or two responses.

With this insight, I am now able to see ways to be more productive—for instance, instead of sending emails back and forth to settle on a meeting time, I could use apps for Outlook like Boomerang to schedule meetings with just one email. Instead of having documents visible only to me in my Inbox, I could share those documents in Office 365 Groups to benefit new team members who come on board. And instead of gathering input via email, I can crowdsource ideas on Yammer.

In this chapter, you will learn about the features in Office 365 productivity boosters. You will also gain an understanding of which tools in Office 365 best serve each purpose.

Understanding the Office 365 Productivity Advantage

You've probably read about the unlimited vacation some big companies have implemented. But have you read the recent statistics that one in three employees do not use all of their paid time off? Or that 49 percent of workers "check-in" when they're on vacation?

The reality is that the cost of overworking is staggering. An overworked, sleep-deprived employee negatively impacts performance, costing U.S. companies $63.2 billion annually in lost productivity.

Microsoft's Finance department has a very cool infographic about productivity stats at the following pdf/link. In it, they recommend automating time-consuming tasks, leveraging productivity tools to get work done faster, and using collaboration software to allow co-workers to pick-up where you left off:

```
http://enterprise.blob.core.windows.net/wordpress/The%20Balancing%20Act.pdf
```

The future of productivity

The world has become a giant network that enables people like me to start my day with a quick check-in on our friends and family on Facebook, catch up on trending topics (while I was asleep) on Twitter, and get up to speed on what's happening in my professional world on LinkedIn.

Imagine what productivity will be like by the end of the decade, when half of the workforce will be millennials, the "always on" generation. This workforce will not be tethered to their desks. They'll require an environment where they can be productive in open spaces, bring their own devices to work. It will completely change the way we think business is done.

Office 365 is built for continuous innovation to meet the changing needs of organizations. Since Office 365 was launched in June 2011, hundreds of new features and innovations have been released to make the technology the obvious choice for productivity. With or without an Office 365 subscription, you can stay informed of these innovations from the Office 365 Roadmap website at `http://fasttrack.microsoft.com/roadmap`. As of February 1, 2016, 266 features have been released, 52 new ones have been launched, 56 are rolling out, and 102 are in development (Figure 4-1).

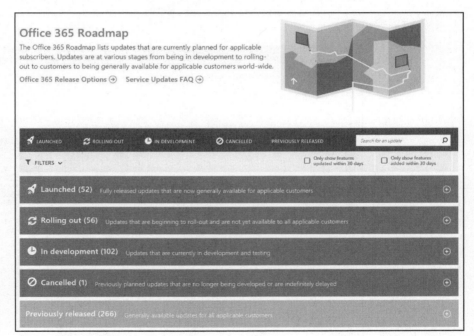

FIGURE 4-1:
Office 365 Roadmap as of February 1, 2016.

Delving into Office Graph and Delve

Your relationships and interactions with the people in your organization are a rich source of data that can be analyzed and acted on to increase productivity.

The problem, however, is that not all of us are smart enough to do that—nor do we have time to do such exercise, even if we have the skill sets of a data analyst.

Office Graph in Office 365 presents a way for people like us to take advantage of our relationships and activities and turn them into meaningful insights. The signals you send from email conversations and meetings in Outlook, instant messages in Skype for Business, social interactions on Yammer, and documents in SharePoint Online and OneDrive are all collected and analyzed by Office Graph to map the relationships among people and information using machine learning. These insights become the foundation for your experiences in Office 365 that are more relevant and personal for you.

Your personalized experiences in Office 365 are presented to you in a Pinterest-like board called Delve. This functionality is available in the E1 to E5 enterprise and government plans, and all plans for nonprofit organizations.

Delve is a great way to search and discover content tailor-fit to your behavior, relationships, and interactions at work. It proactively displays content and information that matters to you as shown in Figure 4-2.

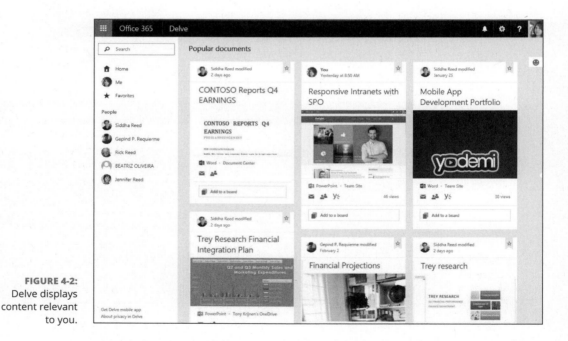

FIGURE 4-2:
Delve displays
content relevant
to you.

You can access Delve from the Office 365 app launcher on the top left corner of the browser and then clicking on the Delve app.

Delve displays the popular documents in a card view on a board (Figure 4-3). The top part of the card is the activity area which tells you who last modified the document, and when. You can click the star on the top right corner to add the document to your Favorites. Or you can see the documents you've added to your Favorites.

FIGURE 4-3:
The Delve card.

Clicking the title on the content card will open the document from its location. The picture displayed on the card is taken from the content of the document. If the document does not have a picture, Delve will display the Office icon of the file type.

Below the image in the card is an icon illustrating the file type. Next to the file type is the location of the document. You can quickly share the document via email by clicking on the mail icon (envelope). To find out who else can access the document, click on the Who can see this? icon (silhouette of two people).

You can create your own boards to find content later. Click on the Add to a board on the bottom part of the card and type in the name of your board.

Understanding Delve Analytics

The new E5 plans for Office 365 take Delve to an even higher level of productivity by providing you with numbers that enable you to make decisions to drive work/life balance, enhance your engagements, and make sense of your time and relationships.

Delve Analytics is an interactive dashboard that tells you how you spend your time in your organization, who you spend it with, and how you're doing related to your goals. You can then use these insights to take control of your time and interactions to improve efficiency and productivity.

Figure 4-4 shows the example of Jenn Reed, who is a Senior Product Marketing Manager. From her dashboard, she is able to see how she spent her time over the course of a week based on a 40-hour work week on a 9 am to 5 pm schedule. From the dashboard, she can set her own goals and prioritize her time at work, based on the insights presented to her.

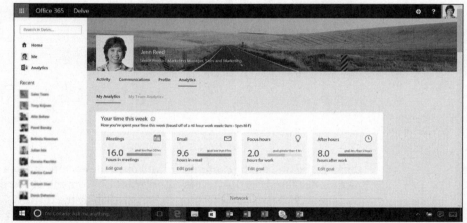

FIGURE 4-4:
Jenn's Delve
Analytics
dashboard.

As Jenn scrolls down the page, she also sees metrics in the Network section that tells her who her top collaborators are, people she needs to get in touch with, and even some insights into how she interacts with her manager (Figure 4-5).

As Jenn scrolls further down, the Email Etiquette section (Figure 4-6) displays the read rate of her emails, as well as the read rate of emails sent to her.

With her personal dashboard, Jenn now has the ability to set and track specific goals to help her become more productive at work.

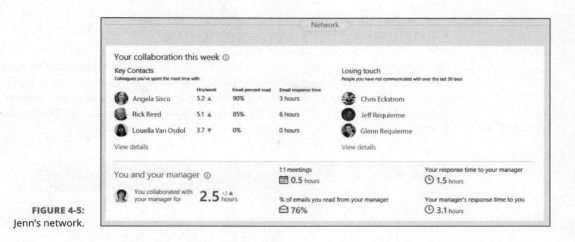

FIGURE 4-5:
Jenn's network.

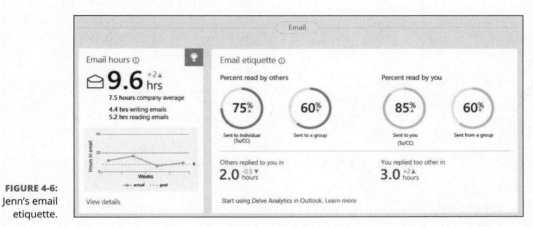

FIGURE 4-6:
Jenn's email
etiquette.

Having a Brilliant Outlook

Email in Office 365 is powered by Exchange Online, the cloud version of the Exchange Server platform, the world's leading e-mail server for business.

TIP

Actually, you don't need to remember that. If all you know is that your emails in Outlook can be synced to your mobile devices whether they're running on the iOS or Android platform, then you're good to go. If you can remember that you don't even need your personal device to check your email—all you need is an internet-connected device—that's even better!

Here are some brilliant new features in Outlook 2016 from the latest version of the Office Suite.

Sending smart attachments

You can significantly reduce the number of clicks to send an attachment in your email with the new functionalities in Outlook. Because Outlook (and the machine learning capabilities in Office 365) pays attention to the files you're working on, your most recent documents will display when you click on the Attach File button (Figure 4-7).

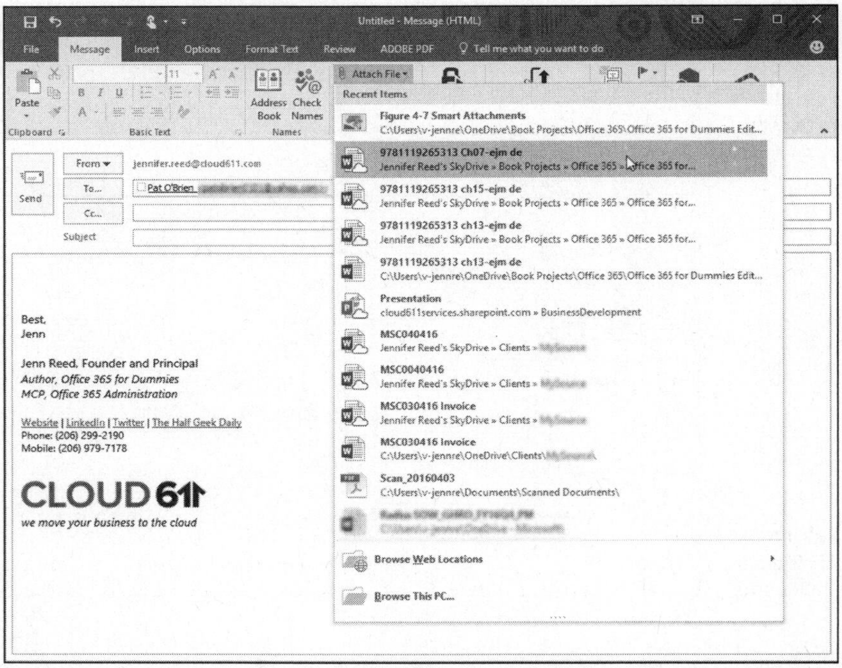

FIGURE 4-7:
Outlook email attachment showing most recent documents.

If your file is saved in OneDrive (personal), OneDrive for Business, or SharePoint, you can either attach the document as a copy or send it as a shared file for you and the recipients to collaborate on. When sending a file, you can set the permission (Edit or View) from the email itself instead of going back to the file location and setting the permissions from there.

Uncluttering your inbox with Clutter

Want an email application that is also a mind reader? Your wish is granted. You can thank Office Graph and Clutter, a new feature in Outlook.

Clutter uses the technology behind Office Graph to analyze the signals you send when you take action on your emails. For example, if you tend to ignore emails from an online shoe store but tend to reply to your manager, Clutter will learn your pattern of behavior. It will start thinking that emails from the shoe store are not as relevant to you, so it will send those emails to the "Clutter" folder so you can focus on the emails that are relevant and important to you. Without any additional actions on your part, your inbox is now de-cluttered. You can also train Clutter to learn your preferences faster by manually moving items in or out of the Clutter folder.

TIP

Enabling Clutter does not mean, however, that you will no longer receive Junk Mail; junk is still there. But at least you will not be flooded with a bunch of not-so-relevant emails every day without losing them to junk mail. So if you decide one day to take advantage of a shoe sale, you can always go to the Clutter folder to find the email with the coupon.

You are in full control of Clutter. If you don't want to use it, you can disable it. Here's how:

1. **Log on to** `http://portal.office365.com`.

2. **Click on the Settings icon (gear icon on top right).**

3. **In the My app settings group, click Mail.**

4. **On the left pane, expand the Mail group, then click Clutter.**

5. **Untick the box next to Separate items identified as Clutter (Figure 4-8).**

Tell Me tells you more

There are three ways to find help in Outlook or any of the Office applications. The easiest way is to use the Tell Me feature, which sits at the top of the Ribbon (Figure 4-9).

To use Tell Me, simply type keywords to find specific functions on the Ribbon. The first time you click on the Tell Me what you want to do box, you see a list of commonly used search functions. After using the feature, the list will show the last five commands you ran.

The other two ways to find help in Outlook are

>> Click the File menu, then click the ? (question mark) icon on the top right corner to launch the Help Viewer.

>> Use the F1 function key on your keyboard to open the Help Viewer.

FIGURE 4-8:
Turning off
Clutter.

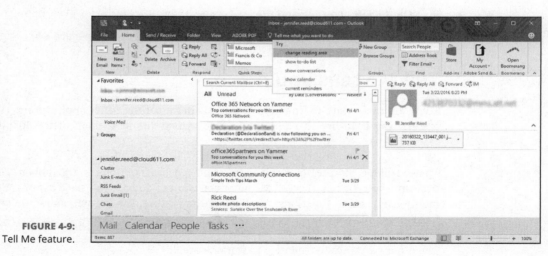

FIGURE 4-9:
Tell Me feature.

Using Outlook apps to streamline work

Outlook apps (similar to add-ins for the desktop version of Outlook) are third-party versatile applications integrated into Outlook not only to streamline work, but also to extend its functionality.

For example, you may have an Outlook calendar item for your company's happy hour. You typically ride the bus to work, so you use Uber to get around during the day. With the Uber app, you can set up an Uber ride reminder without leaving Outlook. Based on your reminder settings, the app will send a notification to your smartphone; with one swipe, you can quickly request a ride.

There are a number of productivity Outlook apps and the list is growing every day. Visit the Office Store at the following link, and then click on Outlook from the left navigation to see the latest list of Outlook app. Click on the app and follow the instructions to install the app:

```
https://store.office.com/appshome.aspx
```

TIP

My favorite productivity add-in is the free Boomerang add-in for sending emails at optimal times, setting reminders for follow ups, and scheduling meetings with people outside of my organization (whose calendar I can't see) without a lengthy back and forth. The add-in works in both the desktop version of Outlook and in Outlook Online. Figure 4-10 provides a glimpse of how Boomerang behaves in Outlook Online.

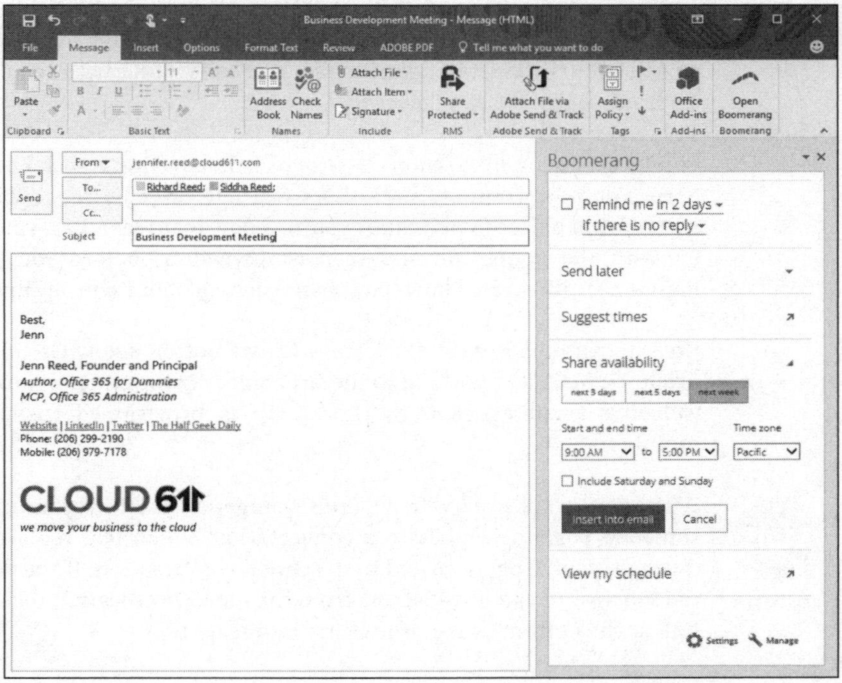

FIGURE 4-10:
Boomerang
Outlook app.

Unifying Teams with Built-In Tools

Two great new collaboration tools in Office 365 E1–E5 plans (and their corresponding government and academic) are Groups and Planner. Their integration with the rest of Office 365 services with familiar user interfaces greatly increases productivity, as you seamlessly perform actions from one application to another (email to calendar to tasks to document library, and more). While you're using these tools, Office Graph also captures your interactions and behaviors, then adds signals to your data set for machine learning.

The Groups experience

If you've ever taken a stretch assignment to deliver a project (either as a contributor or a leader), you know it can be challenging to keep up with the project-related emails, meetings, conversations, calls, and documents. Groups in Office 365 solves this problem by providing a single hub where project team members can collaborate securely and efficiently.

When you create a Group, a shared mailbox is also created, so you can keep all your group emails in one place. You'll also get a shared calendar, cloud storage in OneDrive for Business, and a notebook. Groups is designed for mobile experiences so you can participate in discussions and collaborate with team members on iOS, Android, and Windows devices.

Conducting team discussions in Groups is like having a social networking experience. You post content, and others can like or reply to it. The conversation is sorted from oldest to newest; if you're a new team member, you can quickly catch up with the goings on and read conversations before you joined the group. Figure 4-11 illustrates how team members collaborate in Groups.

Creating Groups is easy: Click the + Create button below Groups, then follow the prompts. Members you add to the Group during the creation process will receive a welcome email as soon as the Group is provisioned (usually within a few minutes).

REMEMBER

When you're subscribed to a Group, you get an email to your mailbox every time someone posts or replies to a conversation. When you reply to the email from Outlook, your reply is posted in the Group conversation. If the volume of emails is too much, you can unsubscribe from the email notification (click the unsubscribe link at the bottom of the group email message).

Project Managing with Planner

When your project collaboration needs require formal task tracking in addition to documents, mailbox, calendar, project notebook, and conversations, Office 365 Planner is the best tool for you.

Planner is a visual project management solution which allows you to create and assign (or re-assign) tasks, and track progress from an individual level under My tasks all the way across organizational levels from the Planner Hub.

When you create a plan in Planner, you automatically get a Board. From the Board, you can create tasks with due dates, documents, categories, and other relevant information. The task items are presented in a Card that can be color-coded and moved around. Team members can enter comments on the card, similar to how the conversation feature works in Groups (Figure 4-12).

When you switch to the Charts view, you see interactive charts that can be drilled down for more details. For example, clicking on part of the histogram in Figure 4-13 allows you to see what's behind schedule for the plan.

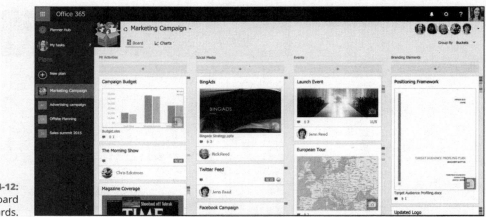

FIGURE 4-12:
Planner Board
with cards.

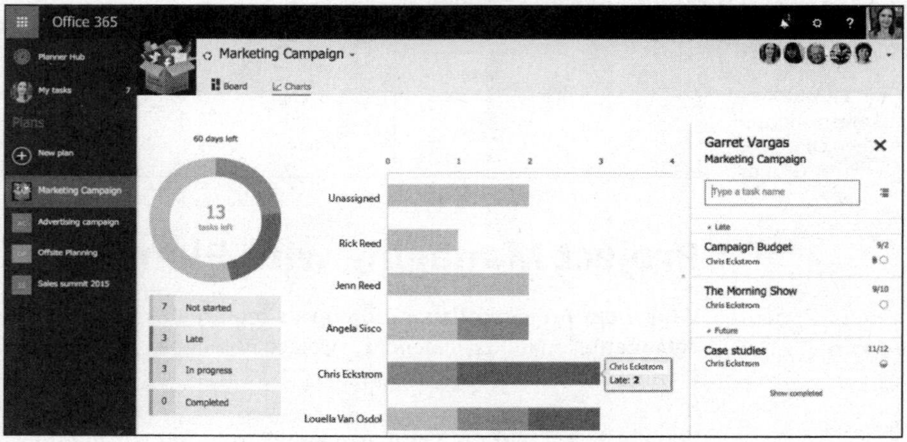

FIGURE 4-13:
Charts view of a
plan in Planner.

The Planner Hub (left side of Figure 4-13) gives you an all-up view of the plans of which you are a member, as well as the plans created as a "public" plan. When you add a plan to Favorites by clicking the ellipses to the right of the plan name, that plan is added to the Favorite plans board with a chart that quickly tells you the status of tasks not started, late, in progress, and completed.

To create a new plan, follow these steps:

1. **Log on to** `http://portal.office365.com`.

2. **From the app launcher, select Planner.**

3. **From the left pane, click + New plan.**

4. **Enter the required information and click OK.**

Getting Social with Yammer

Yammer is Microsoft's answer to Facebook for the enterprise. It helps employees collaborate with everyone in the organization, get up to speed on happenings outside their departments, crowdsource ideas, and even create spaces where they can invite external partners and clients to join.

By default, Yammer is "public" within the boundaries of your organization. This means that when you post something to your Home feed (the default view when you log in), everyone in your organization will see it. This is great for general announcements or crowdsourcing ideas and information without filling people's mailboxes with emails, replies, replies to replies, and replies to replies to replies.

The Home feed displays the latest posts relevant to you, based on projects you've worked on, the files you've posted or interacted with, the Yammer groups you've joined, and the people you've followed.

The Yammer profile page is where you let others know who you are, your areas of expertise, the projects you're working on, and other information you want to share. You will also see the conversations and groups you are part of, the people you are following, and the people who are following you. To get to your profile page, simply click on your picture at the bottom corner of the window (Figure 4-14).

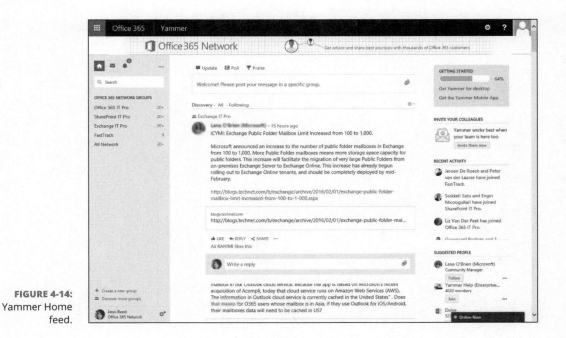

FIGURE 4-14: Yammer Home feed.

The Yammer inbox, which can be accessed by clicking the envelope icon on the top left, is where you keep track of conversations in which you have been mentioned (this happens when people type in the @ sign followed by your name), group announcements, and private messages. You will also see conversations you're following even if you have not been mentioned in the conversation.

If you need to collaborate with people outside your organization using all the Yammer features, the External Network group functionality is your best bet. Here's how to create an external network Yammer group:

1. **Log on to** `http://yammer.com`.

2. **Click + Create a new group above your picture.**

3. **In the Create A New Group window, select External Network and enter the required information.**

4. **Click Create Network.**

3

Exploring SharePoint

Chapter 5

Collaborating Has Never Been This Easy!

I n 1971, computer engineer Ray Tomlinson sent the first email between two computers set side by side. When asked what prompted him to develop such breakthrough technology, Tomlinson's response was "Mostly because it seemed like a neat idea."

More than 40 years later, and over 205 billion of emails sent and received per day in 2015 alone, that neat idea is due for an upgrade. In today's world, where information workers no longer are sitting beside each other but spread out across multiple geographies and time zones, email simply isn't enough to ensure real-time collaboration, self-service information gathering, and robust knowledge management solution.

While email will continue to serve the needs of one-to-one communication and calendaring, SharePoint Online is stepping up to the plate to address team-focused and project-focused collaboration needs. What's exciting about this is that SharePoint technologies deliver collaboration capabilities in a way that enables information that works to be productive anytime, anywhere, and on almost all modern devices.

In this chapter, you get a tour of the SharePoint landscape, understand features for enhanced collaboration, learn social capabilities for better engagements, and get a glimpse of other productivity boosters in Office 365 that integrate with SharePoint Online.

Touring the SharePoint Landscape

As the leading solution for intranets globally, SharePoint is a $2 billion business for Microsoft, with more than 100 million users. If you're new to SharePoint, you might be interested to know that there are a variety of products and services under the SharePoint umbrella:

>> In this book, the SharePoint technology we mostly cover is SharePoint Online, a cloud-based solution that is one of the services in Office 365.

>> SharePoint Server is a solution like SharePoint Online, but it requires buying and maintaining server hardware, installing the software, keeping software or operating system up to date, and hiring people to manage the technology and troubleshoot issues. In SharePoint Online, these tasks are handled by Microsoft.

>> SharePoint Foundation is free software that provides basic, but robust, collaboration solutions, with such features as document sharing, discussions, team workspaces, blogs, shared calendars, and wikis.

>> SharePoint Designer 2013 is a free program that developers use to extend the capabilities of SharePoint, such as creating workflows, customizing the look and feel of SharePoint sites, and connecting to external data sources.

Getting to know the SharePoint personas

At a very basic level, there are four types of personas who use, interact with, and benefit from SharePoint. Although the focus of this book is mostly for end users and SharePoint admins, we want you to know what SharePoint offers to IT professionals and developers:

>> **End users.** If you access your organization's portal or intranet on SharePoint to read announcements or any type of communications, you're an end user. The same is true if your project team uses SharePoint for collaboration.

Throughout this book, you find useful instructions to help you quickly become a productive project team member.

» **Admins.** As you become familiar with the features and functionalities of SharePoint, you may become a super end user and take on administration responsibilities, such as the following:

- *Site collection admin.* This role is responsible for an entire site collection, which may have many SharePoint sites. A site collection admin can control which features are available for the site collection, including workflows, custom branding, and search settings.

- *Site owner.* When you create a new site from the Sites page (instructions are provided later in this chapter), you automatically become the site owner. As a site owner, you can provision sub-sites, manage permissions for the site, change the look and feel, and enable or disable site features according to what's available from the site collection, and more.

» **IT professionals.** SharePoint has built-in capabilities that cater to professionals in an IT department or IT consultants who serve the needs of their clients. Typically, these IT professionals administer SharePoint Online to ensure the technology meets business needs. They can act as the system or **SharePoint admin** with access to the SharePoint admin center in Office 365 where they configure SharePoint settings, such as

- Enabling/disabling Yammer as the enterprise social collaboration solution

- Allowing external sharing of SharePoint sites

- Configuring compliance and data loss prevention policies

- Restoring deleted sites

» **Developers.** These are the technical people who create applications and customizations to extend SharePoint functionalities beyond what Microsoft offers . SharePoint has rich features for the hundreds of thousands of developers focused on this platform. There's even a marketplace for these developers to publish and sell their apps and solutions: the SharePoint Store.

Navigating the Sites page

The Sites page shows all the SharePoint sites you can access in Office 365. If your SharePoint admin (see preceding section) has enabled the functionality, this is also where you create new sites.

To access the Sites page, follow these steps:

1. **Log in to Office 365 from** `http://portal.office365.com`.
2. **Click the app launcher (the icon that looks like a waffle on top left).**
3. **Click sites from the list of tiles.**

Figure 5-1 shows the user interface the Sites page:

FIGURE 5-1:
The Sites page.

>> **New icon.** Create a new team site by clicking this icon and following the prompts.

>> **Search Box.** Search for content or people in Office 365 from this box.

>> **Featured Sites.** This section displays the sites and portals promoted by the Site Collection Admin.

>> **Followed Sites.** A listing of the sites you've followed.

    You can follow a site by clicking on the **Follow** icon (Figure 5-2) on the menu bar from the top right corner of the site.

>> **Recent Sites.** A listing of sites you've recently visited. It also tells you recent activity on the site.

>> **Recommended Sites.** Powered by Office Graph and machine learning, this section lists recommended sites you should follow.

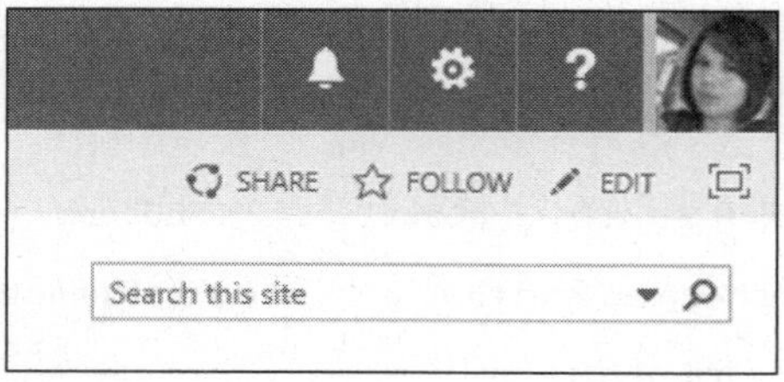

FIGURE 5-2:
The Follow icon.

Enabling/Disabling external sharing

If you are an IT professional with SharePoint admin privileges, you have control over whether SharePoint sites and their content can be shared with users outside your organization. The functionality that allows this to happen is called *external sharing.* Sometimes this becomes necessary when you want people you work with who don't have an Office 365 license (referred to as external users) in your organization to collaborate with you. For example, if you are running a marketing campaign and you're working with an ad agency, you might want to give your contacts in the ad agency access to your project site in SharePoint so you can co-author documents.

By default, external sharing is enabled in SharePoint Online. This means that all sites created from the Sites page can be shared with external users. You can disable this feature globally for the entire SharePoint Online environment or enable/disable any individual site collection.

To disable external sharing globally, follow these steps:

1. **Log in to** `http://portal.office365.com`.

2. **From the Admin group on the left pane, click SharePoint.**

3. **From the SharePoint admin center, click settings from the left pane.**

4. **Scroll down to find the External sharing section and select Don't allow sharing outside your organization (Figure 5-3).**

5. **Click OK.**

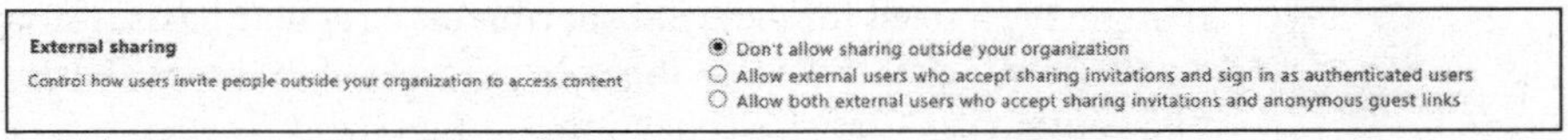

FIGURE 5-3:
Enable/Disable external sharing globally.

External sharing

Control how users invite people outside your organization to access content

- Don't allow sharing outside your organization
- Allow external users who accept sharing invitations and sign in as authenticated users
- Allow both external users who accept sharing invitations and anonymous guest links

To disable external sharing for a site collection, follow these steps:

1. **From the SharePoint admin center, click site collections from the left pane.**

2. **Select the site collection then click the sharing button from the Ribbon.**

3. **From the sharing window that pops up (Figure 5-4), select Don't allow sharing outside your organization.**

4. **Click OK.**

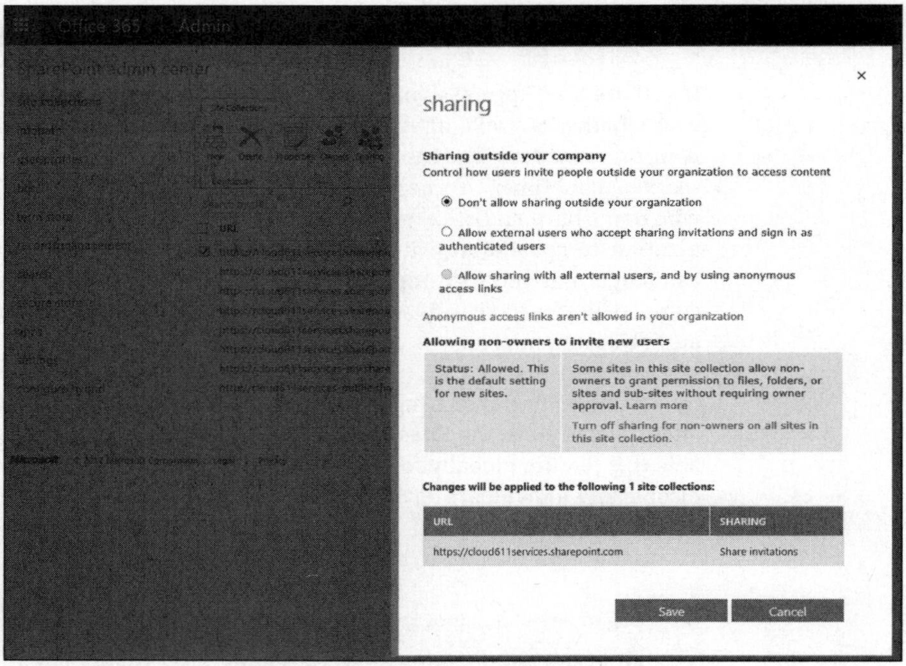

FIGURE 5-4:
Enable/Disable external sharing for a site collection.

WARNING

When you create a subsite, it inherits the permissions of the parent site by default. If you don't break the inherited permission, then external users can access to the subsite, because external users have the same rights as the internal user who invited them to collaborate. Plan your external sharing strategy so you don't inadvertently overshare and potentially expose confidential content to the wrong people.

TIP

If you have a need for external sharing on a regular basis, it may be best to create an entire site collection for the sole purpose of external sharing, and keep sensitive content off that site collection.

Knocking Down Collaboration Barriers

Good collaborators *contribute, take responsibility, cooperate,* and *listen.* Great collaboration happens when you give good collaborators the tools and techniques to automate and simplify their work.

SharePoint Online is chockfull of features to do just that. It knocks down common barriers for collaboration such as document versioning nightmares, lack of content discoverability, scheduling confusion, and misalignment on project goals and objectives.

Setting up and using your Team Site

SharePoint sites using the Team Site template keep teams in sync with shared document libraries, task lists, calendars, and a site mailbox that can be synced to Outlook, and much more. These sites are mobile-friendly, so even when you aren't in front of your computer, you can still collaborate with your team from your mobile device such as a smartphone or a tablet.

Setting up your team site is easy; from the Sites page, click on the new + icon (refer to page 4) and follow the prompts.

When your site is provisioned, you will be taken to a landing page pre-populated with the basic collaboration features, as shown in Figure 5-5:

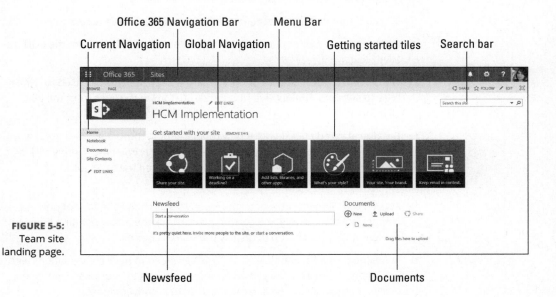

FIGURE 5-5:
Team site landing page.

>> **Office 365 Navigation Bar**. While logged in to Office 365, this navigation bar will persist as you move from one service to another:

- On the left, you'll find the app launcher (looks like a waffle), and the breadcrumb that tells you which Office 365 service you're currently viewing.

- On the right, you'll see these icons: alerts, settings icon (looks like a gear), help, and your profile picture.

>> **Menu Bar**. Just below the Office 365 navigation is a narrow strip called the menu bar:

  ● At the right side of the menu bar are icons that allow you to share or follow the site. If you're a site owner, you will see an icon to edit the page.

  ● At the left side of the menu bar are icons to help you interact with the page. Clicking the Page icon will display the Ribbon, and clicking the Browse icon will hide the Ribbon.

>> **Current Navigation.** Displayed on the left, it shows the following links:

  ● Home (takes you back to the home page)

  ● Notebook (opens the shared OneNote notebook in OneNote Online)

  ● Documents (displays the shared document library)

  ● Site Contents (displays the content of the site you have access to)

If you have site owner permission, you can quickly add links from the EDIT LINKS icon.

>> **Global Navigation.** Shown at the top of the page, it's typically used to display links to subsites. Site owners can quickly customize the links from the EDIT LINKS icon.

>> **Getting started** tiles. If you're new to SharePoint, these tiles are a great way to accomplish key tasks to get your site ready for prime time. Simply click on a tile and follow the prompts. After you've completed the tasks, click on REMOVE THIS to make the tiles go away.

>> **Search Bar.** This versatile box allows you to search the site for not only content but also people and conversations. Click the arrow pointing down to the left of the search icon to display the search choices.

>> **Newsfeed**. Like Facebook, you can use Newsfeed to have conversations with your team members. You can add photos and links to your post. Everyone with whom you share the site can participate in conversations.

>> **Documents.** You can quickly see the contents of the Documents library on the Current Navigation here. You can also create new or upload existing documents from this interface.

As your need for collaboration grows, you may have to add more document libraries, notebooks, lists or even third-party apps for your site. To see what you can add, click the settings icon from the Office 365 navigation bar (Figure 5-6), click Site Contents, and then click add an app.

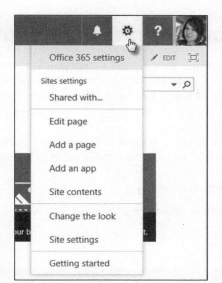

FIGURE 5-6:
Adding more
content from the
settings icon.

TIP

UNDERSCORING IN LINK NAMES

When you share links to files from a SharePoint document library, note that spaces are converted to %20 in the links. Instead, use underscores instead of spaces as separators. As you can see from the following examples, underscores enhance readability. This is true for site names, libraries, lists, and documents.

You can always edit the title to remove the underscore from your sites, libraries, and lists through the Settings section.

Example: Underscores as separators

```
https://cloud611.com/Puget_Sound_Farmers/Shared_Documents/
    Kickoff_Deck.pptx
```

Example: Spaces as separators

```
https://cloud611.com/ Puget%20Sound%20Farmers/Shared%20
    Documents/Kickoff%20Dec.pptx
```

Sharing and co-authoring documents

Rather than emailing documents back and forth between team members, you can streamline the process by loading your documents in a SharePoint site document library. After the document is loaded, you can share it with team members and start co-authoring.

Here's an example: a document that outlines my company's mobile app portfolio. To start collaborating with my team on the document, here's what I need to do:

1. **Load the file in the document library.**

2. **Click the ellipses next to the file to display the callout feature.**

I see a preview of the document, as well as contextual commands (Figure 5-7).

FIGURE 5-7:
The callout feature in SharePoint document libraries.

3. **Click the SHARE command, enter the names of the team members, and select the permission level.**

I can enter a personal message now.

4. **Click the SHARE button (Figure 5-8).**

TIP

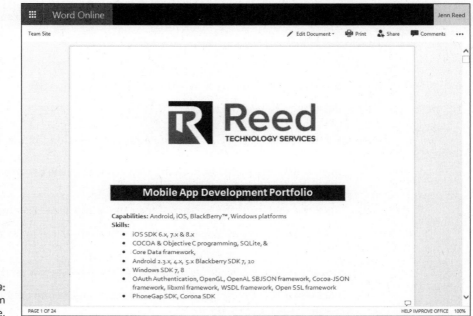

FIGURE 5-8:
Sharing documents and assigning permission level.

Alternatively, I can also click on the EDIT command from the callout feature to open the file in Word Online where I can share the file (Figure 5-9).

Regardless of which devices your co-authors are using, Word Online or Word 2016 allows you and your team to see each other's edits in real time. If you're co-authoring on a PowerPoint file, you will be alerted to changes made by others when you save the file.

FIGURE 5-9:
Sharing from Word Online.

Going back to a previous version

Document libraries in SharePoint are automatically set up for version control. This is particularly helpful when you want to track the evolution of your document. If for some reason the current version doesn't meet your needs, you can always go back to a previous version and not worry about the work you've already done.

By default, new document libraries are enabled for tracking major versions of the document. You can change this setting to track both major and minor versions of the document. (Major version means that every time the file is saved, that version is ready for everyone to see. Minor version means the file is still a work in progress and not yet ready for the broader audience.)

With either a Full Control or Design permissions to the site, you can modify the versioning settings by following these steps:

1. **Go to your documents library.**

2. **On the Ribbon, click Library.**

3. **Click Library Settings.**

4. **In the General Settings group, click Versioning settings to view all available options from the Versioning Settings page.**

5. **In the Document Version History group, select one of the three choices:**

   - No versioning
   - Create major versions
   - Create major and minor (draft) versions

6. **Click OK to save your changes.**

To view the version history and restore a previous version, follow these steps:

1. **In your document library, click the ellipses next to the document to display the callout feature.**

2. **Click the ellipses at the bottom of the callout and then click Version History.**

   The Version History window appears with a list of the versions stored for the file.

3. **Hover over one of the dates until you see the down arrow on the right.**

4. **Click the arrow to bring up the View, Restore, and Delete options for the version (see Figure 5-10).**

5. **Click OK.**

Version History

Delete All Versions | Delete Minor Versions

No. ↓	Modified	Modified By	Size	Comments
0.9	2/25/2016 7:22 PM	Jenn Reed	10.3 MB	
0.8		Jenn Reed	10.3 MB	
	View			
0.7		Jenn Reed	10.3 MB	
	Restore			
0.6		Jenn Reed	10.3 MB	
	Delete			
0.5		Jennifer Reed	10.3 MB	
0.4	2/21/2016 7:09 PM	Jenn Reed	10.3 MB	
0.3	2/15/2016 9:54 PM	Jenn Reed	10.3 MB	
0.2	2/15/2016 8:06 PM	Jenn Reed	10.3 MB	
0.1	1/25/2016 2:01 PM	Siddha Reed	10.3 MB	

Title	Mobile application development
Tags	Marketing; Proposal; Template
Technology	Mobile Apps

FIGURE 5-10:
Restoring a
previous version.

TIP

You restore an item in a list similar to the way you restore a file in a document library except that in a list, there are no minor versions. All versions are saved as a major version.

Getting Social at Work

Working in silos is so five years ago. The clamor in the workplace nowadays is for people to work better together and collaborate more using social tools similar to what we use in our personal (think Facebook) and professional (think LinkedIn) lives.

Office 365 offers more than one tool for social connections, from Yammer to Communities to Office 365 Groups. There are no hard and fast rules for using all, or one over the other but, generally, there are best practices you can apply to ensure you're using the right tool for the right purpose. For each of the tools we cover in this topic, you will find some best practice tips.

Five rules for Yammer success

It took some time, but Office 365 customers now can experience the full benefits of Yammer as an enterprise social networking solution. The service is deeply integrated in Office 365.

In SharePoint Online, you can embed a Yammer feed on your site pages to enable two-way conversations without leaving SharePoint. When you want to use the full

Yammer functionalities, you can easily navigate to Yammer from the app launcher on the Office 365 navigation bar.

Why Yammer?

» If you need to collaborate with others, you must Yammer.

» If you value connections, you must Yammer.

» If you want to share your ideas and benefit from other peoples' ideas, then you must Yammer.

Like most popular social networking sites, there are basic tasks you must complete before engaging with other users in the network. Yammer is no different. If you'll be using this tool for work, here are five rules to set yourself up for success:

TIP

» **Promote yourself by completing your profile.** List your interests and areas of expertise to let your colleagues know who you are. This will also make you discoverable in searches.

Upload a profile photo—it adds a personal touch when people are conversing with you.

» **Let them know you're ready to Yam.** Introduce yourself to the network.

By default, Yammer posts a notification whenever a new member joins the network. You can tack your own introduction from that notification by either replying to it (see Figure 5-11) or creating a new post.

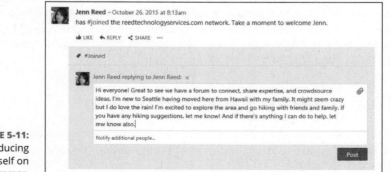

FIGURE 5-11:
Introducing
yourself on
Yammer.

>> **Start Yamming.** Join a group, follow people and topics, post a message, like a post, reply to messages, and even create your own group! Those are just a few of the things you can do to have an online presence.

Yammer is like a gift that gives back. The more you give, the more you receive. Use Yammer to gather feedback but don't be stingy about sharing great ideas.

>> **Stay in the know**. Stay connected with your Yammer buddies via notifications through the Yammer app.

If you become wildly popular, however, you might end up with a bunch of notifications, so adjust your settings from the edit profile page.

>> **Optimize every conversation.** Similar to Twitter and other social tools, you can use symbols as markers:

(hashtags) to mark conversations as topics

@ *(at-mentions)* to alert other users that you've added them to the conversation

Yammer is great for exchanging ideas and two-way conversations around a specific topic. It's an ideal solution for putting a stop to email trees that branch off into multiple replies, forwards, carbon copies, and blind carbon copies just to gather input to arrive at a decision. When you ask a question on Yammer, everyone in the group can see the question, reply to it, and see everyone's replies. You can also conduct a poll as well as praise a colleague on Yammer.

Taking part in Communities

A SharePoint community is a place where you and your colleagues who share the same interests can gather, share ideas, and learn from each other. As a member of the community, you build your reputation through a point system based on your participation. In essence, participation in the community is encouraged via a reward system that acknowledges a member's contribution to the community (see Figure 5-12).

A Community site is simply a SharePoint site with the community template applied to it. The template has built-in features specifically designed for community interaction:

>> **About this community.** Displays a description of the community and date created.

>> **Join.** If you aren't a member of the community, clicking this button will allow you to join.

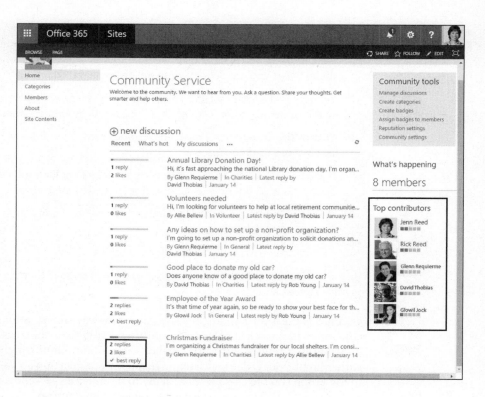

FIGURE 5-12:
Reward system in
a Community site.

>> **My membership.** Displays a summary of your reputation in the community.

>> **Tools.** A set of quick links to make it easy for owners to administer the community.

To create a community site, you must be assigned a Create Subsites permission level. If you aren't the site admin, you automatically have this permission.

If you're the site admin and don't see the Create Subsites permission level, add it by following these steps:

1. **Click the Settings icon from the Office 365 navigation bar.**

2. **Click Site settings.**

3. **Under the Users and Permissions group, click Site permissions.**

4. **From the Ribbon, click Permission Levels.**

5. **Click Add a Permission Level.**

6. **Enter the name and description and then select the box next to Create Subsites under the Site Permissions group.**

   For name and description, you can just enter "Create Subsites" and "Allow user to create subsites," respectively.

7. **Click Create to save your entries.**

To create a community site, follow these steps:

1. **Click the Settings icon from the Office 365 navigation bar.**

2. **Click Site contents.**

3. **Scroll down to the Subsites group, then click the + new subsite icon.**

4. **Enter the Title, Description, and URL name.**

5. **Under Select a template, select Community Site in the Collaboration tab.**

6. **Click Create.**

After you create a community site, the next steps are to start a discussion and invite co-workers to start building your community.

I've seen consulting organizations use community sites to build and foster communities of practice so consultants can collaborate with colleagues who share the same areas of expertise. Ideally, communities should grow organically, not be dictated by management. People will flock to a community if they see value, so it's perfectly okay for a community to die at some point if it has outgrown its purpose.

Becoming a Groupie with Office 365 Groups

SharePoint Online is great for collaborating with project teams, especially when you have to work with cross-functional teams to meet deadlines. But what happens if you just want to quickly band together with co-workers and need an environment to collaborate without the administration responsibilities that come with a SharePoint site?

The answer is Office 365 Groups, or simply Groups. Groups isn't part of Share-Point Online. It's actually a feature in Exchange Online, but it uses SharePoint Online capabilities, such as OneDrive for Business for storing group files and the OneNote notebook.

When you create a group, you automatically get a place for a conversation, a calendar, a location to store shared files, and a OneNote notebook.

Groups can be either public or private:

>> In a public group, anyone in your Office 365 organization can participate in conversations, share files, and view the calendar.

>> In a private group, only members of the group can access conversations, files, and calendar.

To create a group, you start from Exchange Online, not SharePoint Online. Here's how:

1. **Log on to** `http://portal.office365.com`.

2. **Click the app launcher from the Office 365 navigation bar.**

3. **Click the Mail tile.**

4. **From the left pane, in the Groups group, click the + sign to create a new Group (Figure 5-13).**

5. **Enter the required information then click Create.**

6. **Add members to your group by name and then click Add.**

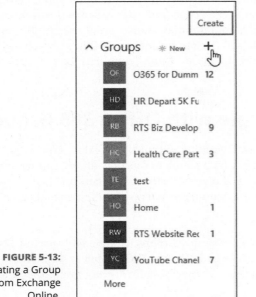

FIGURE 5-13: Creating a Group from Exchange Online.

Your Group will be created and the members will receive a welcome email.

Chapter 4 addresses Groups as part of the built-in productivity tools within Office 365. Check it out to understand the end-user experience for Groups.

TECHNICAL STUFF

Yammer and Groups address similar needs for a feed-like communication platform. Groups has some advantages over Yammer: a shared mailbox, calendar, and a place to share files. Groups also integrates with Planner, a visual task management tool recently added to Office 365 (see Chapter 4 for more about Planner). However, there are plans for Groups and Yammer integration in the future.

Chapter 6

Going Beyond Websites with SharePoint and OneDrive for Business

Finding out what people think about SharePoint is always interesting. Ten different people will often give ten different answers. One thing most people have as a common understanding is that SharePoint focuses on websites. SharePoint definitely handles websites with ease, but there is a whole lot more under the covers.

In this chapter, we explain some of the features SharePoint has beyond websites. In particular, you discover how adept SharePoint is at managing digital content and unlocking the wealth of information contained in that content through the Search feature. Search is the ability to find the digital content you are looking for when you are looking for it. In addition, you find out about the services available in SharePoint Online and get a handle on OneDrive for Business. OneDrive for Business is designed to store your digital documents; under the covers, it's powered by SharePoint.

Managing Digital Content

Imagining a business that functions without using computers is nearly impossible. Computers are used for everything from communication to accounting. Computers definitely speed up business, but this speed has a consequence. The result is that mountains of digital content are produced on a daily, if not hourly, basis. Managing all this content is one of the areas in which SharePoint and OneDrive for Business shine. In the next sections, we examine some nifty SharePoint and OneDrive for Business features, including special online libraries for documents and other media, lists for managing data and tasks, and specialized features, such as Document Sets for working with groups of documents as a single block.

REMEMBER

OneDrive for Business is a place for you to store your documents in the cloud. OneDrive for Business is powered by SharePoint, though. Think of OneDrive for Business as your personal place in SharePoint.

Document libraries

A *document library* is a special folder that you can access through your web browser or directly from within Office applications, such as Word or Excel. If you have ever used SharePoint, then you are familiar with document libraries. With SharePoint Online, these document libraries work the same way they do had you spent the time, energy, and resources of implementing SharePoint yourself. With SharePoint Online, however, you just sign up in the morning and begin using SharePoint in the afternoon.

A document library used to store Word documents, in addition to Excel, and PowerPoint documents, appears in Figure 6-1.

A SharePoint document library takes care of the heavy lifting of managing content, such as the capability to check in and check out a document, versioning, security, and workflow. Each document in a library has a context menu that can be accessed by hovering the mouse pointer over the item and then clicking the drop-down menu that appears to the right, as shown in Figure 6-2.

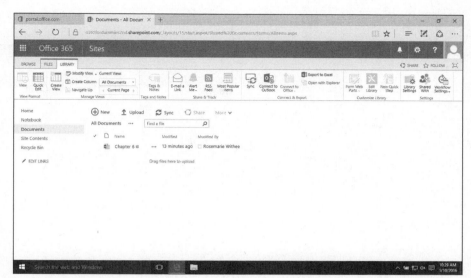

FIGURE 6-1:
A document
library in
SharePoint
Online.

HOW THE CLOUD IS CREATING A LEVEL PLAYING FIELD WORLDWIDE

Notice in Figure 6-1 that presence information with Skype for Business is displayed next to the title of the document. In this case, the presence icon is green (even though you can't see it) which means that Rosemarie Withee is online and available. A SharePoint user can instantly communicate with Rosemarie by clicking on the green presence icon to open her Skype for Business contact card and then click a button to send an e-mail, start a text chat, call directly, or even schedule a meeting. This tight integration between the different products of Office 365 creates a tremendous value. If you work for a very large enterprise, you might already be familiar with this type of integration with Microsoft products. It takes a small army of consultants and specialists to deploy enterprise software. With Office 365, you sign up and begin using the products as a service.

Microsoft has already invested heavily in the required data centers, servers, and well-paid professionals. With Office 365, small mom-and-pop shops all over the world are instantly thrust into the advantages that enterprise software provides. No longer is it only the deep-pocket larger firms that get to experience technological advantages. In this manner, Office 365 is a leapfrog technology. The developing world has not been able to build up the computer infrastructure and expertise required to implement technology like SharePoint, Exchange, and Skype for Business. Now, all of a sudden, no data center and minimal expertise is required to leverage game-changing software. As long as a company has Internet access, employees have access to Microsoft's enterprise software in Office 365.

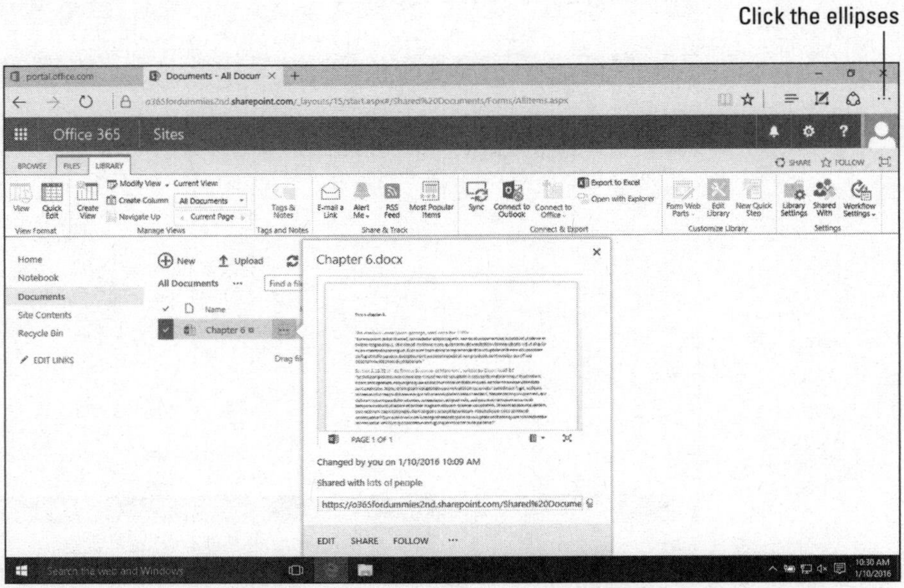

Click the ellipses

FIGURE 6-2:
Accessing the content management functionality for a document in a document library.

A familiar theme in Office 365 is integration between products. In addition to working with document library functionality, such as check in and check out by using the browser, you can also do so from within the Office documents, as shown in Figure 6-3.

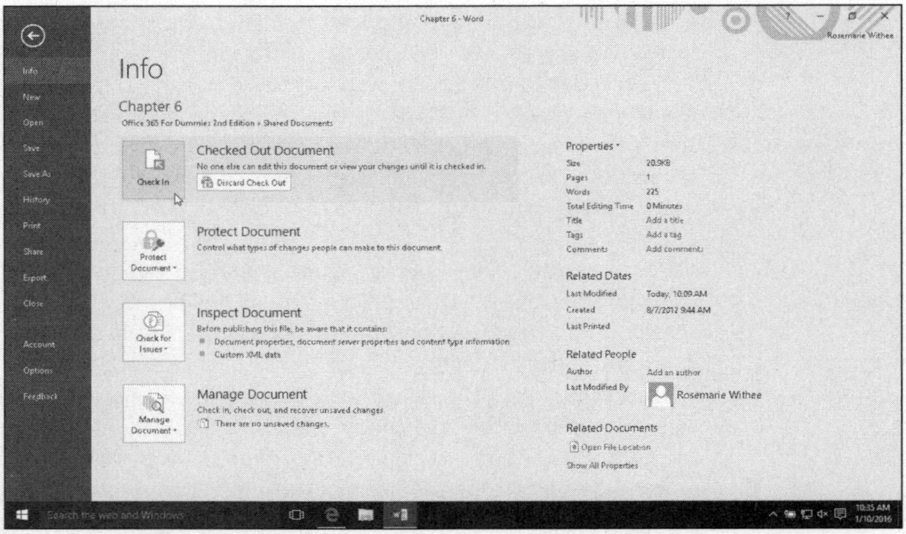

FIGURE 6-3:
Checking in a document from within Microsoft Word 2016.

WARNING

As you can imagine, it takes a lot of space in the database to store multiple versions of documents. For this reason, versioning is turned off by default on new SharePoint document libraries.

To turn on versioning, follow these steps:

1. On the Ribbon, click the Library tab and then click the Library Settings button.

The Library Settings page appears.

2. Click the Versioning Settings link.

The Versioning Settings page appears, as shown in Figure 6-4.

3. On the right, select the versioning settings that are required for your scenario:

- You can choose to have No Versioning, Major Versions, or Major and Minor versions. Major versions are created when you check in a document and Minor versions are created when you save a draft.

- You can also configure a number of other settings, including requiring content approval, the number of versions to retain, the number of draft versions to retain, the level of security, and whether the library should require users to check out the document before they can make changes.

4. Click OK to save your settings.

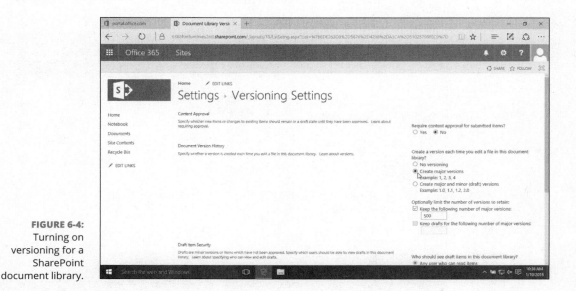

FIGURE 6-4:
Turning on versioning for a SharePoint document library.

Viewing PowerPoint presentations

As you see in the previous section, SharePoint does a great job of handling and managing documents. In addition to working with documents, a number of other features are designed to make you more efficient.

People give presentations on everything from sales to accounting. If information needs to be presented in a meeting, PowerPoint is often the tool of choice.

SharePoint Online includes integration with PowerPoint Online, which is covered in Chapter 13. When you store your PowerPoint presentations in a SharePoint document library, you can open and start presenting them by simply clicking on the title. When you click on the PowerPoint title, your web browser opens the presentation in PowerPoint Online. No need to download the file, save it locally, and open it with PowerPoint on your local computer. SharePoint and PowerPoint Online do all the work for you. This integration lets you keep your PowerPoint presentations in SharePoint, which acts as a sort of slide headquarters. You have probably experienced the problem of looking for a company slide that you know you saw in the past. You might blast an e-mail out asking if anyone has the particular slide deck that you saw presented last year. You may get a reply, but how do you know that is the most recent version of the deck? After you track down the owner of the deck, you might get the right slides you need for your presentation. Using SharePoint, along with PowerPoint Online, provides a one-stop shop for slides.

To upload documents, such as a PowerPoint presentation to a SharePoint library, you simply drag the files and drop them in the browser, as shown in Figure 6-5.

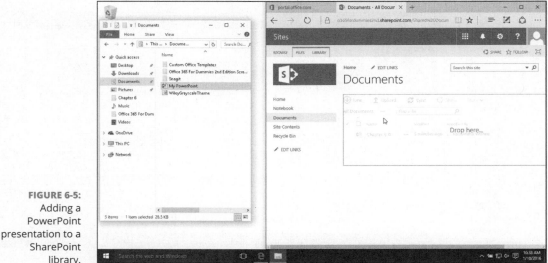

FIGURE 6-5:
Adding a PowerPoint presentation to a SharePoint library.

In addition to opening a PowerPoint presentation from within your web browser using SharePoint and PowerPoint Online, you can also preview the presentation before you open it. To preview the presentation, click the ellipsis beside the presentation's name. A small screen appears showing a preview of the PowerPoint, as shown in Figure 6-6.

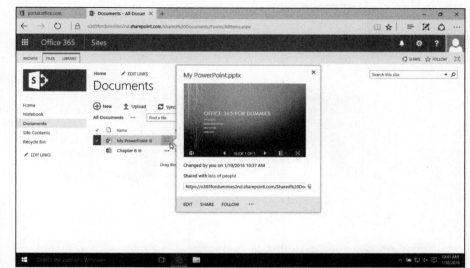

FIGURE 6-6:
Previewing a
PowerPoint
presentation
from SharePoint.

By storing all of your files in SharePoint, you can set up alerts to notify you when anything changes.

TIP

An alert allows you to be notified through either e-mail or a text message whenever changes are made to the file. You can set up alerts to

>> Cover any changes to any file.

>> Cover any changes to a single file.

>> Cover any changes to any file you have created.

>> Cover any changes to any file that you were the last to modify.

A SharePoint library has a number of rich content-management features, such as check-in and check-out, versioning, security, and workflow. Learn more about SharePoint content management features in Chapter 5.

TIP

SharePoint has a specialized library for managing rich media files, such as images, video, and audio files. You can create one of these media libraries by selecting the Asset Library template on the Your Apps page, as shown in Figure 6-7.

REMEMBER

Microsoft also refers to SharePoint lists and libraries as apps. You can access the Your Apps page by clicking the gear icon in the upper right corner, then selecting Add an app.

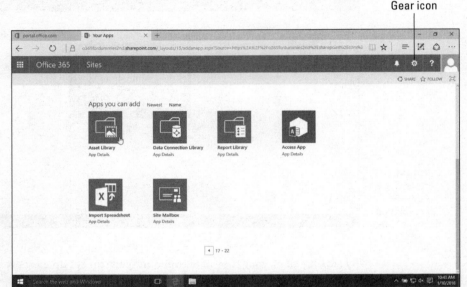

FIGURE 6-7:
Creating a media library by using the Asset Library template in SharePoint Online.

TIP

SharePoint also integrates with other Office products, such as Word and Excel. Just like PowerPoint, you can open a Word or Excel document in SharePoint with Word Online and Excel Online. You can also take a peek and preview a file before you actually open it. Word Online is covered in Chapter 11, and Excel Online is covered in Chapter 12. SharePoint integration with Office is covered in detail in Chapter 7.

Document Sets

A feature in SharePoint is the ability to work with documents in a group rather than individually. In a given day, you might be working on documents for a number of different projects. In SharePoint, a Document Set allows you to group documents together based on some criteria and then work with the group of documents as a single entity. For example, you may have a project you are working on for marketing and a project you are working on for accounting. You can group your marketing documents together and group your accounting documents together. You can then interact with the accounting or marketing documents as a single group rather than individually. Using Document Sets, you can send all your marketing documents through a workflow in a batch simultaneously or view versioning for all the documents as a set at a given point in time. Versioning is covered earlier in the chapter and also in Chapter 5.

To begin using Document Sets, first you need to activate the feature for your Site Collection. To do so, follow these steps:

1. **Click the gear icon and then click Site Settings.**

   The Site Settings page appears showing you all the settings for this particular SharePoint site.

2. **Go to the Site Collection Administration grouping and click the Site Collection Features link.**

   The features page for this specific Site Collection appears.

3. **Click the Activate button next to the Document Sets feature.**

After the Document Sets feature is activated, you can add the functionality to any library. The Document Set takes the form of a Content Type in SharePoint. A Content Type is the grouping of metadata fields into a single group. For example, you may have a recipe that has a content type that includes metadata such as ingredients, cooking times, and required seasonings. The SharePoint Document Set content type includes all the functionality required to group multiple documents into a single entity.

A common document library in SharePoint is the Documents library. You can add the Document Set functionality to the Documents library by following these steps:

1. **Navigate to the library in which you want to add the Document Sets functionality.**

   In this example, we add it to the Documents library.

2. **Click the Library Settings button located on the Library tab.**

   In order to add a Content Type to this library, you first need to enable editing.

3. **On the Library Settings page, click the Advanced Settings link.**

   The Advanced Settings page appears and lets you perform advanced configuration for this library.

4. **On the Content Type section, select Yes to allow the editing of content types.**

5. **Click OK to return to the Library Settings page.**

   Notice that a new section appears on the page now called Content Types.

6. **Click the Add from existing site content types link to add an existing site content type.**

7. **Select the Document Set content type, click the Add button, and then click OK.**

Now that the Document Set functionality has been added to the library, you can create a new document set. To create a new Document Set, click on the Documents tab of the Ribbon and then under the New Document drop-down menu, select Document Set, as shown in Figure 6-8.

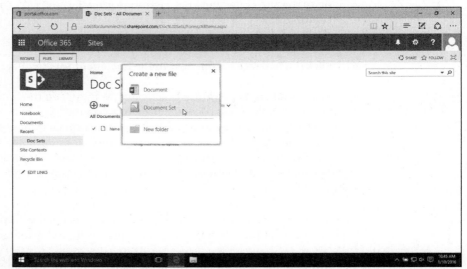

FIGURE 6-8:
Creating a new
Document Set in
SharePoint
Online.

A document set shows up in the Shared Documents library just like another document. You can interact with a document set just like you interact with a single document in the library. The difference, however, is that when you click on a Document Set, you open up the grouping of documents rather than a single document. When the Document Set is opened, a new Document Set tab will appear on the Ribbon. This tab allows you to manage the document set with features such as editing the properties, changing security permissions, sharing the documents, capturing versions, or pushing all the documents through workflow in a batch. Figure 6-9 shows the Document Set tab in the Ribbon.

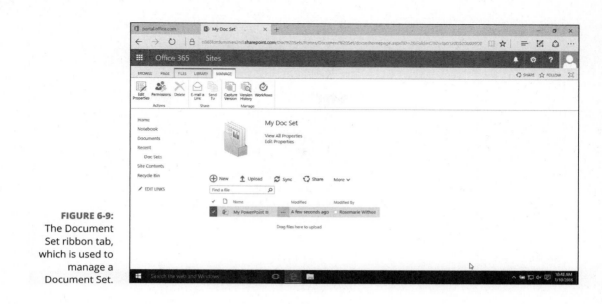

FIGURE 6-9:
The Document
Set ribbon tab,
which is used to
manage a
Document Set.

OneDrive for Business

OneDrive for Business is your personal Office 365 storage location in the cloud.

TIP

If you're already familiar with Office 365 and SharePoint Online, OneDrive for Business is what used to be called SkyDrive Pro; before that, it was called Share-Point My Sites. Along the way, OneDrive for Business integrated a file sync technology called Groove. This winding path has taken us to the current OneDrive for Business.

OneDrive for Business is still powered by SharePoint. If you're familiar with other cloud storage services, such as Dropbox, Google Drive, or Box, then you're already familiar with the concept behind OneDrive for Business. The OneDrive for Business client is shown in Figure 6-10.

TIP

OneDrive for Business is the aptly named business version of OneDrive. The consumer version is just called OneDrive.

To use OneDrive for Business, you simply configure the sync client. When the client is configured, your files will be synced between your local computer and your cloud-based storage in Office 365. If you've never used OneDrive for Business on your Windows 10 computer, it will walk you through configuration when you open OneDrive for Business. You find OneDrive for Business under your Office 2016 folder on the Start menu.

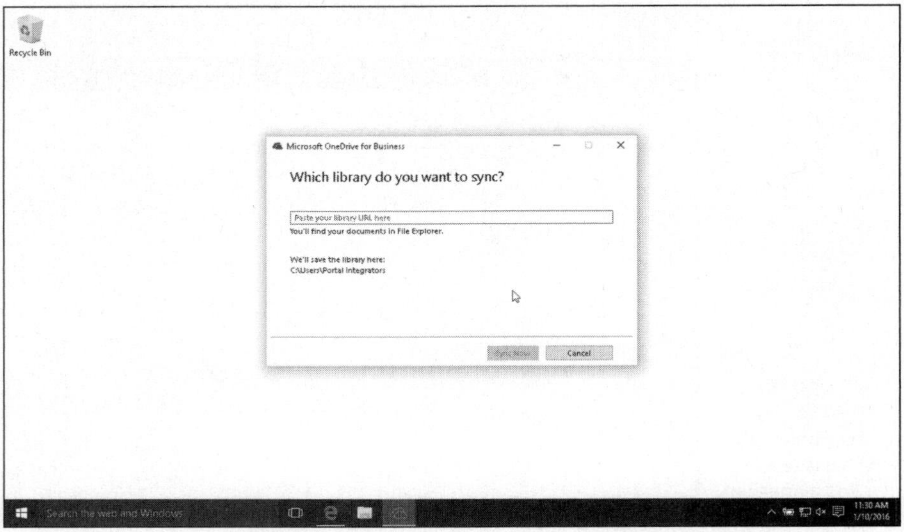

FIGURE 6-10:
Using the
OneDrive for
Business sync
client on
Windows 10.

TIP

If you have Windows 10, you already have the latest version of the OneDrive sync client. If you don't have Windows 10, you need to download and install the latest OneDrive sync client. You download Office 365 software by logging into your account at `http://portal.microsoftonline.com`.

Using Search Functionality

The rich content-management features of SharePoint may be what often garner the most press, but SharePoint is not a one-trick pony. The search functionality of SharePoint is very robust and brings a Google or Bing-type experience to the corporate documents.

Search is one of those things that don't seem important until you really need to find something. You may vaguely remember seeing a presentation done by your colleague a few months ago but have no idea where to even start to look for it in the shared folder. You could e-mail him, but what if he is not available and you need it right away. Search solves the problem of needing to find specific information in a sea of digital data.

SharePoint includes the ability to search across multiple sites. As your organization grows and you have an increasing number of sites, it would sure be a pain to have to navigate to each site in order to perform your search. With SharePoint, you can search in a single location and the search will span across multiple sites.

Sometimes, it can be difficult to get the exact terminology just right to return the content for which you are searching. SharePoint includes the ability to refine a search based on a number of configurable refiners. For example, you might be searching for that document that Bob presented to a client a while back. You type in the search term "onboarding employees" but receive hundreds of pages of content back. You remember that the presentation was a Word document so you narrow the search to only Word files. You still do not see the presentation right away, so you narrow the search down again further to only those presentations where Bob was the author. Bingo! The presentation you were looking for is right at the top of the list. Use the refiners to narrow a search, as shown in Figure 6-11.

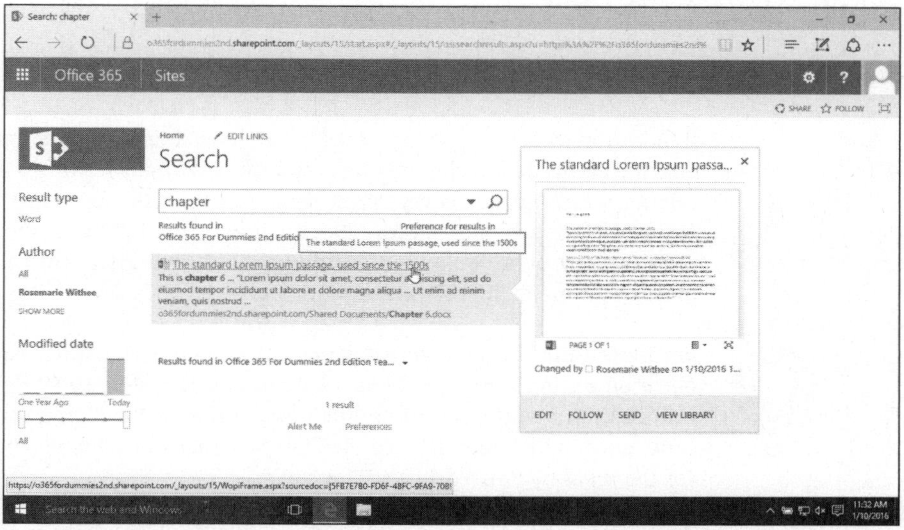

FIGURE 6-11:
Using refiners to
narrow a search.

TIP

You can think of a search refiner as a filter. Your search for a broad topic might return hundreds of possible results. The refiner allows you to filter this information down based on the configured criteria.

Another key aspect of search is finding someone you just met but are not sure how to spell his name. For example, you might meet a co-worker in the hall and he mumbles to you that his name is Kain. You register the name as Kain but when you go to search for him online, you wouldn't normally find him if you type in *Kain* because his name is actually Ken. SharePoint phonetic search allows you to still type *Kain* and SharePoint recognizes that this is phonetically very similar to Ken. SharePoint is smart enough to show Ken in the search results, as shown in Figure 6-12. Because SharePoint also shows Ken's mug shot, or should we say company profile picture, in the search results, you can see that you have found the right person you just met in the hall.

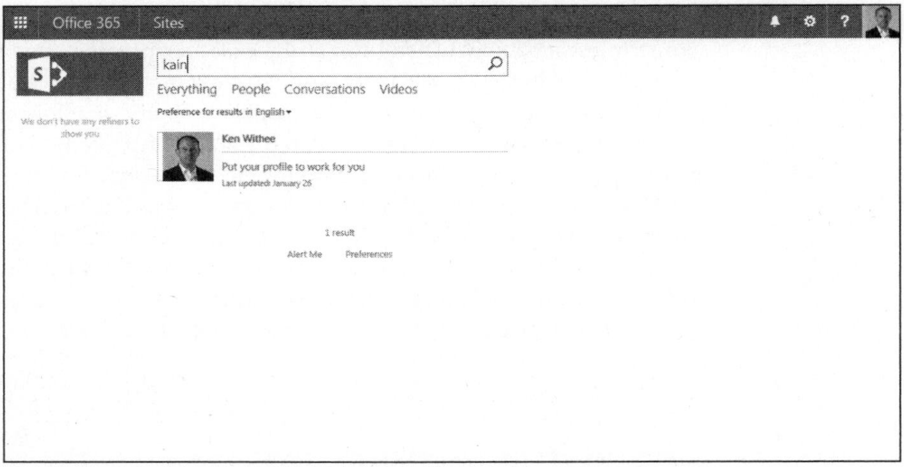

FIGURE 6-12:
Using SharePoint
phonetic search
to find a
colleague.

In addition to Search, SharePoint also includes business intelligence functionality and the ability to develop business solutions without writing a single line of code. Business Intelligence covers such things as reports, scorecards, dashboards, and key performance indicators. The Business Intelligence aspects of SharePoint require their own books, but for now you should know that they are important pieces that make SharePoint so valuable.

TIP

For more information about Business Intelligence by using SharePoint, check out *Microsoft Business Intelligence For Dummies* by Ken Withee (Wiley 2010). For more information about developing business solutions for SharePoint without writing code, check out Chapter 9. To dive deeper, check out *SharePoint 2010 Development For Dummies* by Ken Withee (Wiley 2011).

Using SharePoint with Office Online

SharePoint integrates with Office Online applications, such as Excel Online, Word Online, and PowerPoint Online. All of these services fall under the Office 365 umbrella, so they work together nicely.

Excel Online

The Excel application is a component of Microsoft's productivity suite called Office. Excel is geared toward numbers, lists, and analysis. Excel is widely adopted in the business world and many users probably wonder how they could function in business life without this tool. Excel Online is a service that SharePoint integrates with to cater to Excel spreadsheets. In particular, Excel Online lets you view your Excel data in a SharePoint site.

Using Excel Online, you could have one analyst responsible for the management of the Excel document but share the summary page, graph, or entire document with the rest of the organization. The rest of the members of the organization might not even realize they are looking at an Excel document as the driving force behind the data. From their perspective, they just see a web page on a SharePoint site with graphs, charts, grids of data, and summary data (or whatever part of Excel you decide to include in the page). The person that manages the Excel document doesn't need to learn a new tool. If she has used Excel, then she can simply continue to use Excel with the difference being that her hard work is displayed to the rest of the organization without the involvement of the IT department, developers, or anyone else.

Excel Online is covered in Chapter 12.

Word Online

Word is another application that is part of the Microsoft Office productivity suite. Word provides word processing capabilities. SharePoint integrates with Word Online, which lets you view and edit Word documents from your SharePoint site. When you click a Word document, the Word Online service takes over; you can interact with your document without leaving your browser.

Just like PowerPoint and Excel, you can also preview a Word document that is located in a SharePoint library. To preview a Word document, just click the ellipsis beside the document name; a small version of the document appears. This provides you with a way to peek inside the document without opening it.

Word Online is covered in Chapter 11.

PowerPoint Online

As shown previously in this chapter, SharePoint can also integrate with PowerPoint. PowerPoint is part of the Office suite, and it's designed for building and displaying presentations. SharePoint works closely with PowerPoint Online, so you can view and edit a PowerPoint presentation in your web browser from your SharePoint site.

PowerPoint Online is covered in detail in Chapter 13.

Chapter 7

Integrating the Mobile Experience

The era of personal computing is here. We have crossed over from a time where we personalized our computers with our preferences, loaded them with content relevant to us, or bookmarked sites that interest us to an era where our computers are learning things about us and are therefore able to serve up information personal to us. Through cloud computing and machine learning, artificial intelligence agents like Siri, Google Now, and Cortana are making headway in learning our habits, favorite foods, interests, schedules, and even our personality!

Personal computing is personal because, regardless of the device you're using at any given moment, your personalization is there. It travels with you. It doesn't stay at home in your desktop computer nor is it limited to your mobile devices. And even if your computer crashes or you lose your smartphone, you can have access to your personal content and settings from your devices' automatic cloud backups.

Personal computing then makes you, the user, mobile. It isn't about having mobile devices. Instead, it's about making your experience mobile as you go from one device to another. For example, you can start working on a document from your desktop computer at work, make edits to it from your tablet while waiting at the doctor's office, and finalize it from your smartphone while sitting in a bus.

In this chapter, you see the investments Microsoft has made in making the Share-Point experience mobile. You see how to be productive using the familiar Office applications in Windows devices, and also on iOS and Android platforms. Because the core foundation for being mobile is storing your data in the cloud, this chapter also covers basic data security and privacy in Office 365 and instruction for protecting your documents in SharePoint Online.

Office and SharePoint Integration

The newest version of the Office suite from Microsoft, Office 2016 for Windows and Mac, offers the best set of collaboration capabilities seen so far in the marketplace. For one thing, it removed some of the time-consuming processes in between creating and finalizing documents by enabling real-time co-authoring right from the desktop application for documents saved in a SharePoint document library. In Microsoft Word, for example, by firing up Skype for Business you can initiate instant messaging or voice conversations right from the application with people who are editing the same document simultaneously.

These functionalities are also available for documents stored in OneDrive for Business, a 1 terabyte (TB) online storage solution for Office 365 users. OneDrive is an ideal alternative to your computer's hard drive. Storing your files in One-Drive allows you to access those files from other devices, thereby cutting you loose from your desk.

These new productivity-boosting features are just the tip of the iceberg as Microsoft continues to build a suite of integrated apps and services in Office 365 in much shorter cycles than we were accustomed to in the boxed software days.

Creating a SharePoint document library

A document library in SharePoint is like a folder in your hard drive where you store your files. In SharePoint, there are several types of libraries, but the most commonly used type is the library in a team site. Files stored in the team site document library lend themselves well to sharing, collaboration, version control, and search.

If you have at least an Edit permission level in a team site, creating a new library is simple. Here's how:

1. **From your team site, click the settings icon from the Office 365 navigation bar (looks like a gear).**

2. **Click Add an app.**

3. **Click Document Library from the list of apps.**

4. **Give your library a name, then click Create.**

Upon successful creation, your library will be listed in the Lists, Libraries, and other Apps page.

Version control automatically is enabled when you create a document library. For additional information on how to tweak the versioning settings, refer to Chapter 5.

TIP

If you're creating a library of pictures or mixed media, check out the Picture Library and the Assets Library apps. While a document library can house pictures and videos, you may find the slideshow option for your images helpful in the Picture Library or the built-in video player useful for your audio and video files in the Assets Library.

Encouraging interaction with Ratings

Similar to the Like feature on Facebook, when you find content that resonates with you, SharePoint users can quickly express their opinion of documents in a library through a rating system. Ratings — either a Like or a Star — can be used to create views, such as displaying items with the highest number of stars or likes. If you own the content, the ratings give you insights for improvement.

To set up the rating system in your document library, follow these steps:

1. **From your document library, click Library from the Ribbon.**

2. **Click Library Settings.**

3. **Click Rating Settings.**

4. **Select Yes under Allow items in this list to be rated?**

5. **Select either Likes or Star Ratings for the voting/rating experience.**

6. **Click OK.**

7. **Back in the document library settings page, you will notice that three new columns have been added to the library (see Figure 7-1).**

List Information

Name: Documents
Web Address: https://mod158077.sharepoint.com/sites/contoso/Departments/SM/Documents/Forms/AllItems.aspx
Description: This system library was created by the Publishing feature to store documents that are used on pages in this site.

General Settings	Permissions and Management	Communications
▫ List name, description and navigation	▫ Permissions for this document library	
▫ Versioning settings	▫ Manage files which have no checked in version	
▫ Advanced settings	▫ Information Rights Management	
▫ Validation settings	▫ Workflow Settings	
▫ Column default value settings	▫ Enterprise Metadata and Keywords Settings	
▫ Manage item scheduling	▫ Generate file plan report	
▫ Audience targeting settings	▫ Information management policy settings	
▫ Rating settings	▫ Record declaration settings	
▫ Form settings		

Rating settings

Specify whether or not items in this list can be rated.

When you enable ratings, two fields are added to the content types available for this list and a rating control is added to the default view of the list or library. You can choose either "Likes" or "Star Ratings" as the way content is rated.

Allow items in this list to be rated?

◉ Yes   ○ No

Which voting/rating experience you would like to enable for this list?

○ Likes   ◉ Star Ratings

[OK] [Cancel]

Columns

A column stores information about each document in the document library.

Column (click to edit)	Type
Title	Single line of text
Rating (0-5)	Rating (0-5)
Number of Ratings	Number of Ratings
Number of Likes	Number of Likes
Created	Date and Time
Modified	Date and Time
Created By	Person or Group
Modified By	Person or Group
Checked Out To	Person or Group

FIGURE 7-1:
Setting up the Rating Settings in a document library.

When the rating system is set up, the default view of the document library will display either a series of stars or the word **Like.** Each unique user can vote once. When the vote is submitted, it is averaged with other ratings. Figure 7-2 shows an example of a document library with ratings enabled.

Getting things done from Word 2016

The cloud version of Office is great for on-the-go quick editing and collaboration. When you want to use the robust set of features and functionalities in the Office suite, however, there is no substitute for the desktop application.

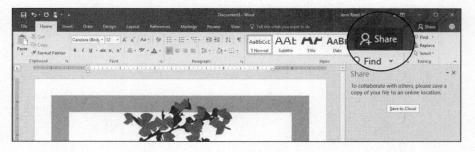

		Name		Modified	Modified By	Checked Out To	Rating (0-5)
✓							
		XT1000 Product Overview	...	January 14	☐ Jenn Reed		★★★★⯪ 4
		International Marketing Campaigns	...	2 hours ago	☐ David Thobias		★★★⯪☆ 3
		New Product Sales Pitch	...	January 14	☐ Jenn Reed		★★★⯪☆ 3
		Q4 Marketing Analysis	...	January 14	☐ Glenn Requierme		★★⯪☆☆ 2
		Sales Invoice Asia Q3	...	January 14	☐ Glenn Requierme		★★⯪☆☆ 2
		Asia Q2 Sales	...	January 14	☐ David Thobias		★★★★☆ 1
		Contoso Denver Expansion	...	January 14	☐ Glowil Jock		☆☆☆☆☆ 0

FIGURE 7-2:
Document library with ratings enabled.

If you spend most of your day sitting in front of your computer and working from the latest version of Word in Office 365, it isn't a stretch to say you've maintained a high level of productivity and managed to stay extremely collaborative.

Let's say, for example, you're working on an international marketing campaign proposal with your team. Word 2016 is installed on your computer from your Office 365 subscription and you're ready to start working. Here's how you can make Word work for you:

>> Create a new document in Word and save it to your OneDrive account or to a SharePoint document library by clicking the Share button (see Figure 7-3) and following the prompts.

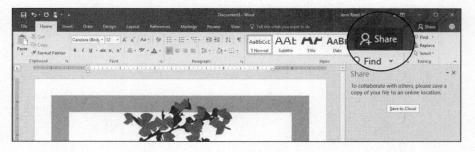

FIGURE 7-3:
The Share button in Word.

>> After saving your document, invite your colleagues to co-author with you by clicking the Share button again and then entering your colleague's email address, entering a note (optional), then clicking Share below the notes box (see Figure 7-4).

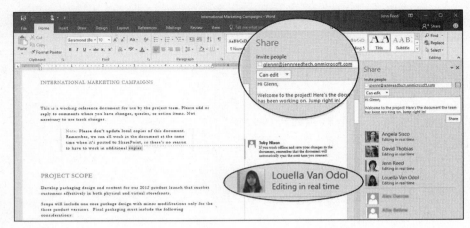

>> Keep track of co-authors who are currently editing the document with you in real-time (as shown in Figure 7-4).

>> If you have a question about a colleague's edits, you can start a chat, make a phone call, have a video conference, or send an email to your colleague by hovering over the user's name and then clicking the appropriate Skype for Business controls (see Figure 7-5).

>> Highlight or annotate a particular text to draw attention to it by using the inking feature in Office. Simply click on Draw from the Ribbon, select the pen style from the Pens group, and start drawing. If you make a mistake, use the Eraser from the Tools group. When you're done, click Select Objects (see Figure 7-6).

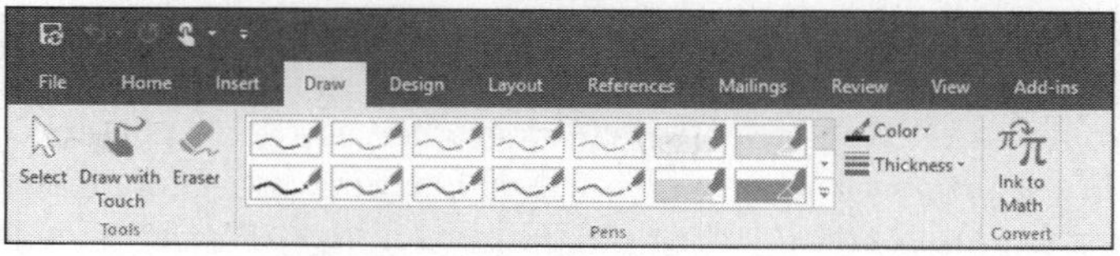

FIGURE 7-6:
Inking in Word.

>> Share a PDF version or a copy of your document as an email attachment by clicking the Share button, clicking Send as attachment at the bottom of the Share pane, then selecting one of the two options (see Figure 7-7).

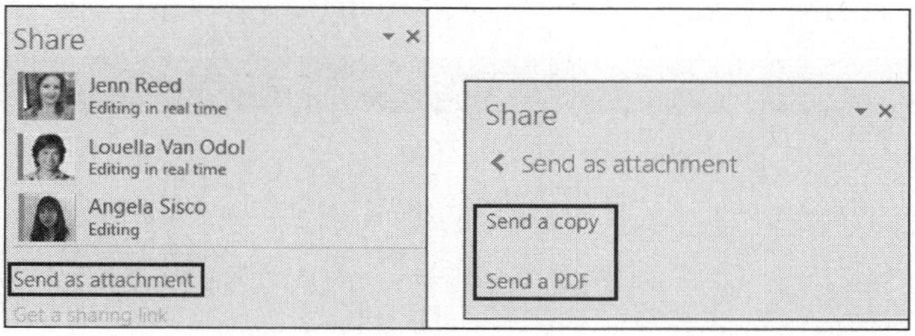

FIGURE 7-7:
Emailing a copy or PDF version of a document.

The sharing and inking features covered in this section also apply to PowerPoint and Excel. OneNote has the same inking feature but no sharing pane as of this writing. You can still share OneNote pages by clicking File from the Ribbon then clicking Share from the options on the left pane.

There are more collaboration features that integrate SharePoint and Office in the works from the Office 365 Roadmap and Microsoft is constantly rolling these out to their Office 365 customers. So don't be surprised if one day you discover a new feature that wasn't there before.

Knowing when to use OneDrive for Business

OneDrive for Business with its 1 TB of storage is your personal online storage for the workplace. It is different from OneDrive, which is 5 gigabytes (GB) of online storage from Microsoft that anyone can use for free with an Outlook.com, Hotmail, or live.com account.

While a document library in SharePoint is great if you're working with a lot of people, OneDrive for Business is ideal when you don't plan to share your files with a broad group of people in your organization. Especially when you need to keep your file longer than you would for project files, OneDrive for Business is the best storage location.

Files you create or save in OneDrive are private by default and available to you only. You can, however, share them with others just like in SharePoint and in Office applications like Word, Excel, and PowerPoint. Figure 7-8 illustrates how a private file is designated by a lock icon, while shared files have the people icon next to them.

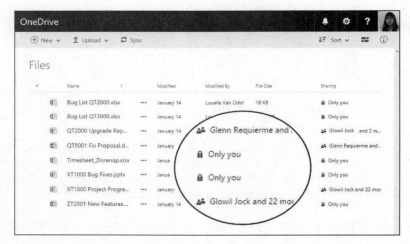

FIGURE 7-8:
OneDrive for
Business
documents
and sharing
indications.

You can sync OneDrive for Business to your computer using a sync app available for both Windows and Mac. This allows you to work on your files offline when you're not connected to the internet.

To sync OneDrive for Business to your computer, click the **app launcher** (looks like a waffle) from the Office 365 navigation bar then click **Sync** from the top menu and follow the prompts.

Once the sync is complete, you will see your OneDrive for Business folder from the Quick Access panel in File Explorer. Figure 7-9 shows my two synced OneDrive folders: OneDrive – Cloud611 which is my workplace account (OneDrive for Business), and OneDrive – Personal which is my free OneDrive live.com account.

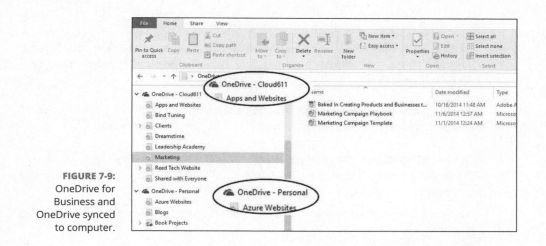

FIGURE 7-9:
OneDrive for
Business and
OneDrive synced
to computer.

Office Mobile Apps Keep You Going

A study conducted by The NPD Group in 2013 revealed that there are now more than half a billion devices in American households connected to the internet. In-Stat, another research firm, predicted that in 2015, 65 percent of the U.S. population (over 200 million people) would have a smartphone and/or tablet. Experts agree that by 2020, people will be outnumbered by the 20 billion devices on the planet. Setting aside all these researches and predictions, I can confirm mobile devices are exploding because in my own household of three people, there are enough computers and devices to support an IT department.

So what do you do when you're sitting by the fireplace playing Words by Post on your iPad with a family member right next to you (who's playing on his Android tablet) and an email comes in from a colleague who desperately needs you to review a marketing proposal or a client presentation? No problem. As Apple puts it: there's an app for that. Or specifically from Microsoft: there's an Office 365 for business mobile app for that.

Mobile documents in the cloud

Each Office 365 subscriber with a qualifying plan can install the Office mobile apps on up to five tablets and five smartphones. The qualifying plans are: Office for Business Premium, Office 365 Business, Office 365 Pro Plus, Office 365 E3, and Office 365 E5 plans.

The core Office apps available in Windows, iOS, and Android devices are Outlook, Word, Excel, PowerPoint, and OneNote. You can also download and install the OneDrive, Skype for Business, Yammer, and Delve apps to round out your Office 365 mobile experience.

The Office mobile apps from an Office 365 subscription come with premium features not available in the free version of Office for tablets and phones:

» **PowerPoint:** Use the Presenter view to see, add, and edit speaker notes; add and edit videos; format images to add styles, shadow, reflection, arrange, and crop.

» **Word:** Track changes; re-orient the page; insert charts; add WordArt; format images.

» **Excel:** Add and modify charts; use pivot tables.

You can save the documents you created from the Office mobile apps to SharePoint or OneDrive. After you connect your app to these cloud storage services, you can quickly access them from the backstage view of the app (see Figure 7-10).

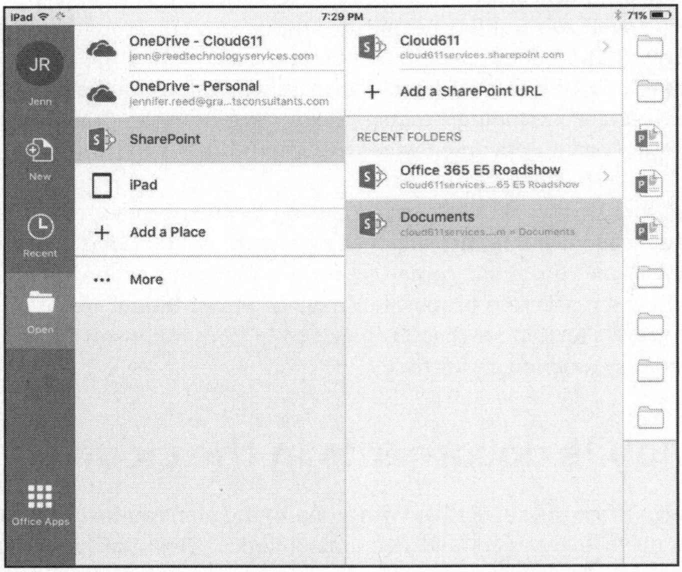

FIGURE 7-10:
Opening a file
from the iPad
PowerPoint app.

Installing the mobile apps

You can find the Office mobile apps in the App Store (iOS) or the Play Store (Android) by searching for "Microsoft Office." On a Windows phone or a Surface (acts as both a laptop and a tablet) device, the apps are pre-installed. Another way to get a summary of the Office mobile apps available for your device is as follows:

1. **From the Home screen in Office 365, click on Settings from the navigation bar.**

2. **Click Office 365 from the Settings pane, and then click Software.**

3. **From the left pane, click Phone & Tablet.**

4. **Choose your device and click the Get app button.**

   You will be taken to the Microsoft products page specific to your device.

5. **Click the Send Mail button, enter your email address, and then click Send.**

   You will receive an email with a list of mobile apps available for your device.

6. **Click the Download link to access the download instructions.**

After the app is installed on your device, make sure to connect your Office 365 cloud services: OneDrive for Business and SharePoint. Here's how:

1. **From the Open menu, click Add a place.**

2. **Select your cloud service (in this example, SharePoint).**

3. **Sign in to your Office 365 account.**

   Upon successful sign in, you will see your cloud service as one of the options with quick links to the libraries associated with it (see Figure 7-11).

Exploring the Word mobile app on an Android tablet

The user interface for Office mobile apps is consistent with the online and desktop versions. Even with the pared down features in the Word app, for example, the app does the job for quick editing. The familiar look and feel optimized for touch screens requires no learning curve earning the Word app the "Best Apps of 2015" title in Google Play.

FIGURE 7-11:
Adding a cloud
service from an
Android tablet.

The Home tab in the Word app on an Android device has basic formatting commands: Fonts, Paragraphs, Styles, and Search. (see Figure 7-12).

The Insert tab gives you options for tables, pictures, shapes, text boxes, hyperlinks, comments, headers and footers, page numbers, and the most commonly used commands for references: footnotes and endnotes (see Figure 7-13).

FIGURE 7-12:
Word app
Home tab
on an Android
device.

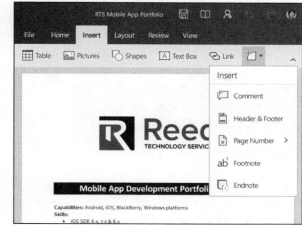

FIGURE 7-13:
Word app
Insert tab
on an Android
device.

The **Layout** tab is where you can adjust margins, change the orientation of the page, choose the paper size, choose the number of columns, and configure page breaks (see Figure 7-14).

FIGURE 7-14:
Word app
Layout tab
on an Android
device.

The **Review** tab has spell check, proofing and language options, word and smart lookup from the references group, commenting, track changes, and options to view the changes in the document (see Figure 7-15).

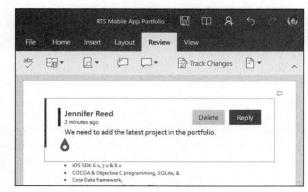

FIGURE 7-15:
Word app
Review tab
on an Android
device.

The View tab allows you to switch between reading and editing mode, zoom in to 100%, display the full page, or stretch the page to fill the width of the screen (see Figure 7-16).

As you can see in Figure 7-16, the app also has a Quick Access Toolbar similar to the desktop version. From this toolbar you can save, view in reading mode, share, undo typing (Ctrl+Z), or redo typing (Ctrl+Y).

The Scoop on External Sharing

SharePoint Online is a great solution for project team members to stay on the same page by giving everyone a one-stop location for team files, calendar, task list, notebook, and more. But what happens when one of your team members is outside your organization? Let's say you're a campaign manager for a statewide election and you want volunteers to access your SharePoint site so they can see the candidate's schedule and download the latest campaign talking points. In this situation, you probably don't want to get Office 365 subscriptions for all of your volunteers.

One way to address this scenario is to use the external sharing feature in SharePoint. Your volunteers in this scenario are considered external users.

Simply put, an external user is someone who does not have a paid license in Office 365 and does not have an email address with your organization's domain name.

When you invite an external user to your SharePoint site, that user will inherit your permissions. In other words, if you can edit or delete a file, the external user you invited will also be able to edit or delete a file.

If your Office 365 license includes the desktop Office application (Office Pro Plus), however, the external user you invited will not have access to those Office applications. The external user will be able to view and edit Office documents through Office Online, the browser version of the Office Pro Plus.

While external users can create new documents and save them back in SharePoint, they can't have their own OneDrive for Business account in which to store files.

When an external user does a search at your site, the search results will be limited to the content they have access to within your SharePoint Online environment only.

There are other advanced features that aren't available to external users, such as accessing site mailboxes, features related to reporting and analytics (Power BI), and open restricted/protected documents.

TIP

External sharing is enabled by default in SharePoint Online. If you want to disable this feature, refer to Chapter 5.

Sharing a site

To share a site, click the Share button on the top navigation, enter the recipient's email address, specify the permission, and then click the Share button (see Figure 7-17).

FIGURE 7-17:
Share a Share-
Point site with
external users.

TECHNICAL STUFF

If you've used SharePoint previously, you may wonder why Figure 7-17 doesn't look like the out-of-the-box SharePoint site you're familiar with. Customizing SharePoint Online to make it look like a WordPress website isn't difficult. You don't need to hire a developer to apply beautiful, modern, responsive themes that adapt to mobile devices. View a collection of ready-to-apply themes at this link:

```
http://themes.cloud611.com
```

To share a file, click the ellipses next to the file, click **Share** from the callout feature (see Figure 7-18), enter the recipient's email address, specify the permission, and then click the **Share** button. These steps are the same for sharing a file from a SharePoint document library or files from OneDrive for Business.

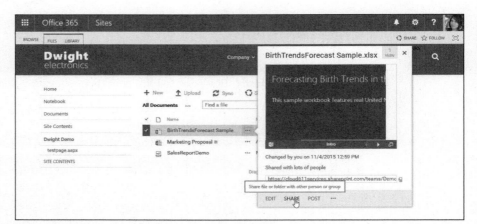

FIGURE 7-18:
Share a file with external users.

Chapter 8

Demystifying SharePoint Online Administration

I f you are working for a small business or a nonprofit organization, or you are a sole proprietor, you likely wear many hats. It's not easy to function as your organization's CEO, CMO, COO by day and at the same time be the IT department also by day! Getting bogged down with data security and protection, patch management, network stability, and a host of other IT-related daily tasks takes time away from your efforts to move your business forward and achieve your goals.

The folks at Microsoft understand those issues and as a result, they've made it so that administering Office 365 and SharePoint Online is not an onerous task.

Office 365 administration is easy, intuitive, and even fun! Setting up a globally distributed organization with a dozen people can be done in 20 minutes. For $12.50 a month per user (as of the date this was written) on an Office 365 Business Premium plan, your business will get Exchange Online, SharePoint Online, Skype for Business Online, Office Web Apps, and a Terabyte of online storage per user.

Best of all, you'll get premium antivirus and antispam security, 99.9 percent uptime guarantee, and 24/7 support from the Microsoft IT department.

In this chapter, you find out how to share the workload with other team members by delegating some administrative tasks, such as enabling access for external users and allowing site collection owners to configure and manage their sites. You explore the similarities and the difference of the roles and responsibilities between the SharePoint Online Administrator and the Site Collection Administrator.

In case you're ever in a SharePoint conference or gathering, we also include some basic information about SharePoint-speak like farms, tenancies, and multi tenancies. The intent is not to turn you into a SharePoint geek, but rather to make you a knowledgeable SharePoint technology user.

Appreciating the Concept of a SharePoint Farm

For the end user, the SharePoint Online experience centers around using the technology to collaborate effectively, secure and share information, upload and download files, track tasks, manage content, and other ways to stay connected with the team. Although you may not think much about what happens to create the SharePoint Online experience, a series of services and applications are running on multiple servers on the backend to give you just the right experience.

Servers are similar to desktop computers but with a lot more power. These powerful computers *serve* up requests from network users either privately or publicly through the Internet, hence the term "server." When SharePoint servers and SQL (a programming language used to communicate with databases) servers come together, they provide a set of services, such as serving up HTML so you can view formatted text on your browser (Web Server), or executing search queries (Query Server), or performing Microsoft Office integration, and much more!

In essence, the infrastructure responsible for your experience as the end user is supported by a collection of servers, each responsible for a set of tasks. That collection of servers is what makes up a SharePoint farm. Everything that happens in SharePoint is administered at the highest level in a SharePoint farm.

REMEMBER

Don't let SharePoint jargon deter you from exploring and using the great benefits this technology has to offer. At its core, SharePoint Online is what allows your organization to round up most — if not all — of your organization's data collection and storage efforts, business processes, collaboration activities, and much more in one web-based application. After you get past the confusion of how farms, tenants, and silos ended up in this technology's dictionary, you'll be on your way to a successful SharePoint co-existence.

Administering the SharePoint Farm and why you don't want to do it

SharePoint farm administration is not for the faint of heart. If you look at the list of typical SharePoint farm administration tasks, your eyes will probably glaze over. Don't fret though. In Office 365, Microsoft manages SharePoint farm-level administration. This is the value of having SharePoint Online as a service hosted in the cloud. In a sense, "putting up the farm" in SharePoint is a risk-free exercise.

The following list covers the SharePoint farm administration tasks:

» **Backup and recovery:** A backup is a copy of a set of data as insurance in case of system failure. You use a backup to restore and recover lost data. Recovery in SharePoint farms enables administrators to quickly restore the farm in the event of a disaster.

» **Database management:** This administration task includes adding, attaching or detaching, and moving content databases, moving a site collection between databases, and renaming or moving service application databases.

» **Security and permissions**: Your organization's SharePoint sites most likely will contain data that you don't want to be publicly available. To restrict access, security and permissions need to be configured. At the highest level, this configuration is done in a SharePoint farm.

» **Service application and service management**: When resources are shared across a SharePoint farm, service applications are deployed. Services that are deployed are named service applications. Service applications are tied to web applications by service application connections. Some services can be shared across farms.

» **Web application management**: In order to create a site collection, such as My Site, a web application must be created first. A web application isolates a site's content database from another. It also defines the authentication method for connecting to the database.

» **Health monitoring:** As with any IT systems, it is important to monitor how the SharePoint server system is running in order to determine issues, analyze problems, and repair those problems. The monitoring feature in SharePoint collects data in a log, which in turn is used to create health reports, web analytics reports, and administrative reports.

>> **Farm administration settings management**: Configuring and customizing the default SharePoint farm settings are part of the farm administration settings management tasks. In addition, these tasks include enabling some key features that are turned off at the initial installation, such as diagnostic logging, e-mail integration, and mobile account connections.

>> **Farm topology management:** At some point, a SharePoint farm will need to be updated to address current needs. Farm topology management tasks include adding or removing a web or application server, adding a database, renaming a server, and managing the search topology.

Multitenancy explained

In a multitenancy environment, a SharePoint farm is architected in such a way that it serves the needs of multiple client organizations. This means that the farm is sliced into subsets and deployed individually for clients and tenants who then manage their own tenancy. As a business owner, this model gives you the ability to run your business the way you want to and leave the IT-related tasks to Microsoft.

For example, as a tenant, you have full control to manage how your content, product, service, marketing collateral, and any other information that you want to manage on the Tenant Administration level (see Figure 8-1), are categorized or classified. In SharePoint-speak, this process defines your taxonomy. Defining your taxonomy upfront establishes naming standards to achieve consistency and content discoverability. After you enter your taxonomy in the Term Store, tagging content becomes easy and intuitive. For example, if you're tagging a content from a SharePoint site and you type in the letters *pro*, terms listed in your taxonomy starting with *pro* (for example, program, project, prospect, and so on) appear, giving you the ability to select the one that fits your needs. The great thing about this is that all the site collections under your tenancy can now consume company-approved, corporate-driven keywords from your taxonomy. This doesn't mean, however, that tagging is limited to the keywords in your taxonomy. Users can always add new tags, which the admin can then add to the Term Store, if appropriate.

In a multitenancy environment, each tenant is separated from all the other tenants with secure "walls" so that one tenant cannot access another tenant's assets. Therefore, if you do a keyword search from any of your site collections, the search results will only pull data from within your tenancy.

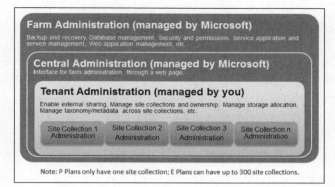

FIGURE 8-1: Breakdown of SharePoint Online Administration levels.

Delegating administration tasks

Delegated administration is pervasive throughout Office 365 and bodes really well for businesses knowing that their cloud solution is not hinged on one person. Can you imagine what it would be like if only one person had the power to grant access, enable features, and block users and then one day that person is somehow not available?

With Office 365 and SharePoint Online specifically, you can delegate administration up and down. By delegating administration and sharing the workload, you can empower the person who knows his business unit best to control who gets access, how much storage to have, and what custom solutions to install in his site collection.

At the top level, the Tenant Administration level, Office 365 enterprise plans offer the following roles in the Office 365 Administration Center:

>> **User:** This role doesn't provide any administrative access.

>> **Global Administrator:** This role is the top-level administrator for your company who has access to all the features in the administration center. Global administrators can assign other administrator roles, including granting someone a global administrator role.

>> **Customized Administrator:** This role allows you to create a customized administrative level so that roles can be divided among multiple people.

The Customized Administrator role can be refined to the following administrative roles:

>> **Billing Administrator:** This role is limited to making purchases, managing subscriptions, support tickets, and service health.

- **Exchange Administrator:** This role is designed to manage the Exchange email service for Office 365.

- **Password Administrator:** This role can reset passwords for users (but not other admins), manage service requests, and monitor service health.

- **Skype for Business Administrator:** This role is used to manage the Skype for Business service in Office 365.

- **Service Administrator:** This role is limited to managing service requests and monitoring service health.

- **SharePoint Administrator:** This role is used to manage the SharePoint service.

- **User Management Administrator:** This role can do everything password and service administrators are empowered to do plus the ability to manage user accounts and user groups. The exception is that this role cannot create or delete other administrators or reset passwords for billing, global, and service administrators.

From the Office 365 Administration Center, the Global Administrator can go down one more layer to the SharePoint Online Administration Center where further tasks can be delegated. The SharePoint Online Administration Center is where site collection administrators are assigned, who in turn can go down one more layer to assign site collection owners.

Understanding SharePoint Online Administrator Responsibilities

The SharePoint Online Administration Center is the hub of activities for the SharePoint Online Administrator, who may be the same person as the Global Administrator.

To get to the SharePoint Online Administration Center, click the SharePoint link in the Admin node on the lower left side of the Office 365 Administration Center.

As a SharePoint Online Administrator, you have control over site collections, InfoPath forms, user profiles, Business Connectivity Services (BCS), the Term Store, records management, search, secure store, apps, settings, and configuration for hybrid environments (see Figure 8-2).

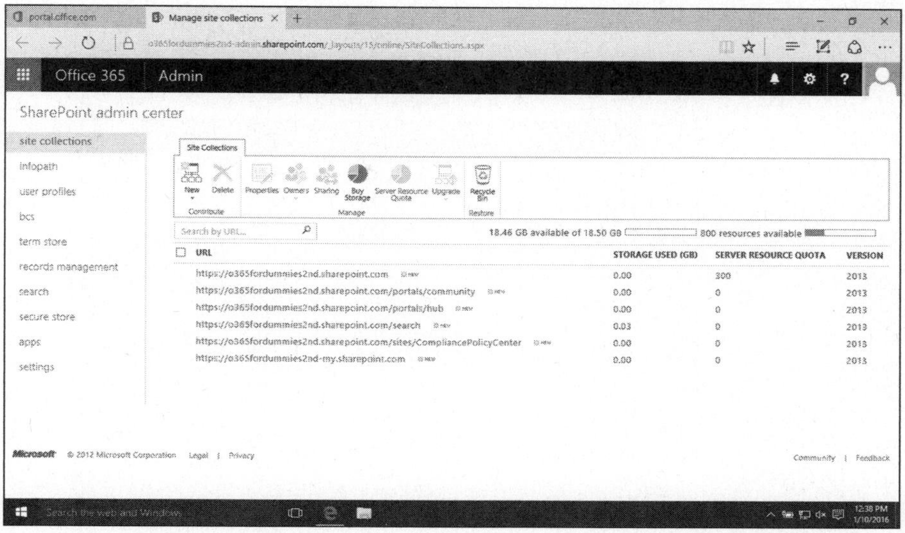

FIGURE 8-2:
SharePoint
Online
Administration
Center.

Turning on external sharing

If you anticipate that any of your site collections or business units that use Share-Point Online have a need for external sharing, the first step as a SharePoint Online Administrator is to turn on external sharing. By turning on this feature, users outside of your organization can be invited to SharePoint Online. This one-time action enables the site collection administrators to grant external access to their individual sites without going through the SharePoint Online administrator.

TIP

Enabling external sharing turns on the feature for all existing and future sites within the site collection for which you activate it. This does not, however, mean that all your SharePoint sites are now publicly accessible. The site collection admin-istrator has to grant someone outside of the company access to a SharePoint site.

To enable external sharing for a site collection, follow these steps:

1. **Click the SharePoint link in the Admin node in the Office 365 Administration Center.**

2. **Click Site Collections from the Administration Center window that displays.**

You see a list of all of the site collections in your Office 365 instance.

3. **Select the checkmark next to the site collection for which you want to enable sharing, then click the Sharing icon in the ribbon, as shown in Figure 8-3.**

The Sharing window appears.

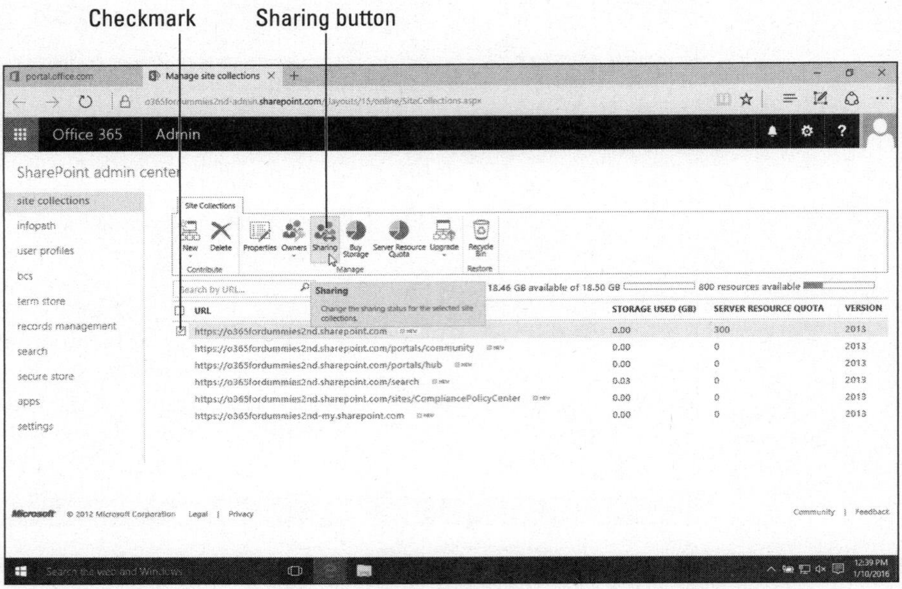

Checkmark   Sharing button

FIGURE 8-3:
FIGURE 8-3:
Selecting a site
collection and
then clicking the
Sharing button.

4. **Select one of the radio buttons to allow sharing to external users who accept sharing invitations and sign in or to allow sharing to all external users by using anonymous links.**

Creating a new site collection

A site collection contains a single top-level site and multiple subsites below it that share common navigation, template galleries, content types, web parts, and permissions.

To create a new site collection, follow these steps:

1. **Click the SharePoint link in the Admin node in the Office 365 Administration Center.**

   The SharePoint admin center screen appears.

2. **Click Site Collections in the Administration Center window.**

   You see a list of all of the site collections in your Office 365 instance.

3. **Click the New button in the ribbon and then select Private Site Collection.**

   The New Site Collection window appears.

4. **Enter the required information.**

5. **Click OK to go back to the SharePoint Online Administration Center dashboard.**

When you create a new site collection, you are prompted to enter a value for the Resource Usage Quota, as shown in Figure 8-4. The value you enter in the box represents resource points that measure the effectiveness of custom applications running inside your site collection. For example, say you uploaded a custom web part that does a lot of calculations and uses up a lot of computing power. Share-Point Online monitors how many resources your custom web part uses. The resource points that you assigned will authorize SharePoint Online to either leave it alone if it's performing within the quota, throttle it if the code is poorly written and starts to hog all the resources, and ultimately kill the web part or make the application stop running if it goes haywire and starts to cause problems. Fortunately, the killing only happens within the affected site collection and has no impact in other site collections within the tenancy.

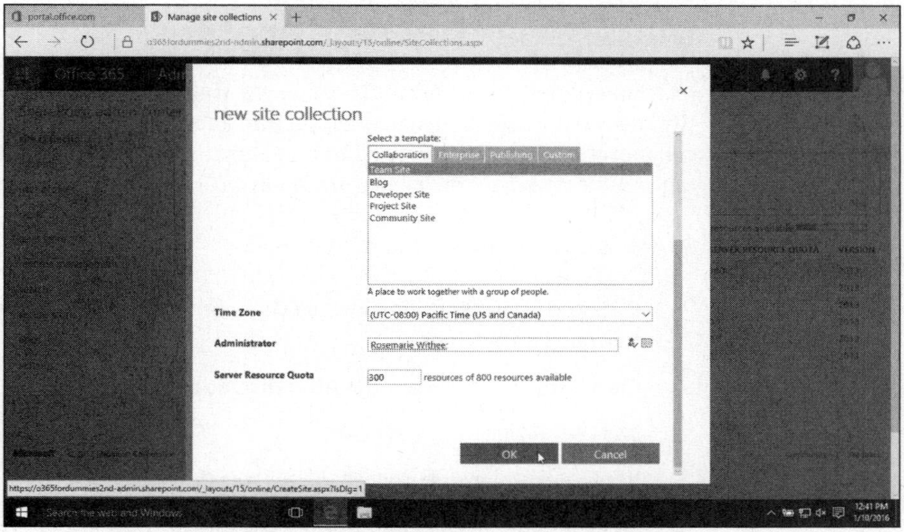

FIGURE 8-4:
Adding a
Resource
Usage Quota.

Assigning a new site collection owner to the new site collection

The idea behind delegated administration is to share power so that you, as the SharePoint Online Administrator, can be relieved of business-unit-specific tasks while at the same time, empowering members of your organization to make the call on tasks related to SharePoint for their business unit.

To assign one or more site collection administrators to your site, follow these steps:

1. **Click the SharePoint link in the Admin node in the Office 365 Administration Center.**

   The SharePoint admin center screen appears.

2. **Click Site Collections from the Administration Center window.**

   You see a list of all of the site collections in your Office 365 instance.

3. **Select the checkmark next to the site collection for which you want to assign administrators, then click the Owners drop-down in the ribbon and select Manage Administrators.**

4. **Enter the name or names of the site collection administrators.**

5. **Click OK to go back to the SharePoint Online Administration Center dashboard.**

Managing the user profiles

As a SharePoint Online Administrator, you may need to edit a user profile to identify the relationship between one user and another, to encourage or enhance social collaboration. Or you may need to edit a user's profile on behalf of someone having trouble updating his or her profile in Office 365.

To edit a user profile, do the following:

1. **Click the SharePoint link in the Admin node in the Office 365 Administration Center.**

2. **Click User Profiles from the Administration Center window that displays.**

   The User Profiles page appears.

3. **In the People group, click Manage User Profiles.**

4. **Enter a name in the Find profiles search box and click Find.**

5. **On the name you want to edit, hover the mouse pointer over to the right of the entry and click the down arrow to display additional commands.**

6. **Select Edit My Profile (see Figure 8-5).**

7. **Enter your edits in the page that displays and then click Save and Close to go back to the SharePoint Online Administration Center dashboard.**

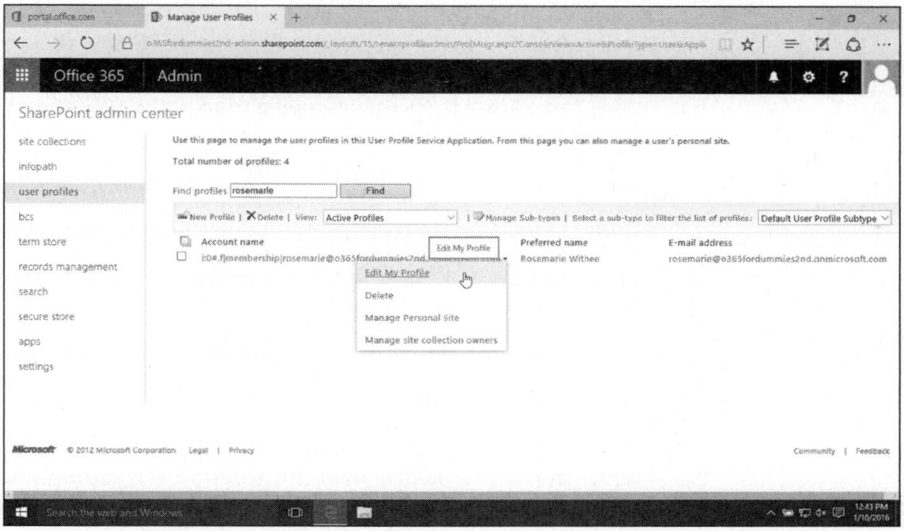

FIGURE 8-5:
Editing a
user profile.

Importing a new custom taxonomy into the Term Store

As a content management system, SharePoint Online provides great out-of-the-box metadata management capabilities through the Term Store. If your organization uses taxonomy to organize data, then you can simply use what you have by importing your custom taxonomy into the Term Store.

If you are a small business, using taxonomy to tag content could mean better governance of how things are described in your company, as well as help build the social fabric of your organization.

For example, say that you require SharePoint users to enter certain information about files they upload to the document library. They have to enter the title, author, business unit, audience, and subject for each file. You can leverage taxonomy so that when a user enters metadata in the Audience field, they can choose from keywords already in the Term Store, such as Internal or External. If the user selects Internal, additional options display to choose from, depending on whether the internal audience is for executives or managers. Under Subject, users can select from keywords, such as HR, Legal, or IT. You can also allow users to enter their own keywords to describe the subject. As you see a pattern emerging of frequently used keywords, it may signal you, as the SharePoint Online Administrator, to move those keywords into the main term set. Not only that, but it may prompt your organization to start thinking about creating a new name for a product according to what words best describe it to your people and what those words mean to them.

To import a custom taxonomy to the Term Store, follow these steps:

1. **Click Term Store from the left navigation in the SharePoint Online Administration Center.**

   Make sure that your name is listed under Term Store Administrators.

2. **Under Sample Import on the right pane, click View a sample import file.**

3. **Download the comma-separated values (.csv) file and make edits to it in Excel to fit your taxonomy.**

4. **In Excel, arrange the terms in hierarchies up to seven levels deep.**

5. **Save the file in its original .csv format.**

6. **Back at the Term Store from the SharePoint Online Administration Center, hover the mouse pointer over the group where you want to load the term set and then click on the arrow that appears on the right (see Figure 8-6) to display additional commands.**

TIP

If you don't see the arrow when you hover the mouse pointer over the group, make sure you've added yourself as a Term Store Administrator and saved the setting.

7. **Select Import New Term Set.**

8. **From the Term set import window, click Browse.**

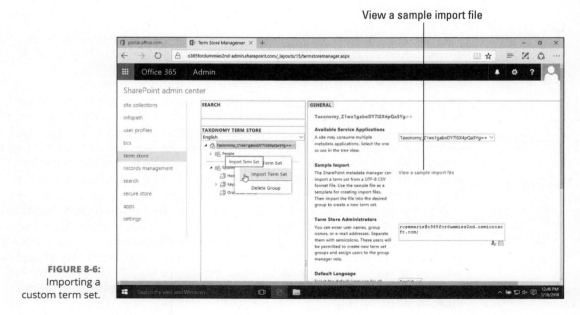

FIGURE 8-6: Importing a custom term set.

9. **Navigate to the .csv file you saved in Step 5, select the file, and then click Open.**

   You are taken back to the Term set import window.

10. **Click OK.**

    You are taken back to the SharePoint Online Administration Center portal where you'll see the term set you just imported listed under the group you selected in Step 6.

Exercising the Powers Vested on the Site Collection Administrator

As a Site Collection Administrator, you have the highest level of permissions in your site collection that allows you to perform tasks that may have routed to your IT team in the past. You also have the power to enable or disable features that are used in subsites within your site collection. Moreover, you have access to all the subsites regardless of whether you've been added as user to the site.

Sharing your site externally

When the SharePoint Online Administrator enables external sharing from the SharePoint Online Administration Center, this does not mean that all site collections are automatically shared externally. You, as a Site Collection Administrator, also need to share the site.

To share the site, click the Share button in the upper right of any site. Once the Share dialog appears you can share the site with others by entering their email address.

If the external users you invite to your site already have an Office 365 account, they can log in by using that account. If not, they will be asked to log in with a Microsoft account. Also, you can share the site with anonymous users using a special link, if the SharePoint Administrator for Office 365 has allowed it for the site collection.

Creating a new team subsite and/or new document libraries

A subsite is merely a SharePoint site under a site collection. It uses the same navigation as the top-level site and has the capability of using all the site collection features that have been activated at the site collection level. Sometimes, it is referred to as the child site, whereas the top-level site is called the parent site.

To create a subsite, follow these steps:

1. **Go to Site Actions (gear icon) ⇨ Site Contents.**

   The site contents page appears.

2. **Scroll down to the bottom of the page and click the New Subsite link under the Subsites section.**

3. **Enter the title of your site in the Title box and enter the URL for your site in the box below if you want a URL different from the title and then select a template.**

4. **Complete the rest of the settings as needed and then click Create.**

   After the request is processed, you are taken to your new site.

About content and content types

One of the many cool features SharePoint Online offers is the ability for users to not only upload documents but also to create a new Word document right from the document library by clicking Documents from the Library Tools on the Ribbon and then clicking New. This action opens a new blank document in Microsoft Word that will be saved online after you give it a filename.

What most new SharePoint users don't know is that you can actually "upload" a link to a document in another library or create new Microsoft Office documents other than Word. In the case of the former, this eliminates duplicate documents that could become a nightmare to sync. For the latter, it streamlines creation of form-based documents.

Uploading a link instead of a file is made possible by SharePoint content and content types features. Think of content as the Word document you uploaded or the new file you created from the document library. The way you defined the settings for your documents is the content type. The geek way of defining content type according to Microsoft TechNet is covered in the next two sections describing scenarios that you're likely to encounter.

Keeping one version of a document in multiple sites

You manage two separate SharePoint sites and you have a document you want to share between the two sites. If you create two documents to upload one for each site, you have to update two documents when something changes. To avoid the extra work, you can upload one document in one site, and "upload" a link to the document in the other site. To do so, follow these steps:

1. In the document library where you want to add the link to, click the Library tab from the Library Tools menu on the Ribbon.

2. Click Library Settings on the Ribbon.

3. Under General Settings, click Advanced Settings.

4. Under Allow Management of content types, select Yes. Scroll down and click OK.

5. Under Content Types you see that Document is already listed as the default content type.

6. Click the Add from existing site content types link below the Document content type.

7. On the Add Content Types page, select Link to a Document below the Available Site Content Types: box.

8. Click the Add button in the middle to add the selected content type into the Content types to add: box on the right.

9. Click OK.

   You are taken back to the Document Library Settings page.

Now that you've added Links as a content type, let's see it in action. Exit out of the library settings view and go back to your document library. To do so, follow these steps:

1. Click the Document tab from the Library Tools menu on the Ribbon.

2. Click the New Document icon to display the available content types. Select Link to a Document.

3. On the New link to a document window that appears, enter the document name and the URL.

4. Click OK.

   You are taken back to your document library.

Viola! Now you can see the link listed as if it were a real document in the library. When you update the original file, the link will always open the latest version of the file it's linked to.

Adding an Excel template in the content type

You want to be able to create not just Word documents from your library but also Excel files. The Excel file you want to use when you create new Excel files is a form template for an invoice that you created. To achieve this, first you need to add your invoice template as a new content type in the site collection. The second step is to then add this new content type to your document library following Steps 1 through 9 in the preceding section, but replacing Link to a Document with the new Excel form template.

To add your invoice template as a new content type in the site collection, follow these steps:

1. **At the parent site, go to Site Actions (gear icon) ⇨ Site Settings.**

2. **Under Web Designer Galleries, click Site content types and click Create.**

3. **Give it a name (Invoice Template), enter a description if needed, and select Document Content Type under Select parent content type from.**

4. **Select Document under Parent Content Type and choose from one of the existing groups or create a new group for your new content type and then click OK.**

5. **Click Advanced under Settings, select Upload a new document template, browse for your template, and then click OK.**

Your new template now displays as an option when you create new documents at your document library.

Managing the look and feel

Sometimes the default look and feel of the site may not suit your needs for one reason or another. You can easily customize your site with out-of-the box features that do not require coding. You can edit the title, description, and icon for your site, give it a new theme, reorder the left navigation, and customize the top link bar (or the horizontal navigation). Go to Site Actions (gear icon) ⇨ Site Settings. The commands are available under Look and Feel.

Managing the web designer galleries

As a site collection administrator, you have the ability to manage the web designer galleries in your site collection. These galleries include site columns, site content types, web parts, list templates, master pages, themes, solutions, and composed looks. You access the web designer galleries by going to Site Actions (gear icon) ⇨ Site Settings.

As with content types, you can create a new site column to represent an attribute or metadata for a list item or content type. When created, the site column can be reused in multiple lists, in multiple sites within the site collection.

One of the handy links in the Web Designer Galleries group is List templates. When you see a SharePoint list that you like and may want to reuse, save the list as a template and then add that template in the gallery. After the template is added, an icon for the list will be displayed as one of the options when you create a new list.

To save an existing list as a template and add to the gallery, follow these steps:

1. **Go to an existing list.**

2. **Click the List tab and click List Settings.**

3. **Under the Permissions and Management group, click the Save list as template link.**

4. **In the Save as Template page, enter the file name, template name, and description.**

   If you want to include the content of the existing list in the template, check the Include Content box. Note that the more data you have in your template, the bigger the file size will be and may cause issues loading the template. We recommend leaving this option unchecked.

5. **Click OK.**

   When the saving process is complete, a notification will be displayed confirming successful completion of the operation.

6. **Click OK.**

   You are taken back to the List Settings page.

When you go to Site Settings (gear icon) ⇨ Add an app, you will see the new template you added as an option.

If for some reason you do not like the master page template that's applied to your SharePoint site, you may need to hire a designer to create a new master page. You then load the new master page into the Master Page Gallery as if it were a document in a document library.

Web parts, themes, solutions, and composed looks require technical know-how to create but after you have them, you can easily add them to the Gallery as if they were list or document items.

Managing permissions and groups

To maintain security and integrity of your site, assign the right level of permission or privilege to the users of your site. As a best practice, create a SharePoint group first, assign a permission level to the group, and then start adding users to the appropriate groups.

An example of a SharePoint group could be the "Executive" group with Contribute access where all your C-level executives are members. Another example is a "Site Owners" group with Full Control privileges, comprised of a few members of your team who are technically advanced.

Grouping your users with similar access needs minimizes the administrative burden of individually adding or removing users from sites, libraries, and lists. Doing this allows you to use those groups in workflows, such as assigning tasks to a group rather than an individual.

In SharePoint, you can assign permissions on the site collection level and have those permissions be inherited or not inherited on the subsite level. You can also further customize the permission on document libraries or lists so even if users may have access to the site, they may or may not have access to certain contents within the site. You can take it even farther down to the granular level by customizing the permission for items in a list or contents in a library so that even though a group may have access to a document library, only certain individuals have access to certain files:

>> To manage your site's permissions, go to Site Actions (gear icon) ⇨ Site Settings and then follow the links under User and Permissions.

>> To manage permissions on a list, library, or item, look for the Share or Shared With buttons. When you share, you can choose to either allow only view permissions or also allow edit permissions.

IN THIS CHAPTER

Using your web browser to develop SharePoint solutions

Understanding how to develop sites

Developing your knowledge of lists, libraries, pages, and apps

Discovering how SharePoint apps work

Chapter 9

Understanding SharePoint Online Development

After you get the hang of SharePoint, you may want to dive deeper into the technology. SharePoint is a web-based product (meaning that you use it with your web browser). Being a user of SharePoint is just the beginning, however. You can develop real-world business apps by using nothing more than your web browser. You don't need to be a programmer and you don't even need to be very technical. You just need some time to find out how to drag and drop components and enter content.

In this chapter, you walk through SharePoint development by using your web browser. You find out about key SharePoint development concepts, such as sites, lists, libraries, pages, and apps.

Going Over SharePoint Development

SharePoint development doesn't mean you need to be a programmer or have any understanding of programming. If you can tweak your Facebook page or update your LinkedIn profile, then you can be a SharePoint developer. SharePoint development begins with nothing more than your web browser.

When you use your web browser to develop new functionality or customize existing functionality, the result is called an *app.* For example, let's say you create a blank SharePoint list, then add some columns and workflow behavior to it and name it an expense manager. You have just created your very own SharePoint app called Expense Manager. Of course, this is a very simple example. Apps can get incredibly complicated. But the idea is the same, regardless of how complex your apps become.

TIP

When you customize a SharePoint list or library, you're creating your very own SharePoint app. Apps are covered in detail later in the chapter.

Using a Web Browser as a Development Tool

To a user, browsing a SharePoint site looks like a regular website — with some fancy SharePoint capabilities. Those SharePoint capabilities enable easy collaboration, access to business information, and a boost to business intelligence, all through the Web. In SharePoint terms, a site is a container for SharePoint pages. This entire ball of functionality, also called a *platform* (because you can build on it), is the Microsoft product called SharePoint. One of the things that makes SharePoint so exciting is that you don't even have to drop out of your web browser to tell SharePoint what to do. As long as you have access to SharePoint and a current browser, you're ready to start developing a site.

When you're first starting out with SharePoint development, you need a site that you can use to practice. When you create a new site you start by choosing a *template site* that already has some stuff built into it — such as lists, libraries, and web parts (also known as apps) developed and configured to do particular tasks. Those templates are available on the Create screen when you create a new site. For example, you may get a request to create a Document Center site in order to manage documents from a central location. Rather than try to configure a Team Site to be optimized for document management, you can use a template specifically designed for this task. In this scenario, the template site you would use is called the Document Center and is shown in Figure 9-1.

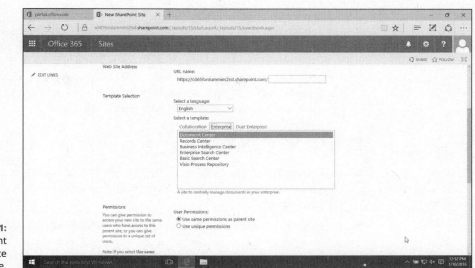

FIGURE 9-1:
The Document
Center site
template.

Developing SharePoint sites

When you need to develop a SharePoint site to solve a problem, be sure that you start with a solid understanding of the available site templates. It's often much easier to start with a site template that almost does what you want and then develop it from this starting point than to develop everything from scratch.

TIP

Before you start building custom applications for SharePoint, having a solid working knowledge of its various components is a good idea. (After all, you wouldn't try to design a house without having some knowledge of how the plumbing works, right?) The best way to get to know SharePoint is to start with a basic Team Site, then further develop it so you understand what the templates are doing. Then you can expand to explore other templates as you build your SharePoint knowledge.

Creating a new site is as simple as clicking Site Actions (gear icon)⇨Site Contents from the parent site and then scrolling down to the bottom of the page and clicking New Subsite. On the New Subsite page, you provide a title and a URL, and select a template (in addition to some other configuration options). The template you choose determines how your new site will be preconfigured. A parent site is simply a site that holds another site.

Site templates are included in SharePoint Online:

- ≫ Some templates are used only for creating a Site Collection (a container for subsites).
- ≫ Some templates are used only for creating subsites.
- ≫ Some templates can be used for both.

REMEMBER

A site collection is a special SharePoint site that allows you to separate key aspects of the sites contained within the site collection. For example, you turn on features at the site collection level, which makes those features available to all sites within the site collection. On a technical level, SharePoint separates site collections by using different databases. This allows for separation of security and users, because two different site collections use two different databases.

Templates for subsites only:

>> **Publishing Site:** A site used to publish content. The site template is used for subsites that need the publishing functionality provided by the Publishing Portal template.

>> **Publishing Site with Workflow:** A site for publishing web pages on a schedule by using approval workflows. It includes document and image libraries for storing web-publishing assets.

>> **SAP Workflow Site:** A site designed to work with SAP that aggregates all business tasks for users.

Templates for site collections only:

>> **Community Portal:** A site that can be used to contain community sites. In other words, an aggregation of communities.

>> **Community Site:** A site where members of the community can come together to discuss topics and interact with each other.

>> **Compliance Policy Center:** Contains policies that are used to manage when documents can be deleted after a certain period of time.

>> **Developer Site:** A site where developers can create, publish, and test apps designed for Microsoft Office.

>> **eDiscovery Center:** A site designed for legal matters and investigations where the preservation and search ability of content is critical. The site is also designed for exporting of content for legal compliance.

>> **My Site Host:** Used to host the personal sites functionality of SharePoint, also known as OneDrive for Business, as well as the personal profile pages of users.

>> **Publishing Portal:** This template offers a starter site hierarchy (grouping of SharePoint sites) for an Internet site or a large intranet portal. You can use distinctive branding to customize this site. It includes a home page, a sample press-releases site, a Search Center, and a logon page. Typically, this site has many more readers than contributors; it's used to publish the Web pages by using a process for approving new content known as an approval workflow.

By default, this site enables content-approval workflows to provide more control over the publishing process. It also restricts the rights of anonymous users: They can see content pages but not application pages.

>> **Team Site – SharePoint Online configuration:** A Team Site that is preconfigured to allow users to share content with external users.

Templates for both subsites and site collections:

>> **Basic Search Center:** This site provides SharePoint search functionality, including pages for search results and advanced searches.

>> **Blog:** This site works like an Internet blog; a person or team can post ideas, observations, and expertise that site visitors can comment on.

>> **Business Intelligence Center:** A site that can be used to present content focused on business intelligence.

>> **Community Site:** A site where members of the community can come together to discuss topics and interact with each other.

>> **Document Center:** You can manage documents centrally for your entire enterprise from this site.

>> **Enterprise Search Center:** This site provides the SharePoint search capability. The Welcome Page includes a search box that has two tabs: one for general searches and another for searches for information about people. You can add tabs, delete them, or customize them with different search scopes or specified result types.

>> **Enterprise Wiki:** You can use this site for publishing knowledge that you capture and want to share across the enterprise. Use this site to edit, coauthor, and discuss content, as well as to manage projects.

>> **Project Site:** A site used for managing, discussing, and collaborating on a project.

>> **Records Center:** A site for managing digital records. The site is optimized to handle the routing of documents and determine whether documents can be deleted or modified or must be retained with their original content.

>> **Team Site:** A site on which a team can organize, generate, and share information. It provides a document library as well as lists for managing announcements, calendar items, tasks, and discussions.

>> **Visio Process Repository:** A collaborative site on which teams can view, share, and store Visio process diagrams. It provides a document library (with version control) for storing process diagrams as well as lists for managing announcements, tasks, and review discussions.

Microsoft is constantly updating SharePoint Online with new features and removing old features. If you see a template not listed here, then Microsoft might have recently added it. Similarly, if you see a template here that you can't find then Microsoft might have removed it.

When you create a new Site Collection, you can also choose the Custom grouping that allows you to choose a template for the new site collection later after you have already created it.

Adding apps (lists and libraries) and pages

In order to develop a SharePoint site (using your browser no less!), you need to understand some of the key components. In particular, these include list apps, library apps, and pages.

When you have an idea of the type of app you want to add, you can add it by clicking Site Actions (gear icon)➪Add an app, as shown in Figure 9-2. You will then see all of the list and library app templates described shortly.

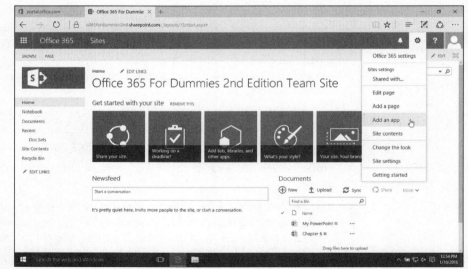

FIGURE 9-2:
Opening the Your Apps page to add a new app to a SharePoint site.

Knowing your list app options

SharePoint Online comes with a collection of standard lists and libraries. Microsoft has already taken the time to develop these in order to make your life as a developer easier, so you may as well use them. The following list introduces the standard SharePoint list apps and provides brief descriptions:

>> **Access App:** This app is used to create browser based Access database applications. If you're familiar with Microsoft Access then you will feel right at home using this web-based SharePoint app.

>> **Announcements:** This app is for brief news items, quick status checks, and other quick, informative stuff.

>> **Calendar:** This calendar is strictly business — deadlines, meetings, scheduled events, and the like. You can synchronize the information on this calendar with Microsoft Outlook or other Microsoft-friendly programs.

>> **Contacts:** If you're a regular Outlook user, you may have developed a list of contacts. If you haven't, here's your chance to list the people relevant to your team (such as partners, customers, or public officials). You can synchronize the SharePoint Contacts app with Microsoft Outlook or other programs that play nice with Microsoft products.

>> **Custom List:** If you're trying to develop a list app but none of the standard list app types does what you have in mind, you can start from scratch with a blank list and drop in the views and columns you want.

>> **Custom List in Data Sheet View:** Here's a familiar twist on the blank list app: SharePoint shows it as a spreadsheet, so you can set up a custom list app as easily as you would in Excel, specifying views and columns as needed. Note that this list type requires an ActiveX control for list datasheets; fortunately, Microsoft Office provides such a control. (Coincidence? I think not.)

>> **Discussion Board:** If you're a seasoned netizen from the heyday of the newsgroup, this list app will be a familiar place for online discussions. Naturally, you want to keep the discussion businesslike, so this list app type helps you manage those discussions (for example, you can require posts to be approved before everybody can see them).

>> **External List:** Use this list app type to create a list of data identified as an External Content Type. An External Content Type is a term used to describe groupings of data that live outside of SharePoint. An example might be data that lives in a backend system, such as SAP.

>> **Import Spreadsheet:** If you have data contained in an existing spreadsheet (created in Excel or another Microsoft-compatible program) that you want to use in SharePoint, you can import it into a list app of this type. You get the same columns and data as the original spreadsheet.

>> **Issue Tracking:** If you want to organize your project team's responses to a problem associated with (say) an important project, this is the type of list app you use to set priorities, assign tasks, and keep track of progress toward resolving the issue.

>> **Links:** This list app type helps you organize links. The user can consult a list of web pages and similar online resources — and simply click to go to any of them.

- » **Promoted Links:** You can use this list app type to create a list of items using visual buttons instead of boring old text.

- » **Survey:** This list app type is for gathering information, specifically by crowd-sourcing. Here's where you put a list of questions you want people to answer. A survey list app helps you formulate your questions and can summarize the responses you get back. The responses to the survey are stored in the list and can then be analyzed, charted, or exported.

- » **Tasks:** This list app type is essentially a to-do list for a team or individual.

Checking out the available library apps

When you need a way to organize files so that they're accessible via a SharePoint site, you find a selection prebuilt for the most common types of library apps in SharePoint Online. Take a gander at these standard library apps and the brief descriptions of what they do:

- » **Asset Library:** Here's where you store information assets other than documents — ready-to-use information in the form of images, audio files, video files — to make them available and regulate their usage.

- » **Data Connection Library:** This library app type is where you can put and share files that specify and describe external data connections. For example, you might want your users to be able to pull data from a data warehouse. Setting up a connection to the data warehouse and getting all the server names, usernames, and connection information just right can be tedious. Using a Data Connection Library app, an administrator could set up the connections and store them in the library. The users would then just use the connection to the data warehouse whenever they want to pull data and analyze it.

- » **Document Library:** You run across — and create — a lot of these in SharePoint. Such library apps are for storing documents, organizing them in folders, controlling their versions, and regulating their usage with a check-in/check-out system.

- » **Form Library:** Here's where you store and manage electronic versions of blank business forms for everyday documentation, such as purchase orders and status reports. To create and maintain library apps of this type, you need a compatible XML editor. Keep in mind, however, that the form library app is just a place to store the data that has been entered into the form. To build the actual form, you need the XML compliant form editor.

- » **Picture Library:** This library app type is for storing and sharing digital images. The difference between the Assets Library and the Picture Library can be subtle because they both store images. The key distinction lies in the name. The Picture Library is designed specifically to store pictures, and the asset library is used to store images. If you think of a picture as a photo and an image as something like a logo or graphic, the differences start to emerge. For example, the pictures in a Picture Library app show a thumbnail image when they show up in searches, but the images in an image library do not.

» **Record Library:** You store business records in this library app. When you create a Record Library app, you're adding some functionality that allows SharePoint to create record management and retention schedules. This type of functionality is important when you want to make sure that you are doing your due diligence in keeping track of your business records by letting SharePoint do the heavy lifting.

» **Report Document Library:** This library app type is used to store and manage report documents. This library app is similar to the Report Library; however, there are some differences. Explore the Report Document Library and the Report Library apps to see which one you like better and which one best fits your reporting needs.

» **Report Library:** This library app type is dedicated to web pages and documents that keep track of performance (and other such metrics), progress toward business goals, and other information used in business intelligence.

» **Site Mailbox:** This library app type is useful to keep email and your documents closely connected because this app connects your site to an Exchange mailbox. Once connected, you can view your email in SharePoint and view your documents in Outlook.

» **Wiki Page Library:** Library apps of this type have interconnected web pages containing content, such as text or images and functionality in the form of Web Parts that multiple users can edit easily.

Paging through the available pages

You can create and develop three primary types of SharePoint pages (in your browser, no less!) — each with a distinct function:

» **Content page:** Also known as a *wiki page*, this is the Swiss Army knife of SharePoint pages. A content page provides not only a place to put content but also a kind of workshop for collaboration, development, and customization — multiple users can wield a full-featured text editor built right into the browser. A content page is easy to develop and is an extremely powerful and intuitive tool for collaborative authoring, data capture, and documentation. For example, if you're in the business of manufacturing consumer products, then you might have a content page that allows customer service reps to capture common questions that users have regarding your products. The page could be dynamically updated as the reps encounter new questions without the need to call in a programmer.

>> **Web Part page:** This type of SharePoint page provides Web Part zones where you can drag and drop various Web Parts (reusable pieces of functionality) right onto your pages from the SharePoint Web Part gallery. Although a set of Web Parts comes standard with SharePoint, you can also custom develop Web Parts to meet your specific business needs. Imagine developing a Web Part for your company that ventures forth to become an everyday tool for nearly all the users in your organization — on their own sites — and to get the tool, all they have to do is simply drag and drop the Web Part right onto their pages. For example, you may have Web Parts that you have developed for your call center reps. When new Web Part pages are developed, the Web Parts that are used by the call center can be added to the page. This lets a programmer package up web functionality into a reusable component (Web Part) that can be reused on multiple pages.

>> **Publishing page:** This type of SharePoint page is designed to serve two functions: managing content and managing the look and feel of the page. A publishing page lives in a document library that provides version control and the SharePoint workflow feature. It's designed for the management and distribution of content — the essence of publishing content to SharePoint.

TIP

For more information on developing in the SharePoint environment, check out the still relevant *SharePoint 2010 Development For Dummies* by Ken Withee. The book was written for SharePoint 2010, but the development concepts still are relevant.

Figuring Out SharePoint Apps

As you have explored throughout the chapter, there are many different types of SharePoint list apps and library apps. Developing a new app is as simple as choosing one of these app templates, giving it a name, and customizing it to meet your specific needs.

Don't be confused by the term SharePoint app. In past versions of SharePoint, these were just called lists and libraries. In the future, they might be called add-ins. Microsoft is continually refining the terminology around SharePoint functionality, but the concept doesn't change. A SharePoint list, library, app, or add-in is a self-contained component of SharePoint that you can customize to fit your specific business needs.

4

Diving into Office Online

Harness the power of Office with nothing more than your web browser.

Gain fundamental knowledge about what an online app is and how it differs from the desktop version of Office.

Dive into each component individually by looking at Word Online, Excel Online, PowerPoint Online, and OneNote Online.

Chapter 10

Introducing Office Online

Office Online (formerly Office Web Apps) is the cloud version of Microsoft Word, Excel, PowerPoint, and OneNote. The apps allow users to create high-quality documents, simultaneously make changes to the documents with coauthors, share these documents from a browser without the need for the desktop application, and more. With Office Online, you're no longer tethered to your office desk to be productive. As long as you have an internet connection, you can use any of the popular browsers from most common devices to access your documents, and even quickly pick up from where you left off in your last session.

You don't have to give up beauty when you create documents on Office Online — your visual-rich documents look identical to documents created with the Office desktop application. Formatting styles, graphs, charts, and data are retained when you open and share documents from Office Online. Flat, boring documents have no place in Office Online.

In this chapter, we'll show you the experience of using Office Online with several cloud storage services. We'll also touch on recently added features and functions to enhance your productivity.

Experiencing Office Online

Office Online as a cloud service is a browser-based productivity solution that includes the core Office apps: Word, Excel, PowerPoint, and OneNote. It's a free service, but it requires a cloud storage account for storing documents.

There are several options for cloud storage that integrate with Office Online:

>> OneDrive for Business and/or SharePoint Online through an Office 365 for business subscription

>> OneDrive.com consumer version through an Office 365 Home subscription or with the free Microsoft account (live.com, Hotmail, or outlook.com)

>> Dropbox

The Office 365 for Business experience

Office Online is included in all Office 365 for Business subscriptions. Whether in OneDrive for Business or in a SharePoint document library, opening a Word, Excel, PowerPoint, or OneNote document will start Office Online from the browser in reading view by default.

Storing documents created from Office Online in SharePoint is subject to the storage boundaries and limits for SharePoint. In OneDrive, each user has up to 1 TB of cloud storage.

To get the latest information on storage allocation in SharePoint Online, search for "SharePoint boundaries and limits" through this link:

```
https://support.office.com
```

When you open a document in Office Online, the browser will render your document exactly as you would expect to see from the desktop application (compare Figure 10-1 and Figure 10-2). You will notice, however, that there are fewer ribbon commands in the online version than the desktop version.

OneDrive.com experience

With either a Hotmail, outlook.com, or a live.com account, you can have up to 5 GB of free OneDrive cloud storage. If that isn't enough, you can upgrade the free account to 50 GB for $1.99/month.

In the Office 365 Home subscription, you can have 1 TB of cloud storage for one user for $6.99/month on the Personal plan. On the Home plan, you can have 1 TB of cloud storage per user for up to five users for $9.99/month.

There is a slight difference in the Office Online apps that display when you click on the app launcher in Office 365 and OneDrive.com (see Figure 10-3) because the Office 365 version is geared for the work environment; the OneDrive.com version is geared for personal use.

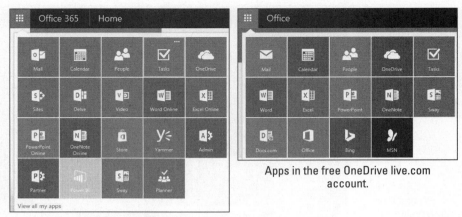

FIGURE 10-3:
Office Online
apps in Office 365
E3 plan vs.
OneDrive.com.

Apps in Office 365 E3 plan.

Apps in the free OneDrive live.com account.

Opening an Office document from OneDrive is pretty much the same as in Share-Point Online or OneDrive for Business. The high-fidelity rendering of the document in the browser is as expected. There is, however, one bonus in the OneDrive. com experience: a Skype button on the top navigation. It allows you to quickly connect with your Skype contacts (see Figure 10-4). As of the time of publication, this feature doesn't appear in the Office 365 business subscriptions; an enterprise version of that button may be available when you read this.

FIGURE 10-4:
PowerPoint
Online from
OneDrive.com.

Dropbox experience

Integrating Office Online with Dropbox is pretty straightforward. There are a few steps to complete when you integrate the two technologies for the first time, but nothing complicated. Here's how to view or edit a document in Dropbox with Office Online:

1. **Log in to your Dropbox.com account.**

2. **Click an Office document (Word, Excel, PowerPoint, or OneNote).**

   When the document opens with the Dropbox native app, you might notice some formatting issues (see Figure 10-5).

3. **Click the ellipses on the top right, then select Microsoft PowerPoint Online (refer to Figure 10-5).**

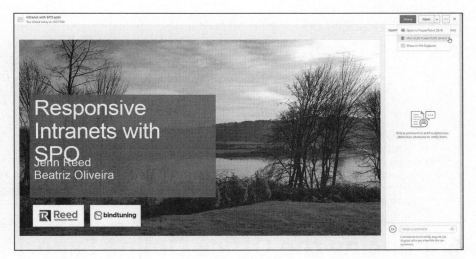

FIGURE 10-5: Office document with formatting issues in Dropbox.

4. **If you've never integrated Dropbox with Office Online before, simply follow prompts to allow Microsoft Office Online to access your Dropbox documents. Click Allow (see Figure 10-6).**

   Your document will now open in full fidelity in PowerPoint Online similar to SharePoint Online or OneDrive. Notice that the formatting issue now is gone in Figure 10-7.

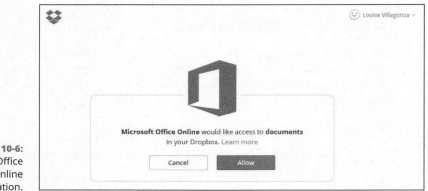

FIGURE 10-6:
Dropbox/Office
Online
integration.

FIGURE 10-7:
Full fidelity
document in
Dropbox with
PowerPoint
Online.

Enhancing the Office Online Experience

The advantage of Software-as-a-Service solutions (SaaS), such as Office 365, is that SaaS vendors can roll out enhancements and updates in shorter cycles and require minimal actions from the end user. If you visit the Office 365 Roadmap page (see `http://fasttrack.microsoft.com/roadmap`), you'll notice a number of features and updates in development to the service. When Microsoft launches these items, they may just show up in the service or application without the user installing anything. So don't be surprised if you're using Office Online one day and come back the next day to find new features to help you get the job done.

The subsequent chapters in this part of the book dive deeper into the functionalities of each of the core Offline Online apps. We think you might be interested to know about new features recently rolled out in Word Online.

Smart Lookup makes you smart

In the consumer version of Office Online, there's a really cool feature that allows you to look up information from Bing, Wikipedia, the *Oxford English Dictionary,* and the web itself, without leaving the screen or page you're on.

Let's say, for example, you're writing a blog in Word Online that mentions Paul Revere. You want to look up more information about Revere, or even embed a likeness of him. Unlike in the past, you won't have to leave the current screen to open a new window or application to look up that information.

With the *Smart Lookup* (also known as *Insights)* in World Online, you can simply select the word or phrase while in Editing View, right-click the selection, and then select Smart Lookup. You will then see on the right pane more information about the word or phrase (see Figure 10-8). Isn't that smart?

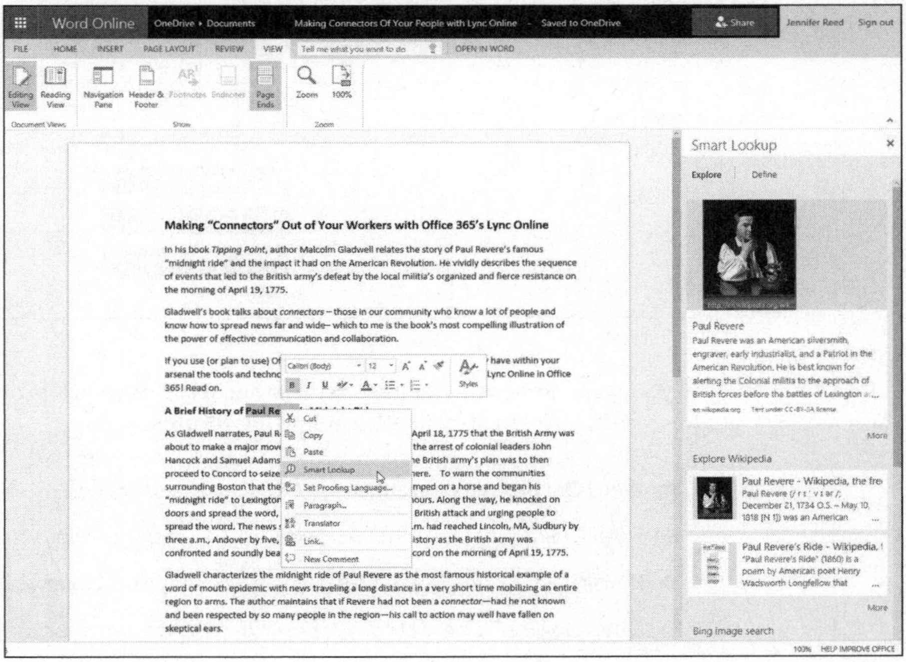

FIGURE 10-8:
Smart Lookup in
Word Online.

TIP

This feature isn't available in Office Online when you're using Office 365 for business yet. It is, however, available when you're using the Office Pro Plus desktop application.

Getting your voice heard

Microsoft is eager to get your feedback on Office Online and other services. If you would like to help improve Office, there are many ways to make your voice heard.

In Office Online, at the bottom right of the screen, you will see a link that says HELP IMPROVE OFFICE. Clicking on that link will open a quick feedback form, which you can then submit (see Figure 10-9).

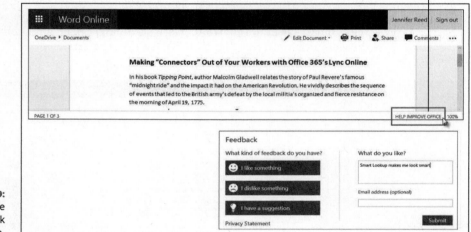

FIGURE 10-9:
Help Improve
Office feedback
form.

If you want to actively engage with other users who are providing feedback to Microsoft, you can also visit the following forums:

>> Word Online UserVoice: https://word.uservoice.com

>> Excel Online UserVoice: https://excel.uservoice.com

>> PowerPoint Online UserVoice: https://powerpoint.uservoice.com

>> OneNote UserVoice: https://onenote.uservoice.com

IN THIS CHAPTER

Finding out how Word Online differs from the regular Word

Wrapping your head around some of the basic features of Word Online

Exploring some of the advanced features of Word Online, such as styles and tables

Chapter 11

Getting into Word Online

With the release of Office 365, an updated version of Word is available that runs as a web application in your web browser. This development may not sound very spectacular, but it has some nifty benefits that we explore in this chapter.

In this chapter, we explore some of the basic concepts of Word Online, such as using the web interface to create, read, edit, and delete documents. We also look at some of the advanced features of Word Online, including working with styles and tables.

Comparing Word Online and Word

Unless you have been living under a rock, you have probably used or heard of a program called Microsoft Word. Word is an aptly named word processing application. In fact, I am writing this text with Word (and looking out at the Seattle sunshine this afternoon). Word is a *thick client*, meaning that you run it from your local computer. In Windows 10, you click Start and then All Apps and you click Word to fire up the program. Word then runs on your computer. A web-based application, on the other hand, runs on a computer in a data center, and you access it over the Internet. If you use Outlook.com or Gmail for email or browse a web page, then you are using a web application. You access a web application by using a web browser, which is a program installed on your computer.

Although Word Online is still Microsoft Word, there are some differences between the two. The biggest difference is that Word runs on your local computer, and Word Online runs in the cloud and is accessed by using your web browser.

GOING BEHIND THE SCENES

The cloud is just a fancy way of describing the act of accessing software and computer resources over the Internet. For example, when you create a Word Online document, it is not some mystical and magical fog that is conjured up from the mists of the Internet. To track down where the actual Word file lives requires a bit of detective work, but it is entirely possible.

Office 365 is nothing more than server software that Microsoft has installed on computers in their data centers around the world. For example, if you are on the West coast, then the physical data center that your Office 365 software is running in might be in the state of Washington. You access this server software over the Internet. Because you don't know, or even really care, where the actual data center is located, you can say it is running "in the cloud".

Now, to track down that physical file you created with Office Online, you need to think about where you saved it. If you saved it to SharePoint, then you saved it into a document library app. We know that SharePoint uses a database product called SQL Server to store all of its content and configuration information. So when you are saving something to SharePoint, you are actually saving it to an SQL Server database. That SQL Server database is running in the Microsoft data center in the state of Washington (or Hong Kong, or Germany — or wherever the closest Microsoft data center is located).

Opening your web browser, pointing it at SharePoint Online, and clicking on a Word document to open or print it is actually very easy to accomplish. Behind the scenes, however, SharePoint Online (running in a Microsoft data center) is contacting the SQL Server program (also running in the Microsoft data center) and requesting the specific Word document. SharePoint then sends that to your web browser, and you see it magically appear.

When you fire up Word on your local computer and create a document, that document can either stay on your local computer or be saved to the cloud. When you click the Save button and save the document, you are prompted for the place where you want to save the file. For example, you can choose to save in a cloud location (such as OneDrive or Dropbox) or you can choose to save the document on your local computer in a location such as the Documents directory or your Desktop. In any case, your creation is a physical file located on a cloud-based storage location or your local computer. When working with Word Online, however, you do not have a local physical file. When you create a document and save it, your document lives out in the cloud. In the case of Office 365, your document lives within a SharePoint Online document library app or OneDrive.

TIP

You can create a document using Word on your local device, save it to the cloud, and then edit it using Word Online. Word Online works even if you are at a computer that does not have Word installed locally, because Word Online only needs a web browser. You can even save a Word Online document to your local device using the Download a Copy button on the File menu.

Getting the Basics

You need to know some basic things about Word Online, such as how it differs from the traditional Word application that runs on your desktop or laptop. You also want to become familiar with the Word Online interface and discover how you can easily work with documents right from your web browser.

Using the Word Online interface

The Word Online interface is almost identical to the regular Word interface, except that it runs within your web browser. The interface contains a Ribbon at the top of the screen, which contains such tabs as File, Home, Insert, Page Layout, Review, and View.

The Home tab contains common functionality in groupings, such as Clipboard, Font, Paragraph, Styles, and Editing, as shown in Figure 11-1.

You use the Insert tab to insert objects into your document, such as a table, a picture, add-ins, links, comments, and notes. The Insert tab is shown in Figure 11-2. You can learn more about how add-ins work with the Office products in Chapter 12.

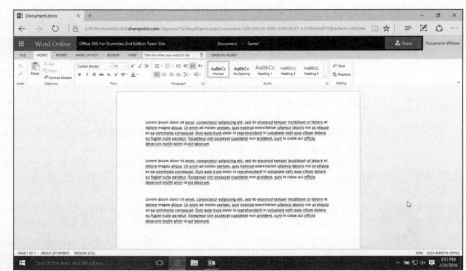

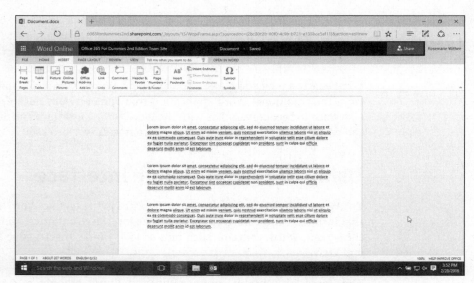

The Page Layout tab is where you can change the formatting of the document. You can change things like the margins widths, orientation (portrait or landscape), the paper size, indentation, and line spacing. The Insert tab is shown in Figure 11-3.

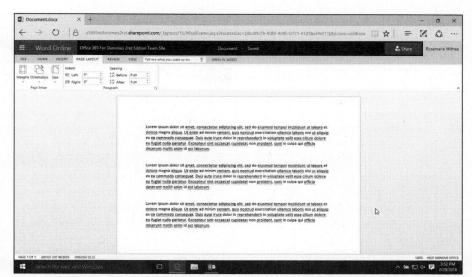

FIGURE 11-3:
The Page Layout
tab on the Word
Online Ribbon.

The Review tab includes such functionality as spell check and comments. You can use the Review tab to add comments and collaborate with others on the document without actually changing the contents of the document itself. The Review tab is shown in Figure 11-4.

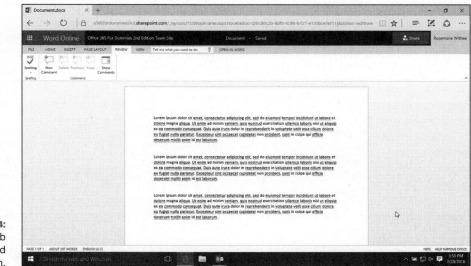

FIGURE 11-4:
The Review tab
on the Word
Online Ribbon.

The View tab allows you to flip between an Editing View and Reading Mode. When in edit mode, you can work with the Home and Insert tabs to modify and develop your document. In addition, you can also find the capability to zoom in on the document and change the view to show page ends and the header and footer. The View tab is shown in Figure 11-5.

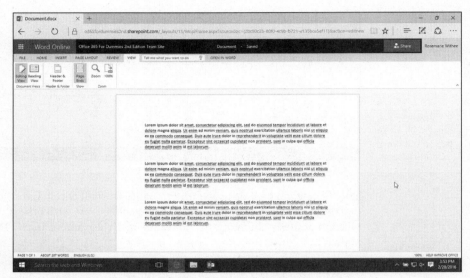

FIGURE 11-5:
The View tab on the Word Online Ribbon.

In addition to the standard tabs in the Ribbon, there are also specialized tabs that only show up when you are working with certain objects. For example, when you select a picture by clicking on it, you will see a new tab — Picture Tools, as shown in Figure 11-6. The Picture Tools tab contains functionality for working with a picture, such as adding alternate text or resizing the image.

In addition to the Ribbon tabs, the interface also includes a File menu. The File menu allows you to save the document, open it by using the traditional Word application located on your computer, or close the document and return to the document library app that houses the document. The File menu is shown in Figure 11-7.

Working with documents

Creating a new Word document in a SharePoint document library app is easy:

1. **Browse to the Documents tab on the Ribbon.**

2. **Click the New button at the top.**

3. **Choose the document type, as shown in Figure 11-8.**

FIGURE 11-6:
The Picture
Tools tab on
the Word
Online Ribbon.

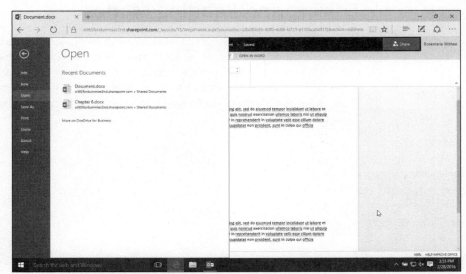

FIGURE 11-7:
The File menu
on the Word
Online interface.

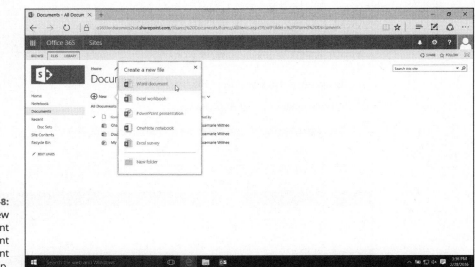

FIGURE 11-8:
Creating a new
Word document
in a SharePoint
document
library app.

When you create a new document, SharePoint is smart enough to create the new document using Word Online, but you can also open the document by using Word installed on your local computer or device.

After you have finished developing your document, you can save it. Doing this automatically saves it to the document library app in which you created it. You can then click on the document to view it and then edit it further by using either Word Online or the local Word app running on your computer, phone, or tablet.

Editing and Reading Modes

The preceding section discussed working with Word documents in Editing Mode. There are times however when you simply want to read the document and not edit it. When you want to only read the document you can switch to Reading View, which looks very similar to a document that is printed on paper. A document in Reading View is shown in Figure 11-9. The Reading View is found on the View tab.

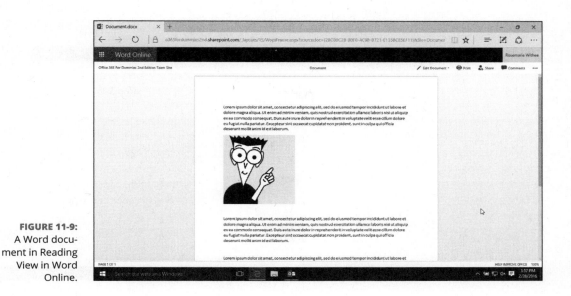

FIGURE 11-9:
A Word docu-
ment in Reading
View in Word
Online.

Working with Advanced Functions

Word Online contains features beyond just adding and modifying text-based content. In particular, you can

>> Manage styles in order to standardize the look and feel of your document.

    You find the styles functionality on the Home tab.

>> Insert Word objects, such as pictures, tables, add-ins, and links.

    You can insert items on the Insert tab.

Styles

The styles let you consistently format a document by selecting a predefined style rather than going through a manual process. For example, you may want your headings to be larger font and a different color. You can, of course, type the text and then highlight the text and make it bigger, and also change the color, but using this method is a lot of work for every heading. A style allows you to simply click the Heading style to make the change, as shown in Figure 11-10.

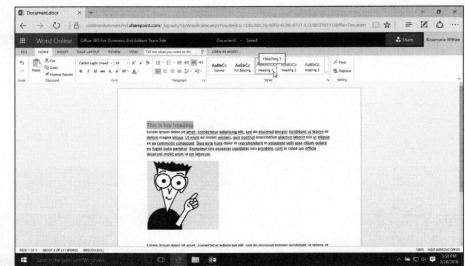

FIGURE 11-10:
Selecting a
heading style in
Word Online.

Tables

A table provides a mechanism for organizing content in your document. A table is divided into vertical columns and horizontal rows. You can insert a table with Word Online by following these steps:

1. **Click on the Insert tab.**

The Insert tab displays the Ribbon that allows you to insert items into your document.

2. **Select the Table button.**

When you select the Table button, you are presented with a grid that allows you to visually choose the number of rows and columns you want to include in your table, as shown in Figure 11-11.

3. **Highlight the number of rows and columns you desire for the table and then click the left mouse button.**

The table is automatically inserted into the document.

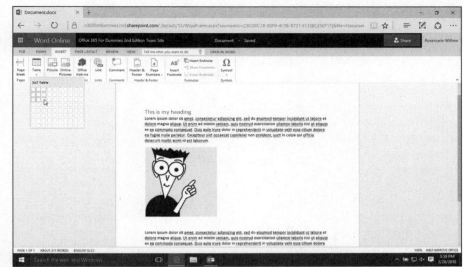

FIGURE 11-11:
Inserting a table
into a document
by using Word
Online.

After the table is created, you can add content to the cells of each column. The table provides a lot of flexibility in the look and feel and layout of the content in your Word document.

Chapter 12

Plunging into Excel Online

E xcel Online is a version of Excel that is part of the Office 365 offering. This version of Excel runs as a web application in your web browser. Working with Excel as a web application has a number of benefits, including the simple fact that you don't need to have the full version of Excel installed on the computer you are using to edit your document. All you need is a web browser and access to your SharePoint site, OneDrive, or another cloud-based storage location (such as Dropbox). You might be on a cruise or using a computer in a café or working from a shared computer at your organization. You can still work with your spreadsheets without having to have Excel installed on the computer you are using.

In this chapter, you explore some of the basic, as well as the more advanced, features of Excel Online and discover how it differs from the traditional version of Excel.

Comparing Excel Online and Excel

Microsoft Excel is one of the most popular data analysis tools on the planet. Using Excel, you can enter numbers into a spreadsheet and use functions to manipulate them and perform analysis. In addition to analyzing numbers, Excel is often used for tracking and managing other data, such as customers, for example. In many organizations Excel has turned into a database-type application where all types of information is stored. Excel is what is known as a thick client in that it runs from your local computer. In Windows 10, you click Start ⇨ All Apps. Then you browse to your Microsoft Office applications and you click Excel to fire up the program. Excel then runs on your computer. A web-based application, on the other hand, runs on a computer in a data center that you access over the Internet. If you use Outlook.com or Gmail for email or browse a web page, then you are using a web application. The way you access a web application is by using a web browser, which is a program installed on your computer.

You will find that Excel Online is still Microsoft Excel but it does have some differences. For one thing, Excel runs on your computer, and Excel Online runs out in the cloud and you access it by using your web browser.

When you create a document on your local computer with Excel, that document traditionally has been stored locally on your computer. When you click the Save button to save a document, you are prompted for the location in which to save the file. You may save the file to a cloud-based storage location (such as SharePoint, OneDrive, or Dropbox) or to your Desktop or any other folder on your local computer. In any case, your creation is a physical file located in cloud-based storage or on your local computer. When working with Excel Online, however, you do not have a local physical file. When you create a document and save it, your document lives on a computer in one of Microsoft's data centers. Because you don't know exactly which computer in which Microsoft data center, you can just say that the document lives out in the cloud. In the case of Office 365, your document lives within a SharePoint Online document library app.

You don't have to be a paid subscriber to Office 365 to work with Excel Online. You can use it for personal use for free with a free Microsoft Office 365 account or Outlook.com account.

Covering the Basics

Working with Excel Online is easy after you find your way around the interface. If you have used the traditional Excel application, then you can recognize that it is extremely similar and you won't have any trouble at all using Excel Online. If you've never used Excel, then you are in for a treat with Excel Online.

Using the Excel Online interface

The Excel Online interface is different from the traditional Excel application in that the web app runs within your web browser. The Ribbon at the top of the Excel Online interface screen contains tabs, such as Home and Insert.

The Home tab contains common functionality in groupings, such as Clipboard, Font, Alignment, Number, Tables, Cells, and Editing, as shown in Figure 12-1.

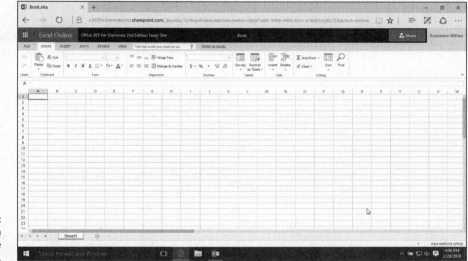

FIGURE 12-1:
The Home tab on the Excel Online Ribbon.

Table 12-1 describes the sections of the Home tab on Excel Online Ribbon.

TABLE 12-1

Features of the Home Tab

Home Tab Section	Description
Clipboard	Allows you to cut, copy, and paste data between cells within the spreadsheet
Font	Allows you to adjust the font size and style
Alignment	Sets the alignment of the data in the cells and allows text to wrap
Number	Changes the formatting of numeric data
Tables	Sorts and filters tables or access the table options
Cells	Inserts or deletes cells in the spreadsheet

The Insert tab allows you to insert objects into your Excel Online document, such as functions, tables, add-ins, charts, links, and comments.

A function performs some calculation, such as summing the values of cells. There are many different functions to choose from in Excel Online. Many would say that the functions are what make Excel so valuable. Adding functions is explored in this chapter.

A table allows you to manipulate data with functionality, such as sorting the data in ascending or descending order or filtering the data based on specific criteria.

An Office add-in is like an app that extends the Excel environment. There is an online store that lists all of the Excel Online add-ins. You access the store by clicking the Office Add-Ins button in the Ribbon of the Insert tab.

A chart is a visualization of data. You can insert many different types of charts into your spreadsheet. Some of the most common types include bar charts, column charts, line charts, and pie charts.

A hyperlink allows you to create clickable text that, when clicked, opens up a new website. For example, you can create a hyperlink with text that says "Learn More" — clicking it takes the viewer of the Excel Online document to a news article.

The comment field allows you to insert a comment into the spreadsheet. A comment is *metadata* because it isn't part of the actual data in the spreadsheet. The comment is data about the data in the spreadsheet, which is why it's called metadata. Comments are useful so that you can leave notes about the spreadsheet without actually modifying the spreadsheet data.

The Insert tab is shown in Figure 12-2.

The Data tab includes data specific functionality, such as connections to data, calculations about data, and sorting of data. After the Data tab is the Review and View tabs. These tabs are designed to provide you various views into your spreadsheet. On the Review tab, you can view and edit comments. On the View tab you can switch between the Editing Mode and the Reading View. The Reading View gives you a preview of how the spreadsheet will look when printed. If you're just reviewing a spreadsheet and not editing it, the Reading View can be much less distracting, which will let you focus on the contents instead of the editing details. The Reading tab is also where you can turn on and off grid lines and headings.

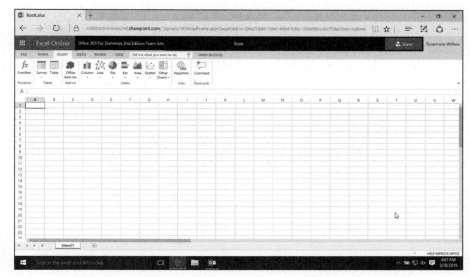

FIGURE 12-2:
The Insert tab on Excel Online Ribbon.

In addition to the Ribbon tabs, the interface also includes a File menu. The File menu allows you to perform functionality, such as saving the document with the same or a different name, opening the document in the traditional Excel application located on your computer, downloading a snapshot of the document or a copy of the document to the local computer. The File menu is shown in Figure 12-3.

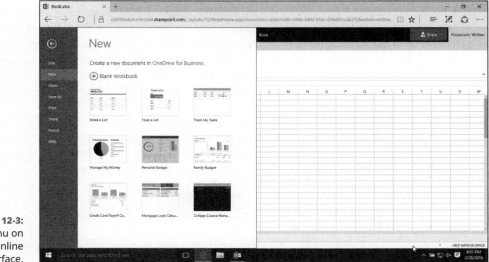

FIGURE 12-3:
The File menu on Excel Online interface.

Working with workbooks

Creating a new Excel Online document in a SharePoint document library app is easy. On the header of the document library app, click the New button and then select Excel Workbook, as shown in Figure 12-4.

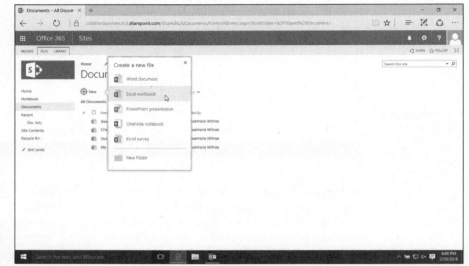

FIGURE 12-4:
Creating a new Excel document in SharePoint.

When you create a new document, SharePoint is smart enough to create the document and place you in Excel Online in edit mode. If you already have Microsoft Excel installed locally on your computer, then you can switch to the Excel client by clicking the Open in Excel button in the Ribbon. This will open up the document in the full-featured application. If you don't have Excel installed locally, you can continue to work on the spreadsheet with your web browser and Excel Online.

After you have finished developing your spreadsheet, you can save it, which will automatically save it to the document library app in which you created it. You can then click on the document to view it and then edit it further by using either Excel Online or the local Excel application running on your computer.

Editing Mode and Reading View

There are times when you do not need to edit a document. For example, you might want to just view the latest spreadsheet report or show a colleague a set of data. Excel Online contains two different modes. When you are editing the document you are using Editing Mode. When you want to read the document, you can simply click it in SharePoint to open it and view it. This is called Reading View, which looks very similar to a document that is printed on paper. A document in Reading View is shown in Figure 12-5.

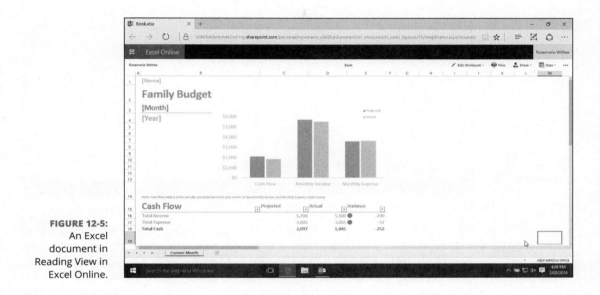

Using Advanced Features

In addition to the basic features that you will use in Excel Online, there are also some advanced features. In particular, you can work with formulas and functions, manipulate data, and even coauthor spreadsheets in real time in the cloud.

Adding functions

One of the primary reasons for the popularity of Excel as a data analysis tool is the seemingly endless supply of functions. A *function* is a bit of logic that performs some calculation or manipulates data in a certain way. For example, you may want a cell to display the addition of two other cells. You can use a simple plus (+) sign to accomplish this addition. Going farther, however, you might want a cell to display the current time. You can use a function, such as Now(), which would display the current time. The power of this function lies in the fact that Excel updates the time each time it recalculates the spreadsheet.

To enter a function in a cell, enter the equal (=) sign followed by the function. For example, to enter the Now() function, you type =Now(), as shown in Figure 12-6.

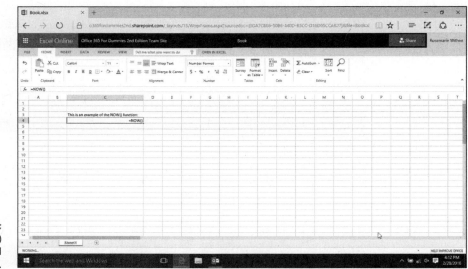

FIGURE 12-6:
Using the Now()
function in Excel
Online.

TIP

To insert a function you can also use the Insert tab and then click the Function button to insert a function. This will provide you a list of functions in case you don't know off hand which function you want to use.

After you finish entering the function and press Enter, you will see the current time rather than the =Now() function in the cell. This simple yet powerful functionality is what lets users create very valuable and complex spreadsheets with minimal training.

TIP

If you are following along, notice that as you begin to type the function, Excel Online automatically starts to show you all the functions and narrows in on the list of possible functions as you continue typing. This feature is useful when you cannot remember the exact name of the function but remember it starts with a specific letter.

An excellent list of the available Excel Online functions listed alphabetically or by category is available on the Microsoft Office website. To find the functions, open your browser and navigate to http://support.office.com. Then search for "excel functions" in the search tool. There are many different functions and spending some time looking through them can save you a lot of time in the future when you are crunching data.

Manipulating data

The ability to manipulate data is a staple of Excel and continues in Excel Online. You can manipulate data by using functions or by creating your own formulas. Functions exist for manipulating numeric data and also text data. You can dynamically link the contents of a cell to other cells. For example, you might have a column for sales and a column for costs and then a third column that denotes profit by subtracting the costs column from the sales column. Using functions and mathematical equations, with nothing more than your web browser, you can quickly whip data into shape by using Excel Online.

Coauthoring workbooks in the cloud

One of the exciting features found in Excel Online is the ability to coauthor spreadsheets with others in real time and at the same time. For example, imagine that you are in Seattle and your colleague is in Manila. You can edit the same document in real time by using the browser. When your colleague enters text or numeric data, you see it appear on your screen. Coauthoring allows for a much more productive experience because you are both editing the same document, which maintains a single version of the truth.

With a spreadsheet open in Excel Online, you can see the other users who are currently editing the document in the lower-right hand corner of the screen. For example, if two people are editing, you will see text that says "2 People Editing." If you click on this text, you will see the two users who are currently editing the spreadsheet.

When one of the users makes change to the document, everyone who is currently viewing the document will see the changes take place in their view as well. This turns out to be an extremely useful feature because the new changes do not have to be emailed to other people in order for them to see the most recent version of the spreadsheet. The spreadsheet only exists in one place, so there is only one version of the truth for this spreadsheet.

Chapter 13

Powering Up PowerPoint Online

Whether you like or loathe PowerPoint, there is no denying that it is here to stay. It has leveled the playing field for anyone who understands his audience — including students, small-business professionals, and big-business executives. The latest version of the application comes loaded with advanced features for animating text and graphics, video editing, ink annotations, presence for real-time collaboration, applying morph effects, and even broadcasting your presentation!

In Office 365, PowerPoint Online is one of the core apps in Office Online. It combines a variety of web services to display high-fidelity presentations in a browser. This is a boon of some organizations that may have users without access to the desktop application.

In this chapter, you will explore the basics of PowerPoint Online, compare the user experience between the online app and its desktop companion, and get started using the online app interface.

After you become familiar with the basic functions, step up to the next level by applying advanced capabilities like the Present Online feature. We don't want you to compromise the quality of your presentations, so in this chapter we include tips and tricks for taming bullets, lists, alignments, and graphics in PowerPoint Online.

Going Over the Basics

Opening a file in the PowerPoint Online initiates a series of processes and services in the backend to render your document in high fidelity, giving you the familiar user interface you experience in the desktop application and giving you the best viewing experience for your presentation.

When you click on a PowerPoint file from SharePoint or OneDrive, PowerPoint Online displays your presentation in Reading View. If the slide has animation or transition, you can see those effects in the Reading View. You can choose to open the presentation in your desktop PowerPoint application, edit the presentation right in the browser, or immediately start the slide show.

Comparing the PowerPoint Online and PowerPoint 2016

PowerPoint Online is designed to be a companion to its desktop cousin, Power-Point 2016. It allows users to collaborate on files and make light edits to a presentation right in the browser, regardless of the user's platform (Windows PC or Mac).

As long as the minimum system requirements are met and a supported browser is used, you can expect to perform most of the basic PowerPoint tasks in the online version that you do on the desktop version.

Due to technological constraints, and because by design PowerPoint Online is a companion and not necessarily a replacement for the desktop version, there are features in the desktop application that are not available in the online version, as follows:

TIP

>> **Password Protection**: If the presentation is password-protected from desktop application, you can't unlock or open that presentation in the online version.

To get around this limitation, set the permission for the document in SharePoint or OneDrive instead.

>> **Printing:** You can only print your slides into a PDF file (not to a printer) when using PowerPoint Online.

>> **Coauthoring:** Multiple people can edit a presentation at the same time.

For the best experience, all coauthors should use either PowerPoint Online or the desktop version, not a mixture of both.

>> **Find and Replace:** This functionality is not supported in PowerPoint Online.

>> **Charts:** You can't insert charts in PowerPoint Online. If you first create the charts from the desktop application, however, they will display with no issues in PowerPoint Online.

>> **WordArt:** Like Charts, WordArt isn't supported in PowerPoint Online, but you can add them first from the desktop app to display them in the online app.

Using the PowerPoint Online user interface

As a default, PowerPoint Online opens files in Reading View and runs animations and transitions that are embedded on the slide. Immediately after the file is loaded in the browser, the top bar gives you quick access to commands to edit the presentation, start the slide show, print to PDF, share with others, and more commands from the settings (ellipses) icon (see Figure 13-1). On the bottom of the screen, you'll see slide navigation controls, as well as commonly used View actions (Notes, Editing View, Reading View, and Slideshow).

FIGURE 13-1:
PowerPoint
Online Reading
View.

The Edit Presentation command gives you the option to edit the document in either the desktop application or the online app. If you select Edit in PowerPoint Online, you're taken to the Home tab on the Ribbon. You see some familiar editing buttons and icons that enable you to format text and paragraphs, navigate and manipulate slides, access the clipboard functions, and use the drawing tools (see Figure 13-2). Editing the file in the rich desktop application is a one-click action from the Home tab with the Open in PowerPoint action from the top bar. You'll also know when others are editing the document as indicated just below the Share icon. You can hide or display the ribbon by clicking the arrow at the bottom right of the ribbon.

FIGURE 13-2:
PowerPoint
Online
Home tab.

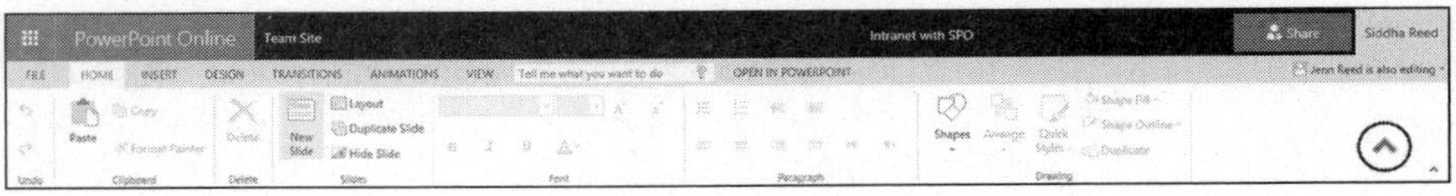

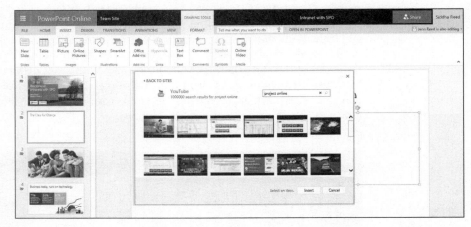

Inserting new slides, tables, pictures, and shapes is done from the Insert tab. Links, comments, symbols, and YouTube videos (see Figure 13-3) can be added from this tab.

FIGURE 13-3:
PowerPoint
Online
Insert tab.

The rest of the tabs (Design, Transition, Animation, and View) are pretty much pared-down versions of the desktop application corresponding tab.

Although there is no Review tab in PowerPoint Online where you would typically check spelling, that functionality is still available in the online app. If you misspell a world while you type, you see a red squiggly line under the word. To correct it, just right-click on the word and choose the correct spelling.

Working with presentations

Creating a new PowerPoint presentation is pretty much the same whether you're in Office 365 SharePoint document library, OneDrive for Business, or the consumer version of OneDrive (see Figure 13-4). Just click on the + New icon and select PowerPoint presentation.

There is no Save button in PowerPoint Online. Whenever you make a change, your work is saved automatically. When you finish your edits, you can close the document by navigating back to your document library (either in SharePoint or OneDrive) from the hyperlinked breadcrumb next to "PowerPoint Online" on the Office 365 navigation bar.

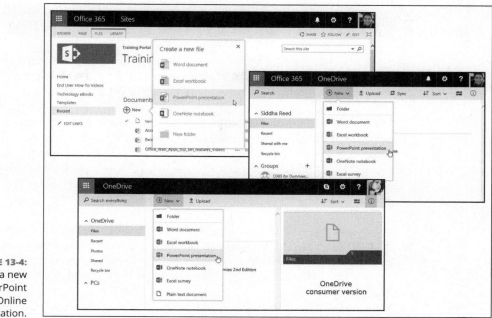

FIGURE 13-4:
Creating a new
PowerPoint
Online
presentation.

Alternatively, while logged on to Office 365 or the consumer version of OneDrive, you can click on the app launcher and then select the PowerPoint tile to create a new presentation. Files created this way automatically are saved in your default Documents folder in OneDrive.

In the consumer version of OneDrive, you will see a notification of new features in PowerPoint Online the first time you create a file from the app launcher (see Figure 13-5). At the time of writing, Skype for Business isn't integrated with PowerPoint Online in Office 365 for business, but it's likely to happen.

FIGURE 13-5:
Skype integration
with PowerPoint
Online consumer
version.

Using Advanced Functions

Despite its reputation for "light editing only," PowerPoint Online is not intended to hamper your creativity or stop you from producing the best-ever sales pitch. When you're on the run and need to spruce up your presentation with text formatting, SmartArt charts, or images, the online app does just fine. In addition, the Present Online feature in the desktop version uses PowerPoint Online technology to run a live presentation to audiences anywhere on their browser or mobile devices.

Presenting online

High speed Internet access is now part of our daily lives, enabling us to easily connect and collaborate efficiently with our colleagues. The advantage of having high-bandwidth networks is to deliver almost full-fidelity slide shows for remote presenters and attendees. This means you can conduct ad hoc meetings and presentations with your colleagues, regardless of location. It could also mean savings for your business as you reduce the cost of travel, training, and conference services.

As the presenter, you need to initiate the Present Online feature from the desktop application. As a participant, you need either a Skype for Business meeting invitation or simply a link (provided by the presenter) and an Internet-connected device.

To initiate Present Online, follow these steps:

1. **Open your presentation in PowerPoint 2016.**

2. **From the Ribbon, click Slideshow, then click Present Online.**

3. **Depending on your attendees, choose either**

   - **Skype for Business** (for attendees within your organization only)

     Choosing Skype for Business will allow you to use an existing meeting or create a new one. After you've made your selection and clicked OK, the Skype for Business application will run. Your session will automatically initiate screen sharing and load your presentation. If you created a new meeting, you can add participants by inviting more people.

   - **Office Presentation Service** (for attendees with an Internet-connected device including people outside of your organization)

     The Office Presentation Service is a free, public service from Microsoft. There's no need to set up an account to use this service (see Figure 13-6).

FIGURE 13-6:
Present
Online
options.

Choosing Office Presentation Service will display a window where you can opt to enable remote viewers to download the presentation. When you click the Connect button, you're connected to the presentation service and your presentation will be processed to be used for the service. When processing is complete, you will be presented a link that you can share by email or instant message (IM). At this point, clicking the START PRESENTATION button will start the online presentation (see Figure 13-7).

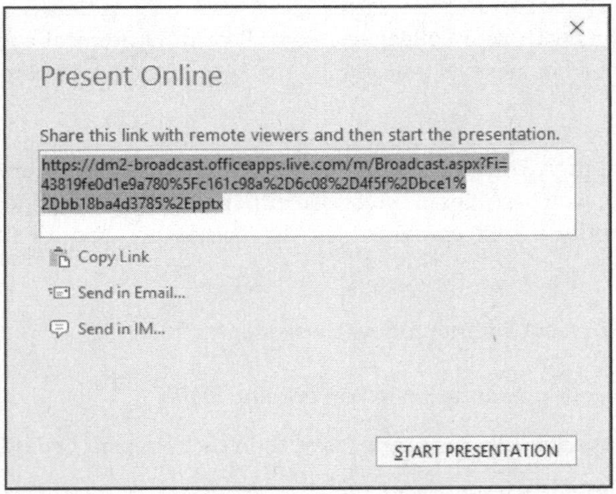

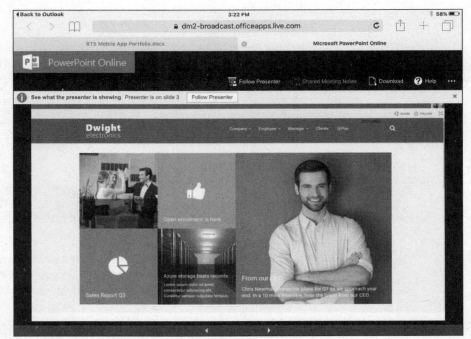

FIGURE 13-7:
Presenting Online
with the Office
Presentation
Service.

To attend the online presentation, simply follow the link provided by the presenter. Your browser will fire up PowerPoint Online so you can view the presentation. As an attendee, you can either follow along with the presenter or click through the slides to move ahead or go back. Figure 13-8 is a screenshot of a user's experience from an iPad.

FIGURE 13-8:
Present Online
attendee
experience from
an iPad.

Adjusting alignments, bullets, and numbered lists

You will find alignment, bullets, and numbering commands on the Home tab under the Paragraph group. Don't be alarmed when your bulleted or numbered list displays characters other than your template's styles. As soon as you click outside of the content placeholder, the default formatting you saw while editing the text is replaced with your template's style.

Two shortcut keys that may come in handy are the Tab and the Shift+ Tab keys. The Tab key indents your list to the right and the Shift+Tab key indents your list to the left.

Adding pictures and Smart Art graphics

To add pictures to your presentation from the PowerPoint Online, click the picture icon in an empty placeholder on your slide. You're prompted to select a file from your hard drive. As soon as the picture is added to your slide, the Picture Tools Format tab displays, allowing you to further customize your picture.

You can also insert a picture through the Picture command on the Insert tab on the Ribbon.

To add a Smart Art graphic, click the Smart Art icon on an empty content place-holder and make your selection from the choices on the Ribbon. You can also add Smart Art graphics directly onto your slide through the Smart Art command on the Insert tab on the Ribbon.

Chapter 14

Figuring Out OneNote Online

Microsoft OneNote is a digital notebook perfect for gathering and storing all your notes, scribbles, emails, digital handwriting, audio and video recordings, research materials, links, and other types of digital information. When you use OneNote, you get the benefit of powerful search capabilities so you can quickly find the information you need from a single location. In addition, OneNote allows you to share your notebooks with others for easy and effective collaboration.

OneNote Online is Microsoft OneNote's cloud cousin that comes bundled with Office Online in Office 365. Like Word, Excel, and PowerPoint, OneNote Online allows you to create, view, and edit notebooks from a web browser.

In this chapter, you find out about the basics of Microsoft OneNote. To set the right expectations, a comparison between the desktop application and the online version of OneNote is covered in this chapter. Instructions for tagging your notes, managing pages and sections, and restoring the previous version of a notebook are covered in the "Using Advanced Features" section of this chapter.

Exploring Basic Functions

Microsoft OneNote is a beefed-up word processing program. You can enter text and graphics to gather, organize, search, and share literally anything you can think of, such as meeting notes, ideas, references, instructions, and brainstorms. Unlike word processors, however, OneNote lets you input free-form sketches, add unbound text, insert screen captures, and record audio and video directly into any section of the application's page. It's a great way for storing digital sticky notes so you can have a clutter-free desktop.

Introduction to Microsoft OneNote

Think back to a time when you had a spiral-bound notebook. It had sections, and the sections had pages. You organized your stuff by writing on a page that belonged to a particular section.

OneNote is like that, but much better, handier, and smarter. If you put information on a page in OneNote, and decide later that the information belongs in a different section, you don't have to start from scratch and rewrite anything. A few mouse clicks do the trick.

Try adding audio and video in your spiral bound notebook. You can't. With OneNote, you can. Now, ask three people to take notes together with you on the same page at the same with your spiral-bound notebook. You can't. With OneNote, it's no problem. You can even see each other's edits in real time.

In OneNote, you also have sections and pages (see Figure 14-1). In Office 365, you can have more than one OneNote notebook.

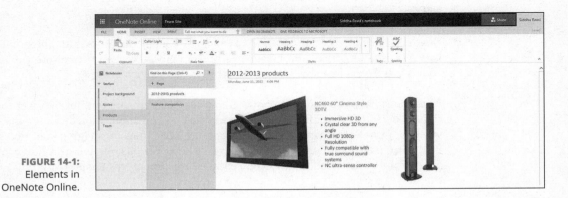

FIGURE 14-1: Elements in OneNote Online.

A great example of how to use OneNote at work is for tracking projects. With a project notebook, you can have a single document to capture project information, such as background, meeting notes, team contacts, and task lists.

One of our favorite features in OneNote is the search capability. Using the search box, you can quickly find content based on keywords, jump to a page based on text within the pictures, and even find your handwritten notes!

Comparing OneNote Online and OneNote 2016

OneNote Online is the web version of the rich desktop OneNote application. Both versions share a similar user interface, making it easy for users to quickly get started using the web app with little or no learning curve. Because OneNote Online is browser-based, most users with light editing and collaborating needs can get by without the desktop version. You can create and edit OneNote documents regardless of your platform (PC or Mac) or your browser (Microsoft Edge, Internet Explorer, Safari, or Firefox). Documents are displayed in the browser in high fidelity, providing users with the same clarity and formatting as in the desktop application. Coauthoring is a snap because users can see each other's entries in real time.

When using the OneNote Online be mindful of the following differences between the online and the desktop versions:

TIP

>> **Audio and Video Capabilities:** Because it is meant as a companion — not a replacement — OneNote Online has limitations. For example, audio or video embedded on a page will not play in OneNote Online but will be preserved for playback in the desktop application.

>> **Shapes, Images, and Tables:** You can't insert shapes on pages in the web app, but you can insert tables, pictures, clip art, and hyperlinks.

>> **Zoom:** This feature is supported only in the desktop version.

You can get around this by using your browser's zoom feature.

>> **Search:** This functionality isn't available in the web app, although you can use your browser's "find" function (CTRL + F) to find keywords on the page that is currently open.

>> **Copy and Paste:** This works for text and images from the web, but such formatting as bold and italics will be lost. However, if you copy and paste from within the notebook, formatting will be retained.

>> **Text Editing:** Basic text editing in the web app is pretty good. You can change fonts, apply formatting, and select styles. Unfortunately, the handy Format Painter feature isn't available in the web app.

>> **Tags:** Custom tags aren't available in OneNote Online, but custom tags created from the desktop application will be displayed. Searching for tags in the online app isn't supported, either.

Despite the preceding limitations, OneNote Online is a robust cloud productivity solution. These key functionalities of the desktop application are available in the online app:

>> Multilevel subpages that can be collapsed.

>> Show authors and version history.

>> Send or copy/paste content from the web pages to a section or page in OneNote complete with links using the universal Ctrl+C (copy) and Ctrl+V (paste) commands!

>> Ability to link to other notes — wiki anyone?

>> Auto link notes to web pages and documents.

>> Quick access to the style sheet for formatting headings.

>> Ability to insert math functions.

>> Embed Office files as attachments or printouts in pages.

>> Format paragraphs: align, indent, change direction.

>> Insert pictures from your local drive or Bing images.

>> Automatic spell check as you type; misspelled words display with red squiggly lines.

>> Easy sharing from the Share button.

>> Ability to quickly create tasks in Outlook from OneNote.

Using the OneNote Online interface

As a browser-based experience, OneNote Online is a pared-down version of the OneNote 2016 desktop version. Accessing more commands and features from the rich desktop application is as easy as clicking the Open in OneNote button on the top navigation or from the File menu.

The five tabs on the Ribbon (see Figure 14-2) give you access to the most commonly used features in OneNote. (There is no Save button — your notebook is automatically saved every time you make a change.)

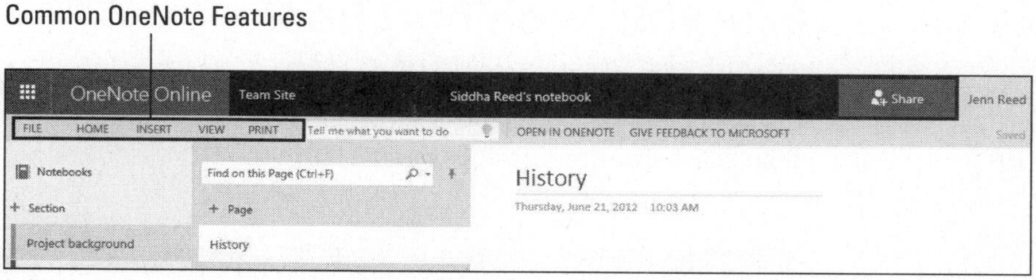

Common OneNote Features

FIGURE 14-2:
OneNote
Online ribbon
commands.

Although most of the commands and functionalities are common in the online and desktop versions, the user interface between the two is slightly different:

>> Sections in the online app are displayed on the left navigation pane; on the desktop version, they're displayed as tabs in the middle pane (see image on top in Figure 14-3).

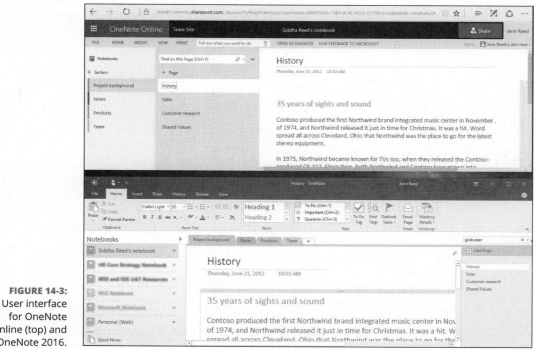

FIGURE 14-3:
User interface
for OneNote
Online (top) and
OneNote 2016.

>> Pages in the online app are displayed on the middle pane next to the sections; on the desktop, they're displayed on the right pane.

Working with notebooks

Creating a new notebook from a document library is the same in SharePoint Online, OneDrive for Business, and the consumer version: Click the + New button, then select OneNote notebook (see Figure 14-4).

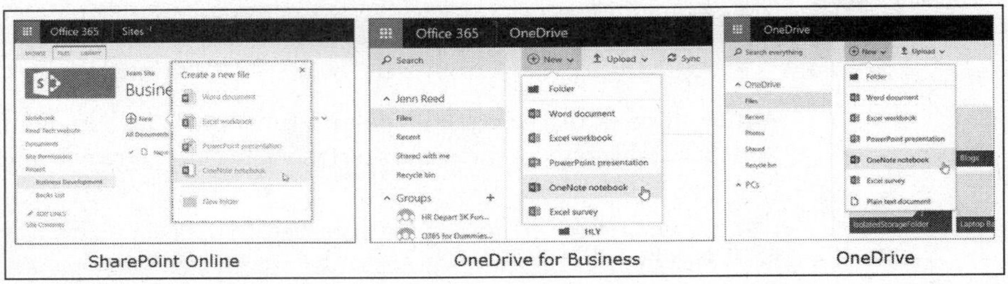

FIGURE 14-4:
Create a new OneNote notebook.

SharePoint Online   OneDrive for Business   OneDrive

REMEMBER

OneNote Online opens a notebook in Edit mode by default. You can immediately make changes to your notebook; as you type, your changes are saved automatically. If another user opens the same notebook in either the online or the desktop application, simultaneous coauthoring automatically begins. Changes made by each of the authors are synchronized almost instantly.

To close the notebook, navigate away from the page by clicking the breadcrumb on the Office 365 navigation bar.

Using Advanced Features

Even if you've never used OneNote before, getting started with the app is easy. The intuitive ribbon commands are similar across all Office apps, so they don't require a lot of training. However, there are some handy features that may not be apparent. Here's the story.

Tagging content for later use

You can use a variety of tags to give your notes another dimension, as shown in Figure 14-5. Tags make your content stand out so you can act on it later. In the desktop application, you can run a Tag Summary to create a page that pulls all the content you have tagged.

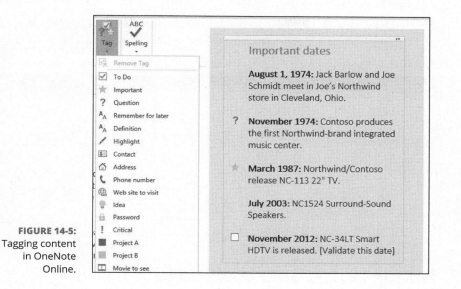

FIGURE 14-5:
Tagging content in OneNote Online.

To tag content, select the text, click Tag from the Home tab, and then click the tag you want to use.

TIP

Similar to Microsoft Word, OneNote Online automatically checks your spelling as you type. A squiggly red underline displays beneath misspelled words and typical Auto Correct actions are applied, including correcting misspellings and converting characters to symbols. If you click the down arrow below the Spelling icon on the Home tab, you have the option to choose the dictionary for the proofing language by selecting Set Proofing Language.

Viewing and restoring page versions

Sometimes coauthoring notebooks with other users can create undesirable results. For example, say a co-worker overwrote your carefully worded instructions in your onboarding notebook for new employees. Not to worry. A page version is saved every time someone edits a shared notebook. OneNote Online allows you to view, restore, or delete previous versions of the page. To do this, follow these steps:

1. **Go to the View tab and click the Page Versions icon.**

   You see a list of all the page versions listed under the page name on the left pane with a date stamp and the author's name.

2. **Click any of the versions to view it.**

3. **After you determine the right version to restore, right-click the versions to display the option to hide, restore, or delete it.**

   When you click on a previous version, you see a notification bar at the top of the page indicating that the version is read-only (see Figure 14-6).

FIGURE 14-6: Viewing and restoring previous versions.

Taking notes on a Web page

It's finally here! With the release of Windows 10, the latest operating system from Microsoft, you can write, annotate, and take notes right on a web page, and share the annotated web page. This is all made possible with the help of OneNote technology.

Windows 10 comes with Microsoft Edge, the new browser replacing Internet Explorer. To start writing on the web, click the Make a Web Note icon on the top right of the Edge browser (see Figure 14-7).

Make a Web Note

FIGURE 14-7: Writing on the web with the Microsoft Edge browser.

You'll see a row of icons on the top left of the web page (see Figure 14-8). From left to right, they're Pan, Pen, Highlighter, Eraser, Add a typed note, and Clip.

FIGURE 14-8:
Make Web Note
tools on the Edge
browser.

When you're done, you can either save your work in OneNote or share it from the icons on the top right (see Figure 14-9). Saving your work will fire up the OneNote native app in Windows 10, but any pages saved in that native app will be synchronized back to your cloud storage and can be viewed in OneNote Online.

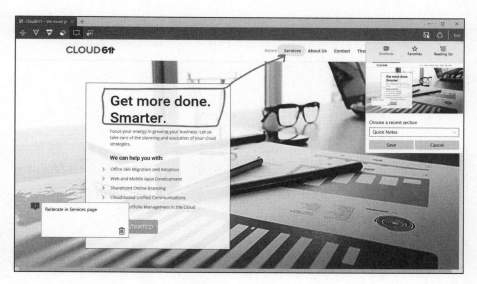

FIGURE 14-9:
Saving and
sharing your web
writing.

5

Instant Messaging and Online Meetings

Chapter 15

Getting Empowered by Skype for Business

You know that little-known tool that people all over the world use to connect with friends, families, and loved ones? Yes, the one that makes 3 billion minutes of calls each day. And yes, the one that more than 35% of small businesses use as their primary communication service.

If you still haven't guessed, we're talking about Skype. This free messaging tool that not only connects people all over the world but also bridges the language barriers with its translation capabilities was acquired by Microsoft in 2011 for $8.5 billion.

True to Microsoft's vision to transform communication and collaboration with software, the business version of Skype is now part of the Office 365 family. Skype for Business takes advantage of all the good things about the Skype we know, as well as Lync, the former communication platform for Office 365.

In this chapter, you will discover the benefits of using Skype for Business as the communication solution for your organization. You'll learn the new meaning of the word *presence* as it applies to Office 365 technologies. As you become familiar with the application, you will be able to take your organization to the next level of collaboration by integrating Skype technologies with Exchange Online, SharePoint Online, and Office applications.

We included a list of best practices for a successful Skype meeting in this chapter, so check it out and impress your colleagues with your efficiency and effectiveness in your next online meeting!

Benefitting from Skype for Business

In the Office 365 small business plans (Business Essentials and Business Premium plans at $5 and $12.50/month/user respectively), users can have unlimited online meetings with IM and HD video conferencing capabilities using Skype for Business.

On the enterprise side, the E1, E3, and E5 plans ($8, $20, and $35/month/user respectively) also enjoy the same benefits as the small business plans but with added capabilities like meeting broadcast with up to 10,000 attendees and even a cloud-based PBX calling services for the E5 plan.

Skype for Business is integrated throughout the Office applications as well as Exchange Online and SharePoint Online. This means that you can quickly view your co-worker's presence or availability status and initiate a conversation without leaving the Office application you're currently using.

When the Office suite is installed on your desktop from your Office 365 subscription, the Skype for Business application is also installed. In most situations, you will enter your Office 365 credentials to log in to Skype for Business to start using the service. On a Windows smartphone, you have to manually download and install the Skype for Business app from the Store.

Skype for Business apps are also available for mobile devices running the iOS and Android operating systems, thus opening the door for users to seamlessly collaborate regardless of their choice of operating system.

By making the Skype for Business apps available on smartphones, users can attend Skype meetings anywhere. When the internet is not available, users can still dial in to a meeting using their cellular connection.

Touring the user interface

Skype for Business helps foster collaboration by enabling users to share their availability, whereabouts, and what they're working on with colleagues. This set of information is called *presence* in the application.

In the Personal Notes section of the user interface (see Figure 15-1), text and hyperlinks are allowed providing everyone with real-time information about the user.

Your picture, *presence* info, and location

Let people know what you're up to with your status in the Personal Note section.

Settings

Tabs: Contacts, Conversations, Phone, Meetings

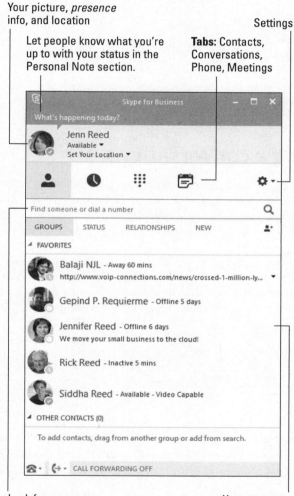

FIGURE 15-1:
Skype for Business user interface.

Look for someone

Your contacts

Skype for Business automatically displays your presence status based on your activity or Outlook calendar.

You can, however, also manually update your status by selecting one of the following options from the presence status drop-down menu (see Figure 15-2).

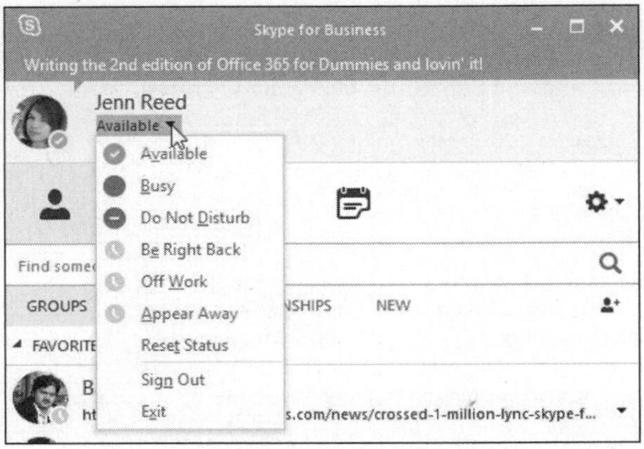

FIGURE 15-2:
Skype for
Business *presence*
indicator.

Starting a conversation

A conversation with a colleague could start as an instant message that turns into a phone call, or a video call, or a web conference where you're sharing screen. It can also start as a conversation between two people and turn into a full-on meeting with the whole team. That's the flexibility that Skype for Business offers.

To start a conversation from the Skype for Business application, hover over your contact's photo. A set of icons will display, allowing you to start the conversation via instant message, phone call, or video call (see the first 3 icons in Figure 15-3). You'll also see the contact card icon and more settings for additional actions.

FIGURE 15-3:
Starting a
conversation
from Skype for
Business.

Everywhere else in Office 365 where you see presence information, in Outlook, Word, etc., you can initiate a conversation by clicking the user's photo to display the icons for IM, phone call, video call, or email (see Figure 15-4).

Unlimited audio conferencing between Skype users within your organization (and federated organizations) is included in all Office 365 enterprise plans. However, if you plan to allow your users to make traditional phone calls, like dialing out or receiving calls from the public switched telephony network (PSTN), you need to subscribe to an Office 365 E5 plan ($35/month). There are also third-party Microsoft partners who can provide traditional phone calling capabilities with just an E3 plan. For example, VoIP Connections recently announced that they crossed 1 million PTSN minutes per month of voice services usage from their customers.

If you manage a small- or medium-size business and would like to try VoIP Connections' service for free for 30 days, please contact Jenn Reed at the following email address for more information and availability of their special promos:

`voicecalling@cloud611.com`

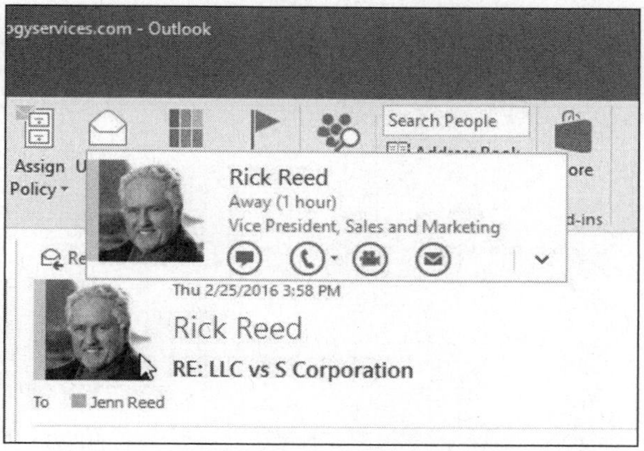

FIGURE 15-4: Starting a conversation from Outlook.

Enhancing the conversation

From an instant message, you can enhance the conversation by using the controls from the IM window. When you click the Share Screen icon (see Figure 15-5) a whole selection of collaboration tools are available at your fingertips, such as: Present Desktop, Present Programs, Present PowerPoint Files, Add Attachments, and More (Whiteboard, Poll, Q&A).

Reviewing past conversations

Sometimes you may need to go back to prior conversations to check your understanding of the conclusion. In Skype for Business, your recent interactions are saved in the Conversations tab. To view older conversations, click the View more in Outlook link. All Skype for Business interactions are saved in the Conversation History folder in your Outlook mailbox.

From the Conversations tab (see Figure 15-6), you can re-connect with your contact and pick up where you left off by double-clicking the conversation.

Add more people

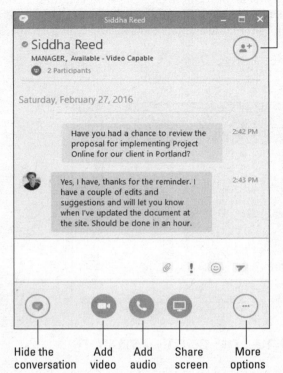

FIGURE 15-5:
Icons with more
actions from the
IM window.

Hide the   Add   Add   Share   More
conversation   video   audio   screen   options

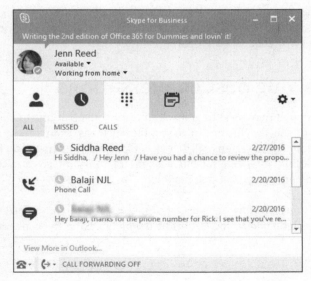

FIGURE 15-6:
Skype for
Business
Conversations
tab.

Conferencing the Skype Way

With Skype for Business and Outlook integration, conducting an effective online meeting regardless of the participants' locations is simple even for those who are not technically inclined. Scheduling online meetings and delivering presentations during the meeting does not involve a steep learning curve.

The meeting experience is pretty much the same from a computer or a mobile device. The buttons and navigation are consistent, whether you're using the desktop application or the mobile apps.

Scheduling a Skype meeting

There are two ways to meet using Skype for Business: from Outlook or from the Meet Now feature in the Skype for Business application.

To schedule a Skype meeting in Outlook, follow these steps:

1. **On the Home tab in Outlook, click New Items ⇨ Meeting.**

   A new window pops up with your untitled meeting.

2. **Enter the necessary information for the meeting (invitees, subject, location, date, time).**

3. **From the ribbon, click Skype Meeting.**

   The body of your meeting invitation will be populated with Skype meeting information and the Skype Meeting button will change to Join Skype Meeting (see Figure 15-7). Depending on your organization's set up, you may or may not see the Join by phone option.

4. **Click the Send button to send the meeting invitation.**

   Alternatively, you can start an online meeting by going to the Calendar view, double-clicking the New Skype Meeting button from Ribbon.

TIP

To start a meeting directly from the Skype for Business application, follow these steps:

1. **Click the arrow next to the Settings icon and click Meet Now (see Figure 15-8).**

2. **From the meeting window that opens, click the Invite More People button at the top-right corner of the window.**

3. Select the participants from your contacts list or add participants one at a
time by entering their email address and then click OK.

The people you invited will be notified to join the meeting.

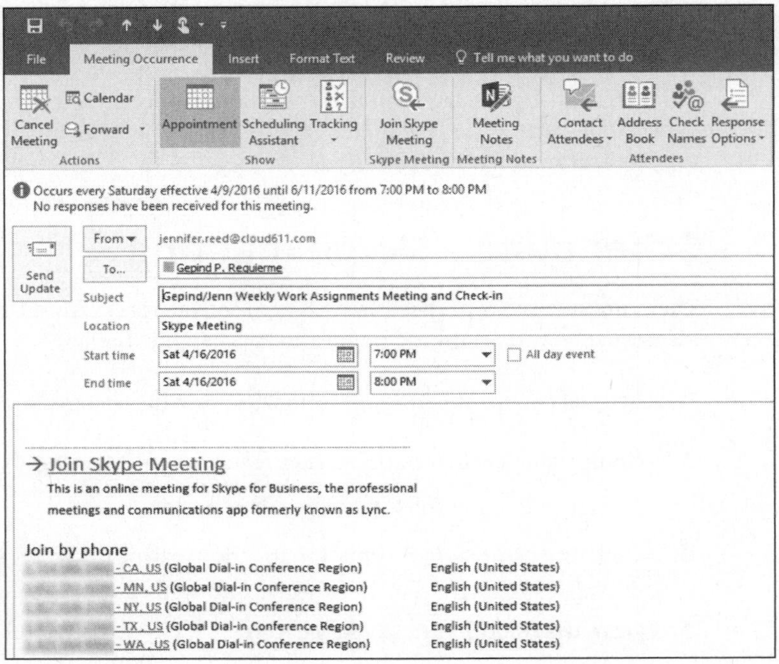

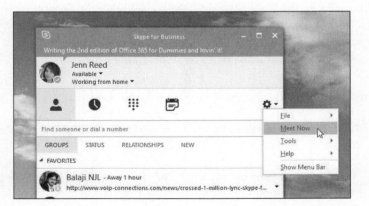

FIGURE 15-7:
Creating a Skype
for Business
meeting
invitation.

FIGURE 15-8:
Meet Now option
from the Skype
for Business
application.

Best practices for online meetings

Using Skype for Business to conduct meetings, especially for participants who are dispersed globally, can result in great savings for your organization. It reduces carbon footprint (Yaay! for the environment) and gives everyone flexibility.

Technology, however, can only do so much. Skype for Business alone is not enough to ensure a successful meeting. Here are some best practices we've compiled from experience that you may want to consider:

>> Wired networks provide for a better meeting experience than wireless connections. Audio quality is not optimal in wireless connections, so if you are speaking a lot, plan to be hard wired. Virtual Private Network (VPN) connections also affect audio quality negatively.

>> Mute your audio unless you are speaking. Hearing a participant typing or a dog barking in the background is not cool.

>> Have alternative means for connection in case you get disconnected. Have the dial-in number handy in case you get dropped from the conference.

>> If you have multiple people in the same room, try to have only one computer logged in to the meeting to prevent audio feedback.

>> If you are a presenter, load content prior to the meeting. Sometimes loading content can take time and you won't want to waste your participants' time by having them wait while the content is loaded.

>> In the interest of respecting the participants' time, set up and test your audio devices before others arrive.

Recording meetings for on-demand viewing

It's inevitable. Sometimes there are forces out of our control that cause us to miss meetings. As the meeting organizer, you have the power to record your meetings and make the .mp4 available for on-demand viewing later. If you do this, however, make sure you inform the participants that the meeting will be recorded. Once the recording is available, you will get an alert from the Skype for Business Recording Manager on your taskbar. You can then load the recording in Share-Point and provide a link to your participants to access the video.

Figure 15-9 illustrates how you can record a meeting from the More Options icon while the meeting is going on.

FIGURE 15-9:
Recording a
Skype for
Business
meeting.

Chapter 16

Making Your Presence Count

S omeone, somewhere is attending a meeting of some sort at the very moment you are reading this page. Studies have indicated that there are 11 million business meetings every day around the world. A white paper released by Verizon confirms that meetings dominate business life in America today, with 37 percent of employees spending their time in meetings.

Imagine what it would be like if your organization had a workforce spread out across the country, or around the globe, and everyone had to attend meetings in person. It simply wouldn't work. It would be too expensive. Even if your organization can afford it, it would be too taxing for your people.

What does work is using the latest conferencing technologies for virtual meetings that give you a face-to-face meeting experience. You stay productive and reduce your travel costs.

Skype for Business is a robust communication and conferencing solution in Office 365. The *presence* feature in the technology alone can translate to substantial time and cost savings by streamlining the process of information exchange between information workers.

For example, let's say, you're working on a project and you need input from five team members. You know that emailing them is not the most efficient way to gather feedback because

>> You know your email will be buried and they won't respond quickly enough.

>> Even if they respond, you'll have to compile all their feedback in several versions until you get the final version, which you then have to finalize to get the final, final version.

So what do you do? You call for a meeting! As soon as you do that, you are now contributing to the 11 million meetings that happen every day (a third of which are unnecessary and unproductive).

In this chapter, you find steps to put a stop to the meeting madness that plagues the workplace. Presence in Skype for Business will play an important role to make this happen. You can make your presence count in meetings even when you aren't there in person.

Understanding Why Presence Drives Productivity

When you're on the go, and especially if you work with a global team, timing isn't always perfect. But just because it isn't perfect doesn't mean you have to miss out on opportunities. Skype for Business allows you to connect with people inside or outside your organization one-on-one through IM, phone call, video call, or virtual group meetings with up to 10,000 attendees. With this technology, you can always get information when you need it to take advantage of business opportunities.

A picture is worth a thousand words

A fundamental element of social interaction is seeing the face of the person with whom you're communicating. But when you're interacting with colleagues who aren't in the same location as you, that can pose a challenge.

Skype for Business is designed to be a beautiful and social experience for the users. The high-quality treatment of profile pictures gives you a sense of actually seeing the face of the person you're talking to. If a picture isn't sufficient, sharing video is merely a couple of clicks away.

The first order of the day when you use Skype for Business is to ensure you have a profile photo. Usually, the photo in Skype for Business is pulled from the About Me page in Office 365. To add or edit your photo, follow these steps:

1. **While logged in to Office 365, click on your photo (or the placeholder photo) on the Office 365 navigation bar (top right).**

2. **Click About Me (see Figure 16-1).**

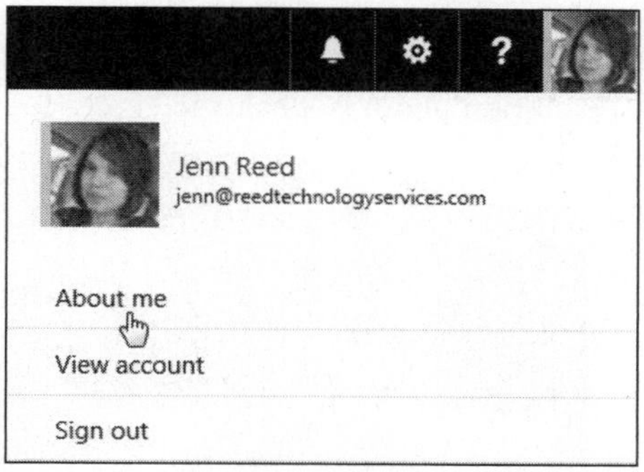

FIGURE 16-1:
Accessing the
About Me page.

3. **From your profile page, click Edit profile (see Figure 16-2).**

FIGURE 16-2:
Editing your
profile.

4. **Click Change your photo from the Basic Information tab.**

5. **From the new window that opens, click Upload photo, find a photo from your computer, and then click Open.**

6. **When your new photo is displayed, click Save.**

Back in the Skype for Business application, your photo should now display at the top along with your presence and location information. When people IM or call you, they'll be looking at your photo while you're interacting with them, giving them a sense of an in-person conversation. During online meetings, your photo will be displayed prominently — bigger than the other participants' — when you are speaking, so a high resolution photo is ideal (see Figure 16-3).

FIGURE 16-3:
Speaker's photo displayed prominently during a meeting.

REMEMBER

Having the system automatically update your presence based on your Outlook calendar is important so people you work with will be confident of your presence state. If presence state were manually updated and people forget to update their presence, then the confidence level would decrease and so would productivity.

Checking your contact's presence

The Contacts tab allows you to immediately know your co-workers' presence. If the person you want to communicate with isn't listed there, search for that contact in the search box. The search will pull information from your organization's Active Directory, your Outlook contacts, and contacts from other organizations that are federated with your organization. You can even search for and add contacts from the consumer version of Skype.

If your contact has entered a personal note, you'll see it below the name. Pay attention to it, as it may help you decide a course of action. For example, if your contact's status says "Looking forward to my vacation in 3 days. . .," you'll probably want to reach out to him or her sooner rather than later.

Tagging contacts for status change alerts

There are times when you need input from team members. The best way to do it quickly is to reach out to your team members, either one-on-one or to all of them at once, via an ad hoc virtual meeting.

Knowing your team members' availability through their presence status helps you decide what course of action to take. If you see that someone's presence is green, it's usually acceptable to start a conversation through IM and then add audio or video if needed. When all you need is a Yes/No answer, IM will suffice. If you need more of a discussion, it's better to add audio or video and even share screen if possible.

But what if your contact is red or yellow and you want to be able to catch that person as soon as he or she is green? The most efficient way to solve this problem is by tagging your contact for status change alerts. When you tag a contact, you get a notification when his or her presence status changes. Here's how:

1. **From the Contacts tab in Skype for Business, right click on the contact.**

2. **Click Tag for Status Change Alerts (see Figure 16-4, left).**

   When your contact changes his status, you get a pop-up alert on your screen (see Figure 16-4, right).

If you no longer want to be alerted of status changes, just right-click on the contact and click Tag for Status Change Alerts to disable the alert.

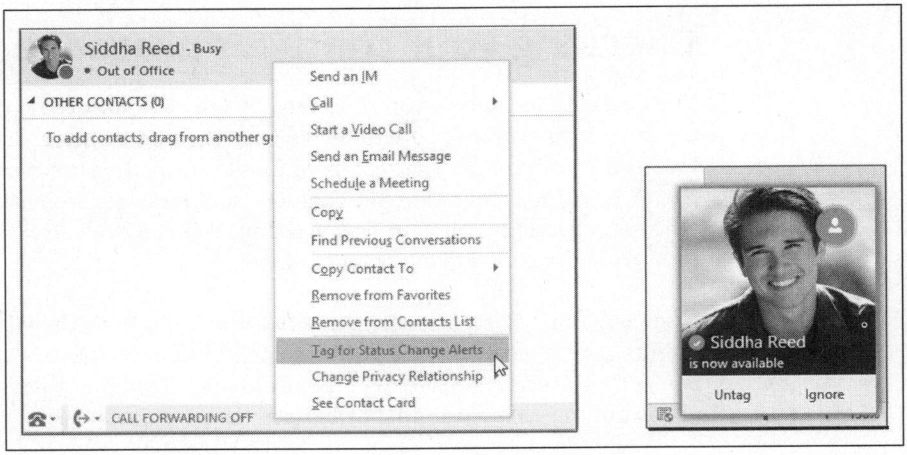

FIGURE 16-4:
Tagging a contact
for status change
alerts.

Presence Indicator Integration

In Outlook 2016 and Outlook Online, presence status also is displayed in emails and calendars items. In other Office applications, you can see presence information usually in the Sharing page or in the document's backstage view. Wherever you see presence information, you can hover over the contact to display the phone and the communication controls to initiate a conversation. You don't need to leave the application to go to Skype for Business to start an IM, for example.

Presence also is integrated in SharePoint Online, OneDrive, and the Office apps:

» In SharePoint Online and OneDrive for Business, hovering over the contact name when it is displayed (usually in a document library) will fire up the communication controls similar to the behavior in Office applications.

» In Office apps, you see the presence status, but the contact card behavior will vary with the operating system.

Skyping from Office applications

For example, let's say you're collaborating on a Word document with a few people. On the Sharing pane, you see the list of people who have access to the document with their presence indicator. When you hover over the contact, the communication controls pop up. You can immediately start a conversation with the contact by clicking one of the available controls: IM, phone call, video call, or email (see Figure 16-5). This experience is also true for Excel and PowerPoint. (In One-Note, the contact card pops up when you hover over the name of the person who made edits to page.)

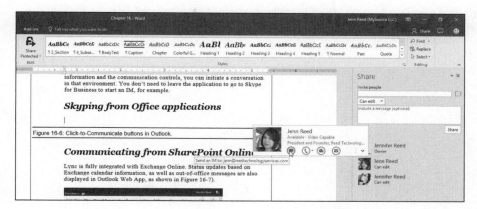

FIGURE 16-5:
Presence status
in Word.

Joining meetings from mobile devices

The Skype for Business app is available for Window, iOS, and Android devices. Once you've downloaded, installed, and logged in to the app, the user interface is very similar.

On an Android device, the main screen will display your upcoming meetings and recent contacts. If you want to see the full list of meetings for today and next day, click on the Meeting icon at the top of the screen (see Figure 16-6). On the Meetings information screen, you will see a button to join the meeting.

After you've joined the meeting, you will be able to interact with the meeting participants, share video, add more participants, and view the presenter's screen if it's being shared.

On a Windows phone, viewing a presenter's screen is impressive (see Figure 16-7) with a high fidelity treatment of the image. Controls can be hidden or displayed to allow you to interact with the participants.

On an iPad, the quality of the screen sharing is the same, but the controls are placed differently to conform to the iOS user interface design (see Figure 16-8).

Screen sharing and video sharing from your mobile device will consume cellular data if you aren't connected to Wi-Fi. You can change the settings in the Skype for Business app for your particular device to allow screen and video sharing only while connected to Wi-Fi.

WARNING

Meeting icon

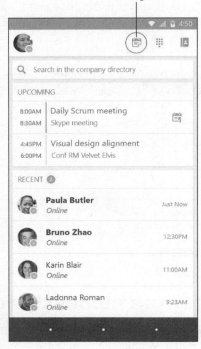

FIGURE 16-6:
Skype for
Business home
screen on an
Android device.

FIGURE 16-7:
Viewing a screen
sharing session
from a Windows
smartphone.

FIGURE 16-8:
Call controls on
an iPad.

6

Preparing to Move

Chapter 17

Meeting Office 365 Requirements

Y ou can think of Office 365 under two broad umbrellas. The first covers consumers, and the second covers businesses, non-profits, schools, governments, and other large organizations.

If you're part of a large organization, then moving from a nice and cozy on-site data center (or storage closet) to the cloud is a big change. You won't be able to walk through the server room and see all the computers with the lights flashing, disks whizzing, and screens glowing. You have a connection to the Internet, and the software and data live *out there* somewhere. To access your software, you begin by using it. You won't need to go through a lengthy installation and deployment process. It can take some time to get used to, but the change can be well worth the effort.

For consumers, the same process holds true. You only need a device (such as a smart phone, tablet, laptop, or desktop computer) and a connection to the Internet, and your data lives *out there*. Of course, you can save your data on your local device, but you run the risk of losing your data if you lose your device or if your device crashes. Also, you can't pick up another device and keep working. You'll be stuck using the device where your data lives. In our new world of mobile phones and tablets the cloud is a very convenient place to store your data.

This chapter covers some of the pros and cons of moving to the cloud for organizations and personal use. We also cover some of the specific requirements of the Microsoft Office 365 offering.

Office 365 constantly is being updated, upgraded, and developed. The user interface on any individual product can change frequently. The concepts are the same, but if you see something a little bit different than what is shown in a screenshot or described in this book, then Microsoft has made some changes.

Cloud Attraction

One of the biggest pain points in the corporate world is the interaction between business users and tech people. The business users couldn't care less about technology and just want the ability to do their job easier and more efficiently. The tech folks want to provide the best solution possible for the business users but get bogged down with time-intensive technical tasks. This concept is illustrated in Figure 17-1.

FIGURE 17-1:
When infrastructure is on premise, IT spends time keeping the lights blinking green, and the business users spend time pestering the IT team for help.

The cloud attempts to alleviate this tension by offloading the infrastructure to someone else — Microsoft in the case of Office 365. This frees up the tech people and lets them spend time optimizing the software for their business users instead of keeping the lights blinking green. Business users are happy because they get a better solution and IT people are happy because their valuable time isn't wasted searching the Internet for instructions on installing and configuring the latest software patch to fix a particular problem. This new paradigm is illustrated in Figure 17-2.

FIGURE 17-2:
Using the cloud lets someone else handle the infrastructure, and lets the IT focus on the needs of the business users.

TIP

Offloading the work it takes to manage and maintain infrastructure allows you to repurpose resources to more valuable tasks, such as providing solutions that use software, including SharePoint to help sales.

On the consumer side, the world has moved on from the tagline *a computer on every desktop*. Today, everyone has a computer in a pocket, a tablet computer on the bedside, a laptop for work on weekends, a desktop at work, and maybe another phone or tablet or Mac for good measure. In short, if you're the average person, you have a lot of devices now. Oh, and you're always on the move. You don't sit still, and you expect to take your work with you.

To accommodate our active and mobile lives where we use lots of devices, Office 365 saves our data in the cloud. The apps you use to work on data can be installed on multiple devices, but the actual data itself is stored only once, up in the cloud. You can work, regardless of where you are or which device you happen to be using at the time.

Looking at the Pros and Cons of the Cloud

As with any decision in life, there are generally pros and cons; moving to the cloud is no exception. Depending on whom you're talking with, the cloud is either the greatest thing since the invention of the wheel or a devilish ploy by big companies to wrestle away control of your data. The truth is that many people find that the benefits of the cloud greatly outweigh the detriments.

Some of the benefits of moving to the Microsoft cloud include the following:

» Outsourcing the hassle of installing, managing, patching, and upgrading extremely complex software systems.

» Having predictable and known costs associated with adoption.

» Keeping the lights blinking green and the software up-to-date and secure falls on Microsoft and is backed by service guarantee.

» Reducing cost is not only an immediate monetary value but also has efficiency and resource reallocation benefits.

» Backing up and securing your data. After all, Microsoft may not be perfect, but its teams of engineers are extremely specialized and are experts at hosting the software that their colleagues have developed.

» Using the software over the Internet — simply sign up and you're ready to go. Without the cloud, a SharePoint deployment could take months.

» Forgetting where your data is located and working on whatever device you happen to have in front of you.

Some of the cons that come along with adopting a cloud solution in general include the following:

» Relying on network and bandwidth. If your Internet provider goes down, then you haven't any access to your enterprise software and data. Microsoft doesn't control how you access the Internet and, therefore, cannot account for any failures. If you live in a location with slow Internet or no cellular Internet coverage, then having your data on a local device might be your only option.

» Having data controlled by someone else. Your data is hosted in Microsoft's data center. That can be both a benefit and a detriment. If you feel uncomfortable with your data *out there* somewhere, then you can either research the Microsoft data centers further or keep your data and applications locally in your own controlled data center or on your local device. In addition, when you sign up for enterprise licensing of Office 365, you also gain licensing rights to On Premise deployments. This capability makes it possible to store extremely sensitive data or user portals on site. For example, you may want your executive, accounting, and human resources portals on site but the rest of your SharePoint implementation in the cloud. Microsoft lets you mix and match this way to fit your comfort level, and terms it a *hybrid* approach to the cloud.

TIP

Microsoft has invested billions of dollars in its state-of-the-art data centers and has gone to great lengths to calm the concern of not knowing where your data is located. For a great video on the Microsoft data centers, check out the video on YouTube by the MSGFSTeam titled "Microsoft GFS Datacenter Tour." You can find this video by searching for "Microsoft GFS Datacenter Tour" on YouTube and then looking for the specific video.

Overall Office 365 Requirements

Although by definition a cloud offering is available to anyone with an Internet connection, there are a few other requirements that must be observed should you choose to use Office 365. In particular, you must be located in a supported country and must have supported software and a high-speed Internet connection.

Geographic requirements

Microsoft has launched Office 365 in over 140 countries around the world, and allows a user license to be assigned to anyone in the world, with the exception of those who live in Cuba, Iran, Democratic People's Republic of Korea (North Korea), Sudan, and Syria.

Software requirements

To get the most out of Office 365, it is best to use Windows 10 with Office 2016 and the latest Edge web browser. Doing this gives you the fully integrated experience. Office 365 does, however, support just about every other popular device including Mac desktops and laptops, Android phones and tablets, and iPhones. In addition, Office Online apps can be run within a browser. If you use a device that doesn't have an app available, you can crack open your web browser and edit Office documents without even installing Office.

When you sign up for an Office 365 subscription, you pay for Office on a monthly basis. The upside is that Microsoft guarantees you the latest version of Office 365 products with automatic updates. Microsoft is quickly moving to a world where requirements won't really matter, because your devices will always have the latest and greatest software.

TIP

As with the rest of Office 365, Microsoft continually is updating requirements. The current version of Microsoft Office is 2016 and others will surely follow. To see whether your existing software will work with Office 365, jump over to your favorite search engine and type "Office 365 requirements". Look for a link to a page on either office.com or microsoft.com and check whether your existing software will work.

TECHNICAL STUFF

A key feature of Office 365 provides the ability for your business's Active Directory instance to sync with your Office 365 account. To achieve this integration, however, your Active Directory domain must be a single forest. What does this mean? It means you can use your existing username and password from work with Office 365. (After it's set up, of course.)

Device requirements

In the old days, you had to use Microsoft Windows if you wanted to use most Microsoft software. The old days are history. Today, Microsoft has Office 365 apps for Mac desktops and laptops, iPads, Android tablets, Android phones, iPhones, plus Windows devices. Microsoft is constantly adding and upgrading Office 365 apps, so be sure to stay up to date on available Office 365 apps for your particular device.

Internet access requirements

Because the Office 365 software lives in a Microsoft data center and is accessed over the Internet, having high-speed Internet access available on a regular basis is important. For some of the components of Office 365, such as the Outlook Web App, high-speed Internet access isn't required, but as a general rule, you want to make sure that you have a pleasant experience and that equals a high-speed Internet connection when dealing with the cloud.

In addition, because Office 365 is a subscription-based product, you will constantly get a stream of updates. This is great because your software is always up to date and you don't have to worry about requirements. However, if you have a slow Internet connection, updates might be more of a problem than a benefit.

TIP

Because Office 365 can be accessed from any computer anywhere in the world with an Internet connection, you have no control over the network connectivity. Most people understand that the speed of their Internet connection directly relates to the speed of a software update or download and will not blame the Office 365 service — that doesn't mean the experience is less painful on a slow Internet connection.

Identifying browser requirements

There are many points of contact with Office 365. Depending on which computer you're using to access the cloud services, you need to make sure that your web browser is supported.

Microsoft guarantees that Office 365 will work with the latest versions of Safari, Chrome, Firefox, in addition to Microsoft's new Edge browser. Although Office 365 will work with the older Microsoft browser, Internet Explorer, it's clear that Edge is the future and it's unclear how long Internet Explorer will be supported.

You can find the latest specifics around supported browsers by cracking open your favorite search engine and typing "Office 365 requirements." Look for a link to a page on either www.office.com or www.microsoft.com and check for specifics around older browsers.

TIP

A light version of Outlook Web App exists when you find yourself using or borrowing a computer that doesn't meet the minimum requirements for the full-featured experience. The light version also loads much faster, and is useful if you're temporarily using a very slow Internet connection. Even though the light version isn't as feature rich as the full version, it accomplishes the basic tasks of email very well.

Skype for Business requirements

As we cover in Part 5, Skype for Business is a powerful communication platform that is used for online meetings and instant communication. Skype for Business installs as a client on your device, and is then used in conjunction with other Office 365 apps (such as Microsoft Word, Excel, PowerPoint, and Outlook) or as its own communications device.

If you're familiar with Skype, then you're already familiar with Skype for Business. Skype for Business is just a business version of Skype with the same great features.

TIP

Skype for Business used to be called Lync. Microsoft acquired the Skype consumer product and dutifully has been merging it with the Microsoft Lync product to leverage the best of both products.

Skype for Business uses a high amount of bandwidth for communication using voice, video, and screen sharing. For these reasons, you should plan on a fairly fast Internet connection to ensure a good experience. We use Skype on our iPhones with regular 4G cellular service all the time and don't have any problems. If you're on a slow connection, your mileage may vary.

UNDERSTANDING BANDWIDTH

It definitely takes some time to get your mind wrapped around bandwidth. What exactly is bandwidth anyway? Trying to understand bandwidth can be like trying to understand warp speed in *Star Trek*. Nobody really understood what it was, but we knew that it made the Enterprise ship go very fast. Punch it, Scotty! Because bandwidth is such a fuzzy topic, it is best to use an analogy in order to understand it.

In a nutshell, bandwidth is the amount of data that can pass over a network at any given time. The best analogy for this is water moving through a hose or pipe. You can think of your data as a pool full of water. If you have a lot of it, such as those massive PDF documents, or 300-page PowerPoint presentations, then you have a lot of water. Say the amount of an Olympic-size swimming pool. If you have just a little, such as a two-page Notepad document, then you just have a small cereal bowl-size of water.

Now, to get that water from Point A to Point B, you need to pipe it through plumbing. If you have a massive 3-foot diameter pipe, then your water will move very quickly. If you have a garden hose, your water will move very slowly. This concept is illustrated in the figure.

The rate at which you can move water through the plumbing and data through the network is called bandwidth. The 3-foot diameter pipe provides high bandwidth and the garden hose provides a small amount of bandwidth. The trick with bandwidth is to remember that the least common denominator always wins. For example, in the water analogy, you might be moving that swimming pool full of water across town, but if the pump siphoning the water out of the pool is only a small hose that attaches to a 3-foot diameter pipe, then guess what — the water will only move as fast as the small hose can move it. The 3-foot pipe will just trickle the water along as it comes out of the small hose. On the other hand if you have a 3-foot pump to go along with that 3-foot hose, then the water will fly through the pipe at a rapid rate.

It is the same with data over the network. If you have a very slow wireless router in your house, then it doesn't matter how fast the Internet speed is coming in and out of your house.

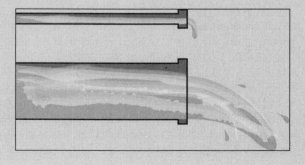

Chapter 18

Planning for Your Office 365 Implementation

Reading this book is the first step of preparing for your Office 365 journey. Throughout the book, we explain how Office 365 can benefit your organization. Now that you're up to speed on the product, you can plan how to get started with Office 365.

Microsoft divides Office 365 into business plans and consumer plans:

>> If you're a business or organization, you need to put some thought into Office 365 and think of it as an implementation.

>> If you're just looking for Office 365 for your family or personal needs, the process is much easier.

In this chapter, you find information to get started with Office 365. Because setting up a business or organization requires much more work than a personal subscription, most of the chapter is geared around planning an Office 365 implementation for your business or organization. You walk through preparing and then planning for deploying Office 365, including such tasks as choosing a subscription plan, cataloging your internal resources, and finding a partner.

Choosing an Office 365 Plan

Office 365 has blossomed over the years. It isn't a one-size-fits-all product. Microsoft recognized this and broke up the product into specific plans to fit the needs of individuals, families, small business, and all the way up to multinational enterprises.

When you're first getting your head wrapped around Office 365, you can think of it as two different products under the same marketing umbrella:

>> If you're a consumer, and you would initially think of buying software at a store like Best Buy, then you're likely looking for one of the Home plans.

>> If you're looking for Office 365 for your business or organization then you're likely looking for one of the Business plans.

When you land on the Office 365 page, this choice is neatly set in front of you with a For Home and For Business button, as shown in Figure 18-1.

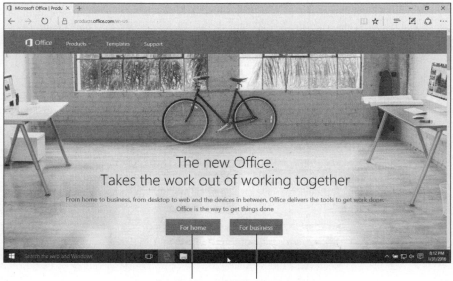

FIGURE 18-1:
The Office 365 landing page at https:// products. office.com.

For Home   For Business

If you're looking for a personal plan and you click the For Home button, the process of purchasing and installing Office 365 is relatively straightforward. Microsoft is constantly changing the terminology so we're hesitant to name the plans. As of this writing, they're offering two plans with the following primary differences:

>> With a Home plan, you have five users that can each install Office products on five devices.

>> With a Personal plan, you have only one user that can install Office products on five devices.

Both of these plans are on a subscription basis: you pay each month and you're constantly guaranteed to have the most up to date software. When a new version of the products comes out you instantly get to install and use it. If you don't like the subscription model, there's a one-time purchase option, but you don't get the updated products as they come out.

The For Home plans are shown in Figure 18-2.

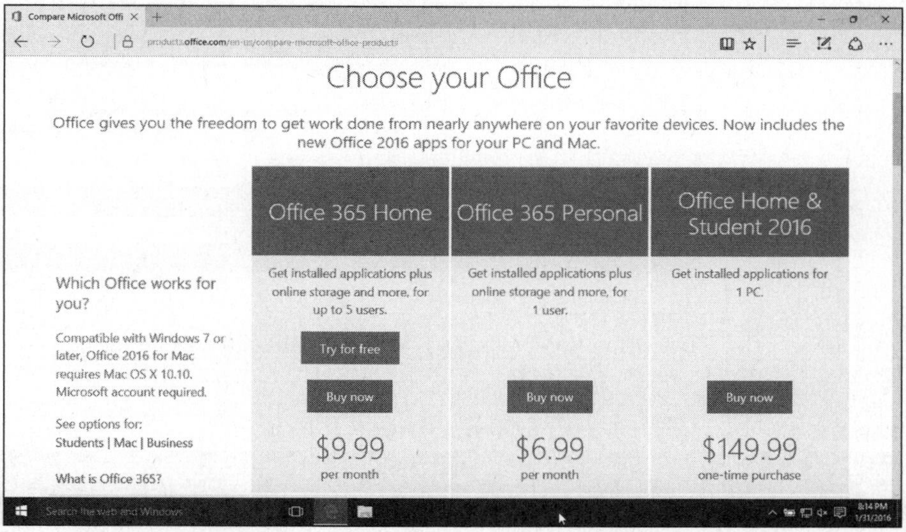

FIGURE 18-2:
The Office 365
For Home plans.

When you're looking for a business or organization plan, the options require much more thought and planning. Again, Microsoft is constantly jiggering the plans to try to segment the offerings in the smartest way for each type of organization. As of 2016, the business plans range from $5 per user per month (the Business Essentials plan) to $35 per user per month (the Enterprise E5 plan).

The For Business plans are shown in Figure 18-3.

The Office 365 business plans have changed over the years and Microsoft has landed on a fairly intuitive grouping. There are small- and medium-sized business plans and there are plans that are geared toward large enterprises. One of the main things to look for is whether a plan includes the Microsoft Office productivity apps that can be installed on your local device (Word, Excel, PowerPoint, OneNote, Outlook, Publisher, and OneDrive).

Plans & Pricing

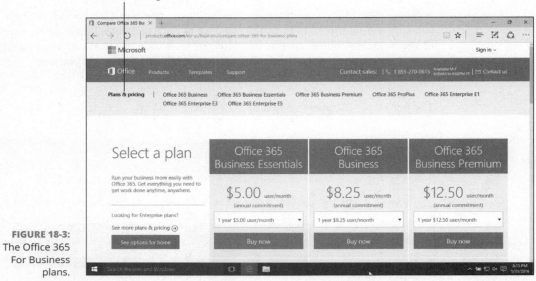

The Office 365 business plans are outlined in Table 18-1.

TABLE 18-1   Office 365 For Business Plans

Plan	Description	Price / User / Mo.*
Office 365 Business Essentials	Online versions of Office. Comes with 50GB mailbox (Exchange), 1TB file storage, and video conferencing. The max number of users is 300.	$5.00
Office 365 Business	Doesn't include email (Exchange) but includes the full versions of Microsoft Office that you can install on your local device. The max number of users is 300.	$8.25
Office 365 Business Premium	Includes both email (Exchange) and the full versions of Microsoft Office. The max number of users is 300.	$12.50
Office 365 Pro Plus	Includes the full version of Microsoft Office and adds Microsoft Access. The Office apps can be installed on up to 5 devices per user. Think of this offering as just Microsoft Office, because it doesn't include email or conferencing. Includes 1TB of online file storage. The max number of users is unlimited.	$12.00

Plan	Description	Price / User / Mo.*
Office 365 Enterprise E1	The entry level enterprise plan that includes features such as business class email, calendar, and contacts (Exchange) with 50GB of space, online meetings (Skype for Business), and a content management system and intranet (SharePoint). Also includes 1TB of file storage. This initial offering doesn't include the full versions of Microsoft Office however.	$8.00
Office 365 Enterprise E3	Similar to the E1 plan but this plan includes the full versions of Microsoft Office that can be installed on your local device and an unlimited email box.	$20.00
Office 365 Enterprise E5	Similar to the E3 plan but this plan adds some additional security and analytics features and the biggest addition is Public Switched Telephone Network (PSTN) calling and Cloud PBX for cloud-based call management.	$35.00

Prices as of this writing. They have been known to change. You can also add various options which affect the price, too.

WARNING

Rather than try to get into the specifics of each plan in this book we recommend that you carefully research each plan option based on what is available at the time you're looking to implement Office 365 for your business or organization. Microsoft is constantly adding new features and shifting things around. Be sure to check the specific plans before basing your decision on Table 18-1.

In addition to the plans outlined for business there are also Office 365 offerings for educational institutions, government institutions, and non-profit organizations. Some of these Office 365 plans are even *free* for qualifying institutions and organizations.

Laying the Groundwork

You should keep in mind that the size and complexity of your organization, as well as the Office 365 plan you choose, will directly affect your implementation. If you're a one-person consultant or small business using a business plan, then your implementation will be very straightforward. If your organization contains thousands of employees with offices around the world, your implementation will be much more in depth and will require extensive planning.

Regardless of your organization's size and the plan you choose, your implementation follows three primary steps — plan, prepare, and migrate, as outlined in this section and illustrated in Figure 18-4. The migration phase is covered in Chapter 19.

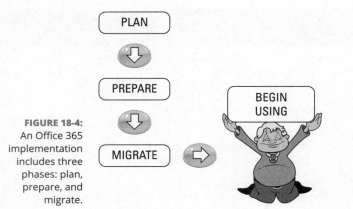

FIGURE 18-4:
An Office 365
implementation
includes three
phases: plan,
prepare, and
migrate.

The best implementation processes follow an iterative cycle in that you continually plan, prepare, and migrate. You need to start somewhere, however, and you always start with a plan. When you get your plan in order, you then move onto preparing to migrate. As you're preparing, you realize some additional things that you didn't include in your plan. As a result, you continually update your plan. Perhaps a better representation of the process is shown in Figure 18-5, even though this might not sit well with organizations that have extensive gating requirements for every project undertaken.

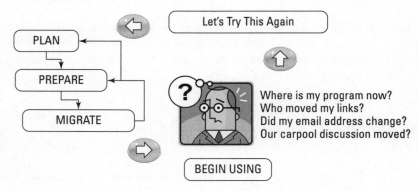

FIGURE 18-5:
The Office 365
implementation
phases in an
iterative diagram.

Planning phase

The planning phase of an Office 365 implementation greatly depends on many factors, including whether you're using one of the business plans or enterprise plans. Regardless of which plan you're using, you want to get a handle on the resources and roles that you will need for the implementation as well as such tasks as

>> Meeting synchronization

>> Issue tracking

>> Strategies around email, such as mailbox size and emailed integration with SharePoint

>> Account provisioning and licensing

>> Internet bandwidth consideration

>> Software and hardware inventories

>> Administrator and end-user training

>> Communication planning

Getting a handle on resources you will need

The in-house, human-based resources that you need for an Office 365 business or enterprise implementation are outlined in Table 18-2. Note that if you're implementing one of the business plans, then a single person or hired contractor might play all these roles with a negligible amount of work required for each role. If you're a large organization implementing the enterprise plan, then you may contract out these roles to a partner or have a team of in-house staff assigned to specific roles.

TABLE 18-2   **Human-Based Resources**

Resource	Description
Project Manager	The Project Manager is responsible for making sure that each resource is on the same page as the Office 365 implementation proceeds.
Office 365 Administrator	Responsibilities include managing the Office 365 interface with such technical tasks as domains, security groups, users, and licenses.
SharePoint Administrator	Responsible for administering the SharePoint Online platform, including creating sites, installing solutions, and activating features.
Exchange Administrator	Responsible for maintaining the settings for user mailboxes and email, including the settings required for connectivity with Outlook.
Skype for Business Administrator	The Skype for Business Administrator is responsible for all configuration with the Skype for Business program.
Network Administrator	Responsible for maintaining the Internet connection for the organization. Because Office 365 is in the cloud and accessed over the Internet, the connection is critical.
Trainer	Takes on the role of learning how the software works and then teaching others the best practices as they relate to your organization.

The enterprise plan includes a number of additional roles that can be used to create a very granular distribution of duties. Chapter 8 outlines the administrative roles in further detail. In addition, SharePoint administrators can control the SharePoint Online environment to the site and even individual lists and library level. For example, you may have an accounting department that has very sensitive data. The SharePoint administrator for that accounting site can add or remove user rights for different parts of the site. All this SharePoint administration is done within SharePoint and isn't part of the Office 365 administrative interface.

Synchronization meetings

With any Enterprise software adoption, maintaining open lines of communication is important. If everyone is on the same page, then it is easier to navigate issues as they arise rather than at the end of the project. Pulling a page from Scrum methodology, it is a good idea to have daily stand-ups where the teams stand in a circle and quickly announce what they're working on and which obstacles are blocking them from continuing with their tasks.

The software development methodology known as SCRUM is a process for completing complicated software development cycles. The term comes from the Australian sport of rugby where the entire team moves down the field as one unit rather than as individual players. If you aren't familiar with SCRUM, then we highly recommend you check out the Scrum Alliance website at www.scrumalliance.org and Jeff Sutherland's site, the father and co-founder of Scrum, at www.scruminc.com.

Issue tracking

Tracking issues as they arise is critical, and you need a process in place. SharePoint is ideal at issue tracking, so you may want to use a pilot implementation of Office 365 that includes SharePoint Online to track your issues for your Office 365 implementation. Isn't that tactic a mind bender?

E-mail strategies

E-mail plays a very important role in nearly every organization. When moving to Office 365, you will be moving your email system. Email can be widely spread and integrated into many different nooks and crannies of your infrastructure. You want to make sure that you do a thorough audit to find out which systems and applications are using email, and which you want to move to Office 365. In addition, you need to be aware of the size of users' email boxes and the amount of email that will be migrated to Exchange Online (which is the email portion of Office 365). In particular, take note of how you're using SharePoint and how SharePoint is using email. If you're new to SharePoint, then you're in for a treat because you gain an understanding of how the product integrates with email.

For more on SharePoint, check out Part III or check out *SharePoint 2010 Development For Dummies* by Ken Withee and Rosemarie Withee (Wiley).

Account provisioning and licensing

The good news is that Office 365 is very flexible in licensing, user provisioning, and administration. With that said, however, you want to plan out the number of users and the licensing requirements you need for your organization. You may choose to adopt Office 365 all at once or as a phased approach by moving a single group over to Office 365 as a pilot. In either case, you need to understand your licensing requirements so that you can plan resources and costs accordingly. The plus side of a subscription-based model is that you can add licenses as you need them or remove them when you don't. Before subscription-based pricing, you had to spend a lot of money for licensing whether you used it or not. Those days are gone.

Internet bandwidth consideration

Because Office 365 lives in the cloud and is accessed over the Internet, your connection must be top-notch. Your network administrator or IT consultant can use a number of different network bandwidth testing tools so that you have firsthand reports on how much bandwidth you're currently using in your organization and how moving to the cloud will affect the users.

Software and hardware inventories

Undertaking an audit of your current software and hardware resources is important. Fortunately, Microsoft has a tool available for just such a task. It is called the Microsoft Assessment and Planning (MAP) toolkit, and it can be downloaded by searching for it in the Microsoft Download Center located at

```
www.microsoft.com/download
```

After you have a handle on the software and hardware in your organization, you need to reference the requirements for Office 365 to determine if you need to make changes. Refer to Chapter 17 for Office 365 software and hardware requirements.

Administrator and end-user training

As with any new system, training is a required element. Office 365 has been designed with intuitive user interfaces for both administration and end users, but without a training plan, you're rolling the dice. A popular and successful approach to training when it comes to intuitive designs is called train the trainer. The idea being that you invest in formal training for a power user and then that user trains the rest of the company. This strategy is very effective even for large organizations because the training scales exponentially. As people are trained, they then train other people.

Communication planning

The best communication is clear, transparent, and all-inclusive. Everyone in the organization has ideas and an opinion. By garnering as many thoughts and as much brainpower (crowd sourcing) as possible, the organization will accomplish two clear objectives.

The first is that you will shed light on problems, issues, and risks early and often and can adjust early in the process rather than down the road when it is too late. The second big win an organization achieves involves ownership and engagement. In order for a project to be successful, you need for the users to be engaged and take ownership of the solution.

Microsoft has taken great effort to make the adoption of Office 365 as painless as possible but, in the end, it will still be a change. It can be argued that it is a change for the better in moving to Office 365 and taking advantage of all the cloud has to offer, but any change at all involves discomfort, apprehension, and stress. Having a good communication plan keeps everyone in the loop and feeling a part of the process. When you effect change at a grassroots level and let the wave of adoption swell up from great user experiences, then the organization as a whole wins.

Migration needs

One of the biggest aspects of moving to Office 365 will be migration of content, including mailboxes and other content. The ideal situation is that your organization has been living under a rock and has no document management system in place or custom portal functionality. In this scenario, you simply start using SharePoint in all of its glory and bathe in the efficiency and productivity gains of a modern portal environment.

The chances are, however, that you already have a number of systems in place. These systems might be SharePoint, or they might be a custom developed solution. In any case, you need to plan to migrate the content and functionality of these systems into Office 365. The good news is that Office 365 is definitely a product worth spending the time, effort, and resources in adopting.

Preparing phase

After you have a good handle on what you plan to do, you need to prepare to do it. Keep in mind that because every organization is different, you should only use these steps as a guide. If you're a small organization, then moving to Office 365 might be as easy as a walk in the park. If you're part of a thousand-person multinational organization with offices around the world, then the process will be much more involved.

TIP

As you begin preparing, you will inevitably realize some deficiencies in your plan. Think of these steps as iterative. When you know more about what you should include in your plan, go back and update your plan. As you walk through the preparation phase, you will know more than you did during the planning phase. This is why an iterative process is so very important. You don't know what you don't know, and to think that you could plan everything without being all-knowing is a ridiculous thought.

DNS

The Domain Naming System (DNS) is a standard used to let computers communicate over the Internet. For example, Microsoft manages the domain microsoft.com. All the Microsoft computers that are accessed over the Internet are part of this domain, and each is assigned a specific number, known as an Internet Protocol (IP) address. When you send an email to someone at Microsoft, your computer asks the microsoft.com DNS server which computer handles email.

When you move to Office 365, you must make changes in DNS so that network traffic understands where it should be routed. In essence, what happens is that when the DNS is changed, anyone sending you an email will have that email routed to your Office 365 implementation rather than to the current location.

Mailboxes

As you just discovered in the preceding section on DNS, there are specific computers responsible for hosting your email. If you keep your email on your local computer, then you won't have any email data to migrate. However, if you leave your email on the server, then all that data will need to be migrated to the Office 365 mailboxes. This migration can be one of the most technically difficult parts of moving email systems, but with guidance from a partner, it can be pain free.

Portals

A web portal, also known as an Intranet site, can be as simple as a static web page, or as complex as a fully integrated solution. SharePoint provides a tremendous amount of functionality, and it has seen massive adoption in the last decade. Office 365 includes SharePoint Online, which is nothing more than SharePoint hosted by Microsoft. During the migration phase of an implementation, you need to decide which content you want to move to SharePoint and which you can leave where it is currently located. In addition, you need to decide which functionality you want to integrate into your portal and which systems are better left in place.

Logins and Licensing

If you're a part of a very large organization, then your IT team probably manages your users with a Microsoft technology called Active Directory. For large organizations, you can sync this on-site management of users with the Office 365 users, which results in a single login and simplified access to the cloud environment. If you're part of a small organization, then you might manage all your users in Office 365 directly. In either case, you need to come up with a list of the people who need to have access to Office 365 and the associated licensing.

Training

Even the best software is useless unless people know about it and know how to use it. Microsoft has created a wealth of documentation and user training that can be had for little or no cost. In addition, any partner you decide to work with will have training plans available and can conduct training for Office 365.

Support

After users start adopting Office 365, they're bound to have questions. You need to have a support system in place in order to accommodate even the simplest questions. The support system should include power users as a first point of content and then a formal support system that escalates all the way up to Microsoft supporting Office 365.

Office 365 Online Documentation

This chapter alone isn't intended as a complete guide for implementing Office 365. Your primary source of information about all things Office 365 can be found at

```
http://support.office.com
```

On the Office Support site, you will find navigation at the top of the page for Apps, Setup, Training, and Admin, as shown in Figure 18-6.

These links are your key to learning about Office 365. Spend time going through this content. If you're implementing Office 365 for a business as we discuss in this chapter, then you will find the Admin → Office 365 For Business is a great place to dive into right away.

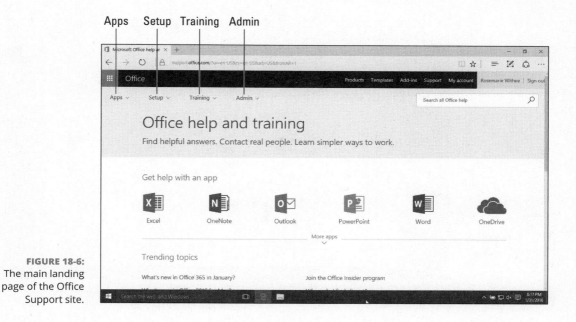

Apps Setup Training Admin

FIGURE 18-6:
The main landing page of the Office Support site.

In addition, Microsoft has released a number of downloadable guides for Office 365. Search the Microsoft Download Center for Office 365 at the following URL:

```
www.microsoft.com/download
```

Choosing a Partner

Throughout the chapter, we cover planning and preparing for an Office 365 implementation. As noted, the process isn't linear but is iterative. For example, you don't plan and then stop planning and move into preparing, and then stop preparing and move into migration. Instead, it is an iterative process in that you know what you know at the time and you will know more later on down the road. Luckily, if you use a partner, that partner will have been through this iterative cycle many times with other customers and can make the process much easier than undertaking the process on your own.

Microsoft provides the ability to find a partner on their Office 365 product page. Simply navigate to http://partner.microsoft.com, then type Office 365 into the search link about halfway down the page. The results will show you information about the partners and reviews for each partner, as shown in Figure 18-7.

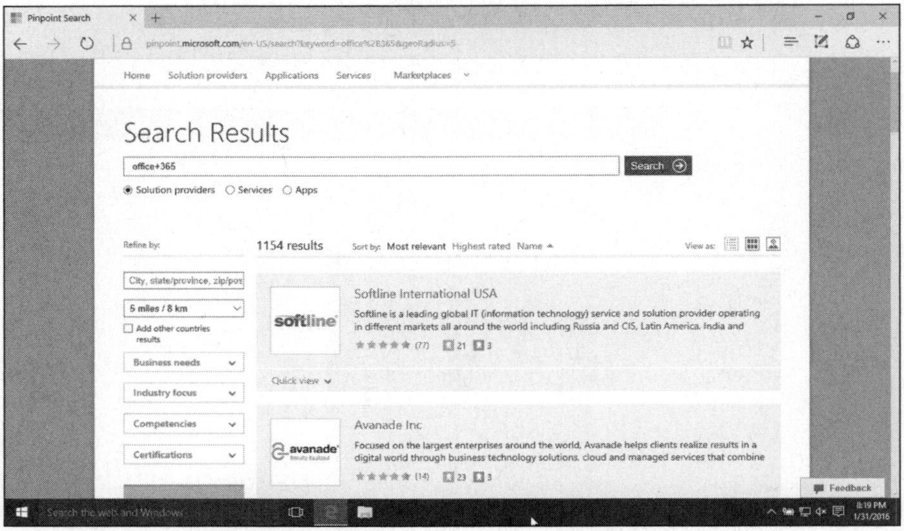

FIGURE 18-7:
Finding a
Microsoft
partner.

TIP

Reading the reviews and doing your homework can pay huge dividends when it comes time to implementing Office 365. An experienced partner can make the process seem like a dream, whereas an inexperienced partner can taint your view of the Office 365 product forever.

Chapter 19

Implementing Office 365

I n Chapter 18, we detail how to prepare and plan for an Office 365 implementation. In this chapter, you get to throw the switch and make the move to the Microsoft cloud.

Office 365 is designed for nearly every type of organization — ranging from a one-person mom-and-pop shop, to a stay-at-home dad tracking chores, to a student, and all the way up to a multinational enterprise. Because of this massively different audience, every implementation is different, both in complexity and in time.

This chapter covers the general process and gives you some pointers on where to go for more information. If you're planning to use one of the Office 365 For Home plans, you're in for a treat. Its implementation is simple and straightforward. The challenge with Office 365 can be when you're implementing it for an organization. If you're a small organization, then some of the steps in this chapter may be overkill. If you're a very large enterprise, then you will surely want to work with a partner, such as an IT services firm specializing in Office 365, that can guide you through the process.

This chapter provides a high-level overview of the steps required to implement Office 365, including preparing users through training, activating licensing, providing a support mechanism, and migrating data and custom portal functionality.

It also provides a quick section on getting started with the For Home plans. Microsoft has gone out of its way to keep the consumer plans simple; with Windows 10, the process is a snap. For this reason, this chapter focuses mostly on implementing the For Business plans.

Getting Started with Office 365 For Home Plans

If you're choosing an Office 365 For Home plan, the process is very straightforward. You just buy it and start using it. If you purchased a plan with the full version of Office, you also install those apps. The process is simple and straightforward.

To get started with Office 365 For Home, follow these steps:

1. **Open your favorite web browser and navigate to** `https://products.office.com`.

2. **Click the For Home button to see the consumer-based Office 365 plans.**

3. **Decide which plan fits your needs and click the Buy Now button.**

   The main choices (which may change) are the Home plan and the Personal plan:

   - The Home plan allows you to install Microsoft Office on up to five PC/Mac computers and up to five tablet or phone devices.

   - The Personal plan allows only a single PC/Mac and a single tablet and phone device.

4. **Follow the purchasing wizard to complete your purchase.**

5. **Open your Office 365 consumer portal at** `https://products.office.com`.

6. **Click the sign in in the upper-right corner, then select For Home to sign in with your Microsoft account.**

   After you sign in, the portal is displayed, as shown in Figure 19-1.

After you purchase Office 365 For Home, you can begin using it. Your main landing page is always `https://portal.office.com`, which you can open in any browser. For help, open `https://support.office.com` in your browser and check out the excellent documentation for the apps and the products contained within your Office 365 subscription.

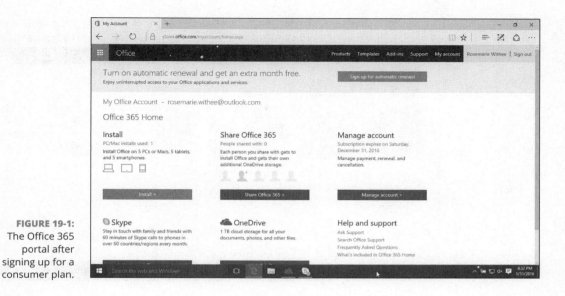

FIGURE 19-1:
The Office 365 portal after signing up for a consumer plan.

Getting Started with Office 365 For Business Plans

The initial process for purchasing a For Business plan is very similar to the process for purchasing a For Home plan. However, the similarities end there; many of the For Business plans contain advanced software that you will need to plan for and administer. This is such software as SharePoint, Exchange, and Skype for Business.

To purchase a For Business plan, follow these steps:

1. **Open your favorite web browser and navigate to** `http://products.office.com`.

2. **Click the For Business button to see the business-based Office 365 plans.**

3. **Decide which plan fits your needs and click the Buy Now button.**

   Within the business plans, a major choice you will need to make is whether to go with the small and medium business plans or the enterprise plans. For more information on these plans, see Chapter 18.

4. **Follow the purchasing wizard to complete your purchase.**

5. **Head over to your Office 365 portal at** `http://portal.office.com` **and sign in with your Microsoft account as shown in Figure 19-2.**

   Here, you can read about your Office 365 subscription and get things set up.

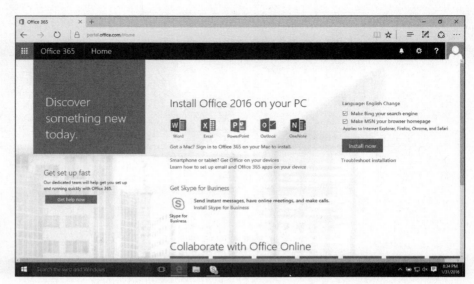

FIGURE 19-2:
The Office 365
portal after
signing up for a
business plan.

Purchasing an initial Office 365 For Business plan is just the beginning. Because you're managing a business, you will need to add users, add licensing, configure the services you're planning to use, migrate data, add your organization's domain, build out your intranet portal, train people, and generally get everything set up and ready to go. You do all of this from your main Office 365 portal at http://portal.office.com.

Getting Users Ready for Office 365

Microsoft Office 365 is easy to use and has very intuitive interfaces. However, that doesn't mean that you can just turn it on and tell everyone to "go wild." Although you may be familiar with the Microsoft Office products, understanding how these same products integrate and the value that results from that integration is critical in increasing productivity and boosting efficiency. To get users ready for the plunge, you need to start with training and follow up with a support system so that everyone knows where to go when they need help.

Training

We recommend using a simple formula known as the *tell, show, do* method. Here's what you do:

1. **Tell people how Office 365 works.**

2. **Show everyone how it works with a live demo.**

3. **Let people get their hands dirty and do it on their own.**

This strategy works great for all types of technology training.

TIP

The Office 365 product is made up of a basket of products. These products include the Microsoft Office productivity suite, SharePoint Online, Exchange Online, and Skype for Business Online. The different plans that make up Office 365 include various permutations of product features. For example, in order to get Microsoft Office with your plan, you need to purchase one of the plans that includes licensing to install it on local devices. For more information about the features that make up the different plans, refer to Chapter 18.

Attempting training for such a broad product as Office 365 can be challenging. For example, providing training on just the Microsoft Office piece can consume a great deal of effort because the product is made up of a number of applications, including Word, Excel, PowerPoint, Outlook, OneNote, Publisher, Access, and Skype for Business. Rather than focus on training for each of these components, a better strategy might be to focus on how to achieve specific business functionality without going into the details of each product. For example, for email you use Outlook, for the company intranet you use a web browser and navigate to it (SharePoint is the technology behind it, but you don't need to worry so much about that), and for instant communication and meetings you use Skype for Business.

TIP

Microsoft has a number of partners that provide training for Office 365. You can search Pinpoint for the word 'training' to find a list of training companies. Access Pinpoint by using the following URL in your browser:

```
https://pinpoint.microsoft.com
```

Support

Even the most experienced and seasoned mountain climbers have a support system, and your organization shouldn't be any different. Establishing a support system doesn't mean spending a lot of money. A support system can be as simple as a go-to power user on the team or as complex as a full-fledged call center. Depending on the size of your organization, your support system can take many different forms. A good strategy, however, is to take a tiered approach by starting with communal support through some of the collaborative features of Office 365, such as SharePoint and Skype for Business. Besides, isn't it poetic to use Office 365 to support Office 365? You can find out more by checking out Part III (SharePoint) and Part V (Skype for Business).

The community can provide base-level support and work together to figure out the technology. When the community cannot help, then you can call in the big guns by requesting support from your partner or even from Microsoft itself.

TIP

By creating a vibrant community that collaborates and supports each other, your organization will have a much better Office 365 experience. The cultural changes that come about from an integrated and connected workforce can add a tremendous return on investment to the organization. With Office 365, you have the tools, but every employee must use them to make the transition effective.

When you need to enter a service request with Microsoft, you can do so from within the Office 365 administrator portal, as shown in Figure 19-3. The admin center is accessed by logging into `http://portal.office.com` and then clicking the waffle in the upper left corner and choosing Admin.

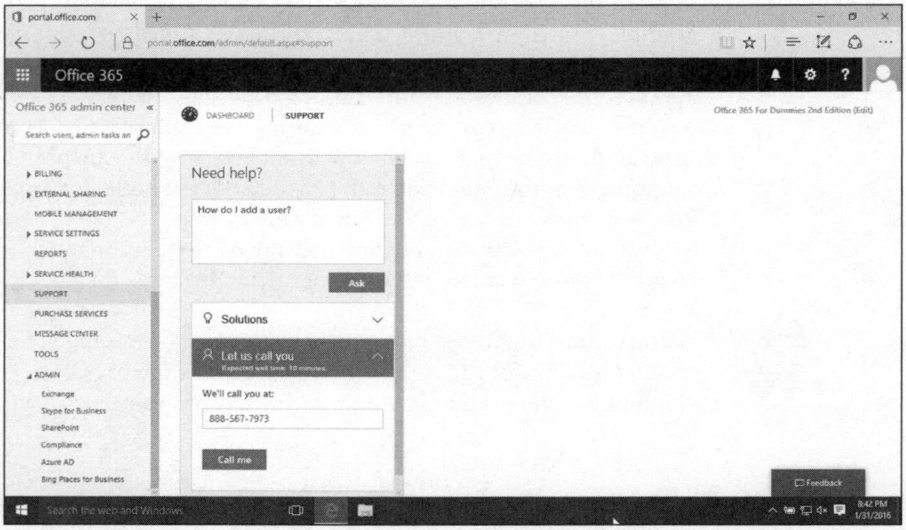

FIGURE 19-3:
The Service Request section of the Office 365 administrator interface.

Migrating to Office 365

The nice thing about Office 365 is that it lives in the cloud and is very flexible. You can migrate small test runs of data to a trial Office 365 subscription and figure out what might go wrong when you migrate the entire organization. In fact, we highly recommend that you sign up for an Office 365 trial right now. The trial is absolutely free, and you can be up and exploring the product in a matter of minutes.

TIP

In the past, it was difficult to gain access to enterprise software, such as Share-Point, because it took an astute tech person to set up the environment. The tech person had to find hardware capable of running the software and then install the operating system, all supporting software, and finally SharePoint. Even if everything went as planned, the process took at least a week and possibly a lot longer. With Office 365, you, as a business user, can go straight to the Office 365 website, sign up for a trial, and explore SharePoint in a matter of minutes!

Activating licensing

The process for assigning and activating licensing has dramatically improved over the last year. In the past, the process was often described as painful. The new process is streamlined and lets you add and remove users and licenses based on your immediate needs.

To add licensing, you need to add users to the plan by clicking on the Users tab, and then selecting Active Users as shown in Figure 19-4.

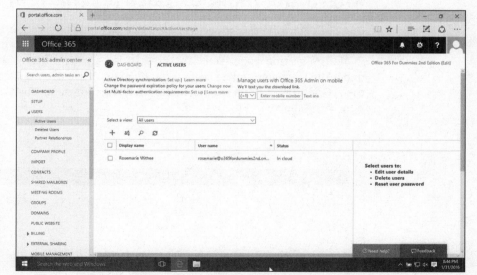

FIGURE 19-4:
The Active Users screen in the Office 365 plan administrator interface.

You begin the process of adding a user by clicking the plus symbol from the Ribbon of the Active Users screen. As you walk through the wizard, you're asked to enter information, such as the user's first and last name and administrative rights the user should be assigned. In addition, you have the opportunity to assign specific licensing to the user, as shown in Figure 19-5.

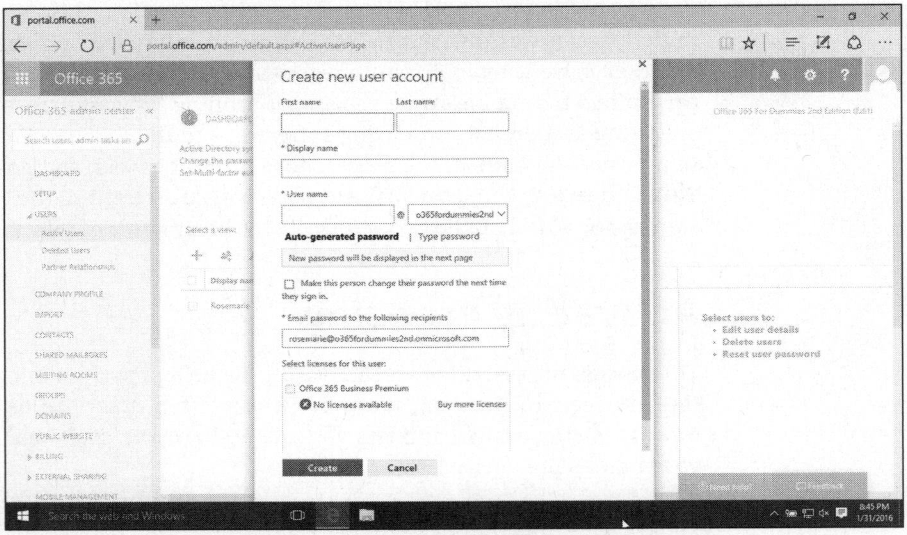

FIGURE 19-5:
Assigning Office
365 licensing to a
new user.

Migrating mailbox data (Exchange)

One of the most visible aspects of an Office 365 implementation is the migration of email data into the Exchange Online system. To begin a migration, you use the E-Mail Migration page. You can access this page by clicking the Manage link under the Exchange Online section on the main Office 365 management page and then clicking the Recipients link in the left navigation pane. Then, click the Migration tab as shown in Figure 19-6.

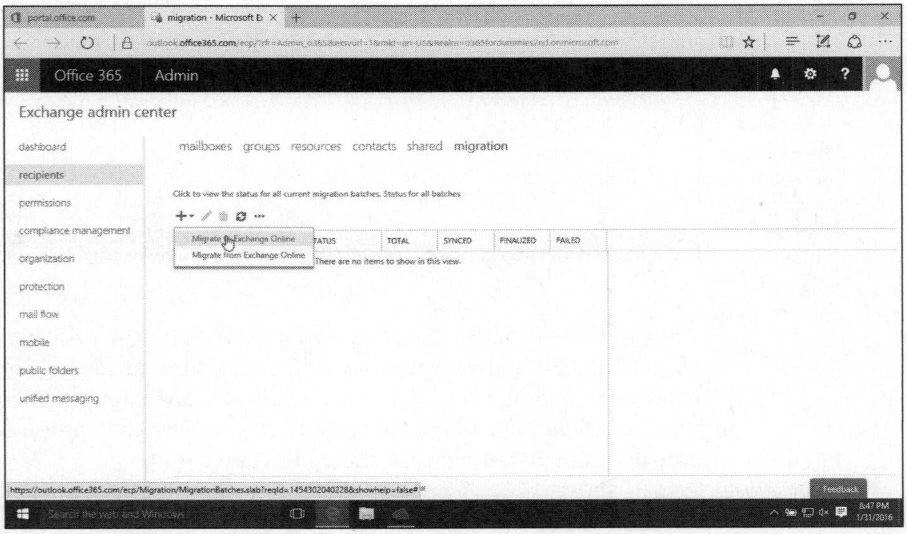

FIGURE 19-6:
Accessing the
E-Mail Migration
button on the
Exchange Online
Management
page.

To begin a new migration, click the plus symbol, then click Migrate to Exchange Online to begin walking through the Migration wizard, as shown in Figure 19-7. The Migration wizard will let you migrate your Exchange settings. If you're migrating from Exchange 2007 or later, the wizard will use Autodiscover to auto detect settings. If you're migrating from Exchange 2003 or IMAP, then you need to enter the settings manually. After completion of a migration, user email will be available in the Office 365 system.

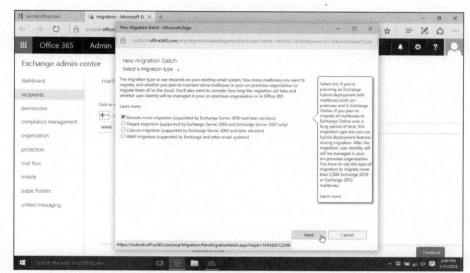

FIGURE 19-7: Beginning a new email migration in Office 365.

TIP

A number of other tools and partners are available to assist in email migration. Find these resources in Pinpoint located at the following URL:

```
https://pinpoint.microsoft.com
```

Migrating portal content and functionality (SharePoint)

The SharePoint platform has become one of the most successful products in Microsoft's history. As SharePoint experts, we have spent countless hours working with clients in every industry on SharePoint projects. SharePoint is a platform and as a result, it tends to get complicated, which often leads to an organization employing the help of consultants. Much of the complexity of SharePoint lies in the infrastructure of the platform. A SharePoint implementation requires a number of different engineers all working in unison to make the platform available to users. The good news with Office 365 is that Microsoft takes over this complexity of building and maintaining the platform, and you, as a user, can focus on just using the product.

Migrating to SharePoint Online (which is part of Office 365) requires you to migrate any content or custom functionality that you may currently be using in your portal environment. As you begin to delve farther into SharePoint, you find that one of the major attractions is the ability to consolidate the functionality of multiple disparate systems into the SharePoint platform. This consolidation creates a one-stop shop for business tasks as compared to logging into multiple systems that rarely communicate with each other.

Migrating content to SharePoint Online

Migrating content to SharePoint can be as easy as uploading the documents you have saved on your local computer or as complex as moving massive amounts of digital content from one Enterprise Content Management (ECM) system to another. If you're a small or medium organization, then you can gain familiarity with content management in SharePoint and in particular with document library apps. SharePoint document libraries are covered in Chapter 6. You can also check out *SharePoint 2016 For Dummies* (Wiley) by Ken Withee and Rosemarie Withee.

Migrating custom functionality to SharePoint Online

One of the best things about SharePoint is that it is a platform and not a specific tool. As a result, you can build just about any business functionality you need to run your business right into your SharePoint implementation.

With so much power at your disposal in SharePoint, you need to think about what you have developed. If you're one of the rare few who has never used SharePoint, then you can simply start using SharePoint Online. If, however, you have already used SharePoint either on premise or through another hosting provider and are moving into SharePoint Online, then you will need to move your custom functionality into your new portal. Migrating functionality that you have developed can be a challenge. One of the best ways to tackle this challenge, however, is to carefully document your current environment and then determine if it is better to try to migrate the functionality or re-create it in the new environment.

If the functionality you have developed is a simple list or library app, then you can go into the List Settings page and save the list as a template with content. This creates a physical file that you download to your computer and then upload to SharePoint Online. After you install the template into SharePoint Online, you can then re-create the list or library app by using the template. The result is that your list or library app is transported into SharePoint Online with only a few clicks of a mouse.

For more advanced functionality, you can either redevelop it in the new environment or hire a consultant to undertake the project under your guidance.

Throwing the switch

After you have migrated both email and portal data, you're ready to throw the switch and direct all traffic to the new Office 365 environment. Throwing the switch is accomplished by updating your Domain Name System (DNS) records in your domain registrar. The results of this simple procedure are enormous. After you update DNS, every user of your current system is directed to the Office 365 system.

A DNS record is a translator from human readable computer names to computer readable computer names. For example, if you type www.microsoft.com into your web browser, the Microsoft web page appears. How does this happen? Your computer sees microsoft.com and knows it is a text entry. Computers talk to other computers by using numbers known as Internet Protocol (IP) addresses. Your computer needs to find out the IP address of the computer running the microsoft.com website. It does this by querying a DNS server. The DNS server looks up the text-based address (known as a domain name) and sends back the IP address. Your computer can now use the IP address to contact the Microsoft computer.

When you update the DNS records for the email, for example, you're telling the DNS lookup system that when someone wants to send you an email, their computer should use the IP address of Office 365 rather than the one you were using before. In essence, after you update DNS you have thrown the switch and are using Office 365 rather than the old system.

Configuring mobile phones

The cloud offers the advantage of being fully connected at all times to your important data and communications. There is no better way to access your Office 365 environment on the go than with your mobile phone. If you're using one of the new Microsoft Windows 10 phones, then you can connect with your SharePoint and Office documents as well.

Microsoft has taken the approach that they will make Office 365 available to people regardless of the device they use. Gone are the days when you needed a Windows device to use Microsoft products. Today you can get Office 365 apps for your iPhone, iPad, Android Phone, and Android Tablet. You can even get Office for your Mac.

Microsoft has worked hard to make Windows 10 a seamlessly integrated experience with Microsoft Office, but that doesn't mean you have to choose Windows 10. Microsoft is taking the approach that they want you to choose Windows 10 because it's a better and more integrated experience. However, if you don't choose it, they're still spending billions of dollars to make Office 365 apps available on Apple and Android phones.

You can find more information about setting up your mobile phone with Office 365 by navigating to the following URL:

```
https://support.office.com
```

For example, for Outlook, you can navigate to the Apps → Outlook support page. You can then browse support for the Outlook app on such topics as getting started, scheduling meetings, working with tasks, and Outlook on mobile and tablet devices. The Outlook help page is shown in Figure 19-8.

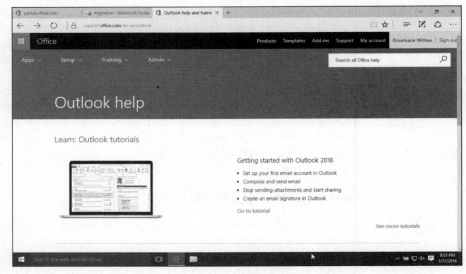

FIGURE 19-8:
The Outlook Help Center.

IN THIS CHAPTER

Finding your way around the Office 365 management pages

Getting a handle on managing Exchange

Figuring out how to manage Skype for Business

Discovering how to manage SharePoint

Chapter 20

Managing Office 365

As you find out throughout the book, the Office 365 product is actually a suite of products consisting of SharePoint Online for portals, Exchange Online for e-mails, Skype for Business Online for instant and ad hoc communication, and Microsoft Office for productivity. When it comes time to manage these components, Microsoft has created a web-based interface that is intuitive and easy to use.

In this chapter, you explore the management interfaces for Office 365. You can gain an understanding of the general Office 365 management pages and then move into exploring the specific management pages for each of the individual services.

Going Over Office 365 Management

Microsoft has taken a great deal of time and put a tremendous amount of resources into developing the management interface for Office 365. Microsoft designed this interface for everyday users with the idea being that it doesn't take an IT expert in order to manage the Office 365 product. The main Office 365 management interface is actually a website you navigate to with your favorite web browser.

A web interface for managing an online product is nothing new. If you have ever used Facebook or LinkedIn, then you are familiar with using your web browser to manage an online product. The Office 365 management interface is no different; it is just the interface designed by Microsoft to manage their business cloud product.

The Office 365 For Business management page can be accessed by navigating to the following URL in your web browser:

```
https://portal.office.com
```

If you're looking for the landing page for the Office 365 For Home plans, navigate to `https://products.office.com`, click the sign-in drop-down in the upper-right corner, then choose For Home. If you choose the Work, school or university from this products page, it's the same as going directly to the portal.office.com page.

You sign in by using the credentials you used to sign up for the Office 365 product. After you have signed in, click the waffle in the upper-left corner of the screen, then select Admin. The Office 365 management website appears, as shown in Figure 20-1.

It is a common theme with Office 365 that things are always changing. The concepts found throughout the book remain the same, but the exact interface is always changing.

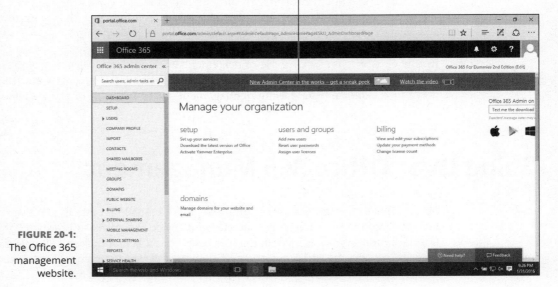

FIGURE 20-1: The Office 365 management website.

TIP

The management interface discussed in this chapter focuses on the Office 365 Business Premium plan. If you are using one of the Enterprise plans, you will have more management options. For example, the Skype for Business Cloud PBX option is only available in the Enterprise E5 plan. Depending on your plan, the options for that plan are available in the management interface.

The management website includes sections down the left-hand navigation for Dashboard, Setup, Users, Company Profile, Import, Contacts, Shared Mailboxes, Meeting Rooms, Groups, Domains, Public Website, Billing, External Sharing, Mobile Management, Service Settings, Reports, Service Health, Support, Purchase Services, Message Center, Tools, and Admin. Wow, that is a lot of options! It can be a bit overwhelming at first but Microsoft is trying hard to make it as organized and intuitive as possible. Keep in mind that Microsoft is constantly changing this interface, so the options you see may be different. The concept for achieving a task is the same, but you may have to hunt around the management interface to find the exact option you want at the time you're looking for it.

In addition, whenever you are logged in to Office 365, you have access to the affectionately named *waffle menu.* The waffle menu is in the upper-left corner of the screen and looks like, well, a waffle. When you click this menu, it expands to show you all of the Office 365 apps you have for your account. For example, if you want to check your email, you can click the waffle menu, then click Mail. Your browser then opens the Outlook Web App (OWA). Likewise, if you select Sites, you see the SharePoint sites.

The waffle is always there when you are logged into Office 365; if you want to go back to the management interface, click the waffle again, then choose Admin.

TIP

The waffle only shows apps for which the user account has access. If a regular user is logged into Office 365, he or she can't see the Admin option in the waffle (unless they have admin access, of course).

Table 20-1 outlines the functionality of the left-hand navigational groups and links.

When you land on the administration screen, you are on the Dashboard. The Dashboard shows you the health of each of the services in your Office 365 plan, as shown in Figure 20-2. Notice the service health for Exchange, Identity Services, Office 365 Portal, Office Subscription, Power BI, SharePoint, Skype for Business, Sway, and Yammer Enterprise. Depending on your subscription, you may see different services listed.

TABLE 20-1 Office 365 Administration Links

Link	Description
Dashboard	The main landing page where you can see the health of the Office 365 services.
Setup	A guided experience that you can use to set up your Office 365 subscription.
Users	Add users and manage partner relationships here.
Company Profile	Set your company profile, such as the name, address, phone number, and contacts.
Import	Import files into your Office 365 subscription.
Contacts	Manage contacts that are available within your organization. You can also do this in the Exchange admin center, but it's a common task, so it's also available here.
Shared Mailboxes	Manage shared mailboxes. You can also do this in the Exchange admin center but it's a common task, so it's also available here.
Meeting Rooms	Manage meeting rooms. You can also do this in the Exchange admin center but it's a common task, so it's also available here.
Groups	Manage groups. You can also do this in the Exchange admin center but it's a common task, so it's also available here.
Domains	Set which domains are assigned to your Office 365 subscription. For example, for Rosemarie's company, her domain is portalintegrators.com. She adds this domain to Office 365 for the Portal Integrators subscription.
Public Website	Office 365 no longer provides a public-facing website through SharePoint, but Microsoft has pursued a partnership with Go Daddy and Wix to fill the gap. You can learn more on this page.
Billing	Manage billing-related tasks, such as your subscriptions, bills, licenses, and billing-related notifications.
External Sharing	Configure external sharing for sites, calendars, and Skype for Business.
Mobile Management	Set up mobile devices with Office 365 on this page.
Service Settings	Settings for specific services, such as for mail, sites, and Skype for Business. Most settings also are available in the specific admin centers (such as for Exchange, SharePoint, and Skype for Business), but some settings are used often, so they're available here, too.
Reports	All the reports you could ever imagine about what is happening in Office 365. There are reports for usage, mail, SharePoint, Skype for Business, and auditing, among others.
Service Health	The current and historical health of the services that make up Office 365, and any upcoming maintenance, are outlined in this section.
Support	If you get stuck, you can open a service request with Microsoft. This section provides information on known issues, documentation, and a way to open a new support ticket.
Purchase Services	If you find you need more services or subscriptions, you can learn about what is available on this page.

Link	Description
Message Center	The message center is a place to view messages and announcements. Make sure to check it often to stay up to date.
Tools	Microsoft has added tools to assist you in your administration duties for Office 365. These include checking your configuration, checking connectivity, and analyzing based on best practices.
Admin	The Admin section has a link for the main administrative pages for each particular service, among some additional admin links. The service admin links include Exchange, Skype for Business, and SharePoint. We explore these management pages later in the chapter.

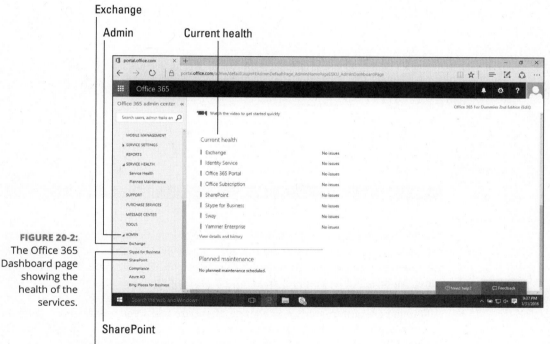

FIGURE 20-2: The Office 365 Dashboard page showing the health of the services.

REMEMBER

Microsoft is constantly adding new services and expanding the Office 365 product. The dashboard is your quick view of the status of all the services you can leverage in your Office 365 plan. The dashboard also announces any upcoming maintenance on the services so you can stay informed and plan accordingly.

In addition to the service health, the dashboard also contains a list of admin shortcuts. These are things like resetting passwords, assigning users, assigning licenses, and downloading software.

Managing Exchange

The management section for Exchange can be accessed by expanding the Admin link in the lower-left of the main Office 365 administration page and then clicking the Exchange link. When you click the Exchange link, you are presented with the Exchange admin center, as shown in Figure 20-3.

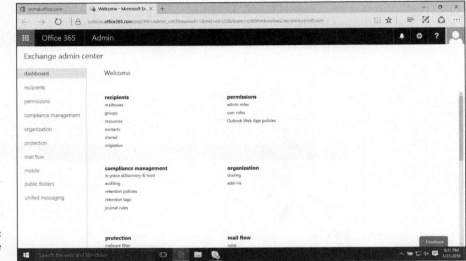

The Exchange admin center follows the same theme as the Office 365 admin center with navigational links down the left-hand side. The links include Dashboard, Recipients, Permissions, Compliance Management, Organization, Protection, Mail Flow, Mobile, Public Folders, and Unified Messaging.

When you are administering Exchange, there are tasks you will find yourself constantly doing. Navigating through a long set of clicks can be a hassle. For this reason, the Dashboard has links to admin pages you find you use frequently. The Dashboard provides a quick place to perform common tasks, such as working with recipients of email, setting permissions, working with compliance and security, and handling mail flow.

The Exchange Online management pages contain a tremendous number of configuration settings that could only fully be covered with a dedicated book on the topic. The following sections provide an overview to managing Exchange for yourself or your organization.

REMEMBER

The standard Office 365 disclaimer also applies to Exchange. Microsoft is constantly updating, changing, and improving the product. You may not find the menus and options exactly as we outline in the book. If things look different, Microsoft has made an update. The concepts remain the same, but you may have to look around to find exactly what you're looking for.

Managing recipients

The management pages for managing recipients include pages for managing user mailboxes, groups, resources, contacts, shared mailboxes, and migration (as shown in Figure 20-4).

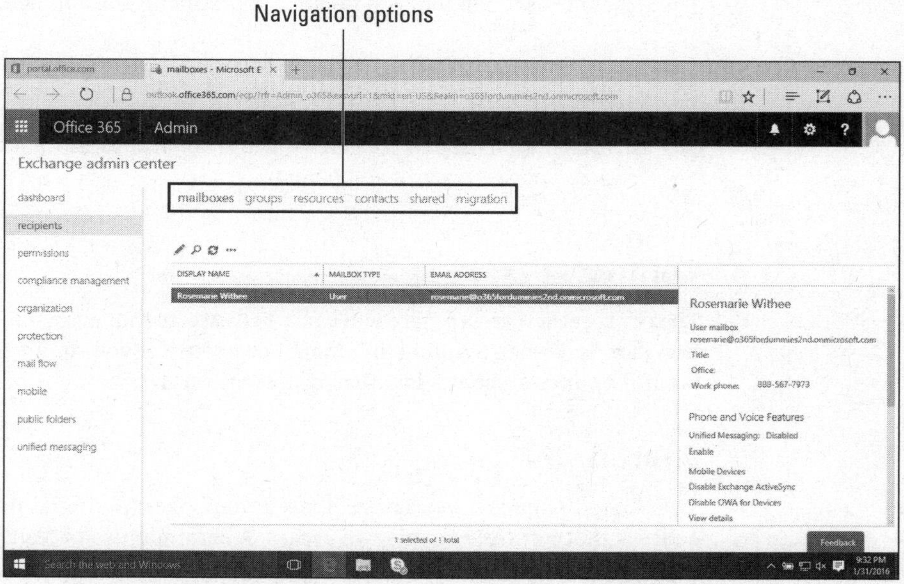

Navigation options

FIGURE 20-4:
The management landing page for recipients.

Mailboxes

The main landing page when you open the recipients link is for managing mailboxes. This is where you will spend most of your time, so it makes sense that this is the landing screen. On this page, you can edit user mailboxes, and also enable or disable features, place holds, configure archiving, and even turn on or off email connectivity for a mailbox. You can click the navigation bar across the top to change to other related management pages for recipients, such as groups, resources, and contacts (as shown in Figure 20-4).

Exchange even lets users connect external accounts so they can view email from other systems.

Groups

The Groups section provides configuration options for managing users in groups. You can create groups for distribution and security:

» A *distribution group* is a collection of mailboxes that all receive a message when an email is sent to the group.

» A *security group* is a collection of security settings that are applied to everyone within the group.

Resources

The Resources section lets you create a room mailbox or an equipment mailbox:

» A *room mailbox* is used for a fixed location, such as a meeting or conference room.

» An *equipment mailbox* is for items that are not in a fixed location, such as a truck or another piece of equipment.

Contacts

The contacts screen is where you can add contacts that everyone in your organization can find when sending an email. For example, you might need to add a contact for your contact at a law firm or a lawn service.

Shared

The Shared page lets you create shared mailboxes. A shared mailbox is an email address that multiple people can access. A common use of a shared mailbox is for support. You may have multiple people, on different shifts, monitoring and responding to email. As long as everyone has access to the shared mailbox, they can check it and reply to messages.

Migration

The Migration page is where you can either migrate email into Exchange, or migrate email from Exchange to another email system.

Managing permissions

You can manage permissions for Exchange by clicking the Permissions link. Once on the permissions page, you can create various admin and user roles:

>> An *admin role* assigns permissions to a user to manage a certain portion of Exchange, such as a help desk or records.

>> A *user role* lets you assign certain user behavior to people, such as allowing them to manage their own distribution groups or associated apps.

The permissions page also is where you find the Outlook Web App (OWA) policies. OWA policies provide you with the ability to customize the behavior of the browser-based OWA email app. You can enable or disable such features as instant messaging, text messaging, LinkedIn contacts sync, and Facebook contacts sync (as shown in Figure 20-5).

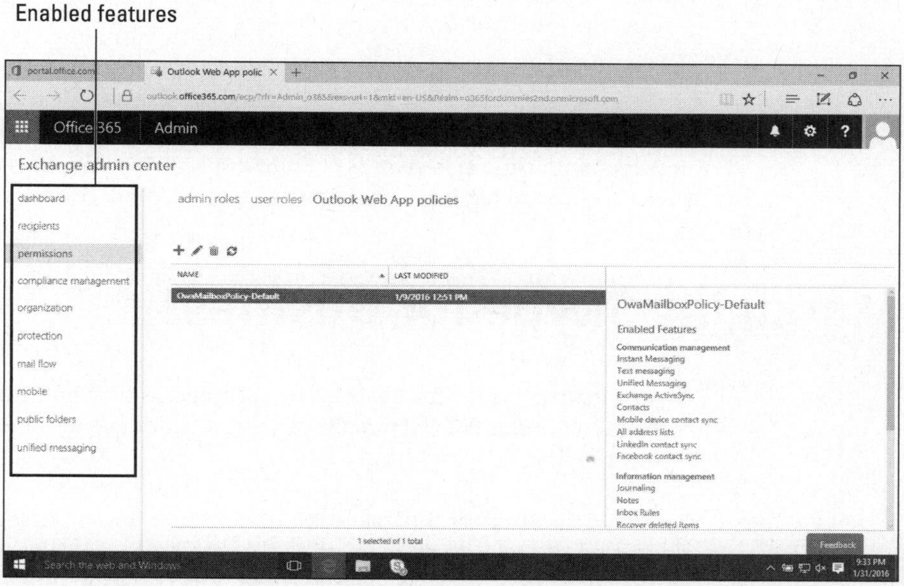

Enabled features

FIGURE 20-5:
The OWA policies admin page.

More Exchange management

In addition to managing recipients and permissions, you can also manage such features as how mail flows through the Exchange system, compliance requirements, mobile connections, and public folders. Each of these features has a corresponding navigational link.

The possibilities for managing Exchange are nearly endless. Whole books are dedicated to the subject. Take some time to explore the Exchange admin center. Exchange is an administrative area that requires a person with dedicated time to conquer.

The Mail Flow page provides the ability to create rules, configure domains, journaling, and reports of email delivery.

Rules let you control the flow of email within your organization. For example, if an email is sent to a mailbox (such as info@portalintegrators.com), then you can have a rule that forwards the email to everyone on the support team.

You can also configure domains and journaling:

>> Configuring *domains* allows you to accept e-mail for specific domains, such as portalintegrators.com.

>> Configuring *journaling* allows you to record email communications in support of email retention or archiving policies.

>> This functionality is critical for highly regulated industries, such as banking.

Delivery reports let you search for specifics on email communication, such as messages with certain keywords or from a specific person. This can be very handy when you need to dig into your email system and understand what is going on.

Managing Skype for Business

You can manage Skype for Business by clicking the Skype for Business link nested under the Admin link on the main Office 365 admin center. Refer to Figure 20-2 to view the link.

The Skype for Business link takes you to the Skype for Business admin center. The admin center is where you manage all things Skype for Business. The admin center includes links for Dashboard, Users, Organization, Dial-In Conferencing, Meeting Invitation, and Tools.

The Dashboard is the main landing page when you open the Skype for Business admin center. The Dashboard includes key user statistics and organizational information, as shown in Figure 20-6.

Managing users and your organization

The users screen is where you manage Skype for Business users. You can set the location of the users and configure whether they can use specific features, such as being able to communicate with people outside of the organization. You can also set features such as external communication, at the organizational level so that it affects everyone.

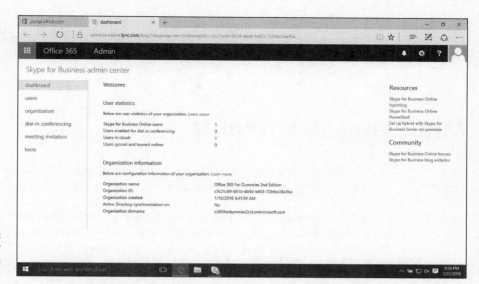

FIGURE 20-6:
The Skype for
Business admin
center.

You can even configure Skype for Business to allow communication with the outside world only when you specifically approve a domain. You might do this for a partner organization so the employees of both organizations can communicate with each other, but not with anyone else in the outside world.

TIP

Skype for Business can be configured to let users communicate with regular Skype consumer users. This opens up the Skype world to your organization — but use this feature cautiously.

TIP

Managing dial-in conferencing and meeting invitations

Conferencing is where you set up group meetings with a common phone number so someone they can call into the meeting, even without a computer. Office 365 lets you set up a Microsoft bridge, or even a third-party bridge.

Bridge is just another name for a shared phone number for a meeting.

REMEMBER

Usually, there's an extra charge for dial-in conferencing. With the latest Enterprise E5 plan Microsoft has introduced a tremendous number of Skype for Business features. In essence, Microsoft has become its own telecommunications carrier.

Explore the Office 365 Enterprise E5 plan if you are interested in advanced telecommunications offerings, such as Cloud PBX and connectivity with the Public Switched Telephone Network (PSTN).

TIP

When you set up a meeting in your Outlook client, an invitation is sent to everyone that you have invited to the meeting. You can customize this invitation with your own logo, help URL, legal URL, and footer information.

Managing SharePoint

You can manage SharePoint by clicking the SharePoint link nested under the Admin link on the main Office 365 admin center. Refer to Figure 20-2 to view the link.

After you click the link, you land on the SharePoint admin center page where you manage site collections, user profiles, the Term Store, and apps, among many other things. The SharePoint admin center is shown in Figure 20-7.

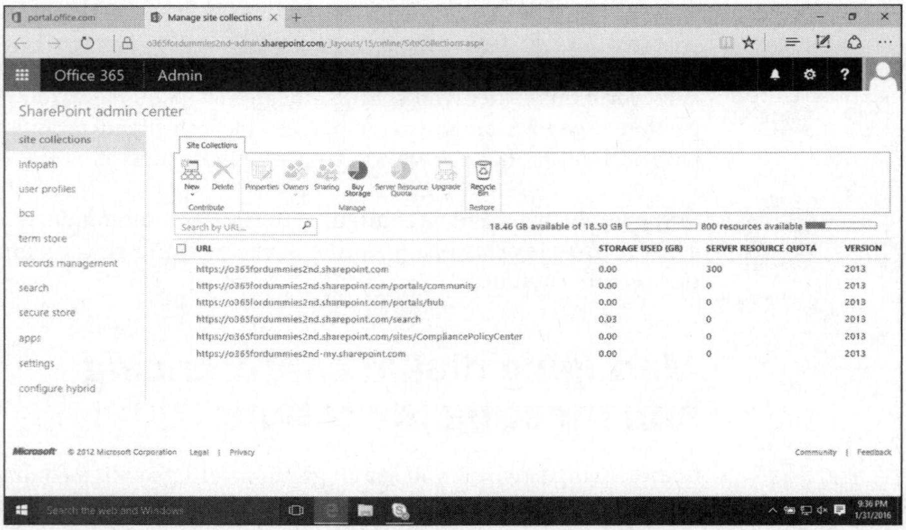

FIGURE 20-7:
The SharePoint admin center.

TIP

The SharePoint admin center is unique to certain business plans in Office 365. If you are using a plan that doesn't have SharePoint included, you won't see the management link for the SharePoint admin center.

Managing site collections

When you first land on the SharePoint admin center page, you are presented with the management screen for site collections. Everything that is user facing in SharePoint is contained within a site collection, so this is a logical landing spot for the SharePoint admin center. In other words, site collections are always front and center in your mind as the SharePoint admin for Office 365.

TIP

A site collection is a unique instance of SharePoint so you can create a site collection for sensitive areas of the organization (such as Accounting or Human Resources), then create a separate site collection for the rest of the organization. Think of a site collection as a logical collection of SharePoint websites. A site collection isolates SharePoint components, such as user permissions, navigational components, and content types.

The site collection management screen lets you create and configure site collections. In particular, you can perform tasks, such as assigning site collection administrators, allocating resources, and setting resource and domain information.

Managing SharePoint site collections is nearly a book unto itself. For more about managing SharePoint, check out *SharePoint 2016 For Dummies* (Wiley) by Ken Withee and Rosemarie Withee.

User Profiles

The User Profile page provides the ability to manage SharePoint components that relate to user profiles, such as the ability to manage people, the organization, and the configuration settings for the personal SharePoint site functionality known as My Site, as shown in Figure 20-8.

FIGURE 20-8:
The User Profiles configuration page in the SharePoint admin center.

People

The People section lets you manage user properties and user profiles. You can create new profiles and edit existing profiles. In addition, you can manage audiences, user permissions, and policies.

TIP

An audience is a grouping of users that match specific criteria. For example, you might create a policy for everyone with the department property of their profile set to Executive. You could then target specific SharePoint functionality for only this audience. A policy provides specific functionality for users, such as the ability to add colleagues to their profiles themselves.

Organizations

The Organizations section of the User Profiles screen lets you manage the properties and profiles of the organization. For example, one of the properties of the organization might be the company logo, and another property might be the physical address or web address. By using this screen, you can create new properties or edit existing properties. The Profiles section lets you manage a separate profile for different departments within the organization.

TIP

An easy way to think of properties and profiles throughout SharePoint is that properties define the fields used in the profiles. For example, a property might be First Name, and the profile would use this property but would associate Rosemarie with the property in the profile.

My Site Settings

A SharePoint My Site is a personal site for every single user. A My Site allows users to create their own SharePoint space without worrying about having the right administrative access to a shared site. The My Site section provides the ability to set up and configure the My Site functionality for SharePoint Online.

SharePoint Term Store

The Term Store is a global directory of common terms that might be used in your organization. The idea behind the Term Store is that you want to create consistency in the way data is entered and managed throughout your SharePoint environment. For example, you might have a Human Resources Department. You don't want people to enter data, such as 'HR', 'HR Dept.', 'Human Resources Dept.', and 'Human Resources Department'.

These are all actually the same thing, but because people enter names in different ways, it becomes difficult to maintain consistency. Using the Term Store, you can enter the term as 'Human Resources Department' and know that every place throughout SharePoint that uses this field will enter it in a consistent way when referring to that specific department.

Managing apps

SharePoint apps are small functionality that can be added to SharePoint. SharePoint apps are also being called SharePoint add-ins, because they add functionality to SharePoint. SharePoint includes a store where you can find and install apps into your environment.

Using the SharePoint apps management page, you can manage the purchasing and licensing of apps and configure SharePoint store settings such as turning off the ability of end users to purchase apps in the store. You can also monitor apps that you have installed, and set permissions on apps so that you have full control on who is allowed to use which particular apps.

The SharePoint apps management page is shown in Figure 20-9.

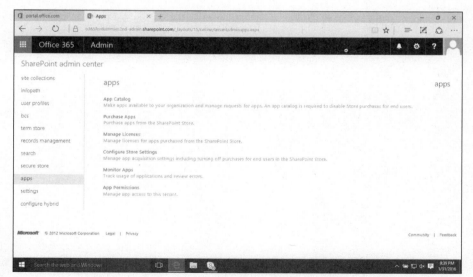

FIGURE 20-9:
The SharePoint apps management page.

TIP

In addition to the configuration information discussed in this section regarding Office 365, you also have full access to configuring the site collection within SharePoint. SharePoint is deserving of a book unto itself. A good place to start is *SharePoint 2016 For Dummies* (Wiley), by Ken Withee and Rosemarie Withee.

7

The Part of Tens

Chapter 21

Ten Signs It's Time for You to Move to Office 365

he Fortune 500 companies have spoken. Cloud computing is in. According to Microsoft, 80 percent of these successful organizations are empowering their businesses using the Microsoft cloud. Between Microsoft Azure, Microsoft Dynamics CRM, and Office 365, the cloud business is good business for Microsoft. It's so good that they have invested $15 billion to build their impressively massive cloud infrastructure which includes more than one million servers sitting in more than 100 data centers around the world. And they aren't stopping there. With Microsoft's recent research investments in underwater data centers, we may in the future get cloud services not so much from the cloud but from the bottom of the seas!

If you're still holding back and hanging on to your in-house servers, dutifully patching and maintaining them, let us give you some good reasons to let go. If you're still using a patchwork of services to stitch together a semblance of enterprise-class productivity solutions, let us break it down for you: that is so last year. It's time to move to Office 365. Here are the top ten reasons why.

Your Team Likes to Collaborate

Cloud and collaboration is a match made in heaven. Using collaboration tools hosted in the cloud allows you and your colleagues to make edits simultaneously to a document online.

In Office 365, co-authoring is a given for documents saved in OneDrive for Business and SharePoint Online. There's something magical about working on a document with team members and automatically seeing their edits appear on your screen in real-time. No more of this emailing back and forth to get people's updates, compiling them manually, and creating several versions. In the new world of Office 365 collaboration, the document you're working on is the latest version. You can even get clarification from your co-author when you see what they're typing simply by starting an IM conversation right from the document itself.

Version history is enabled by default in SharePoint Online, so if you ever need to restore an older version of a document, all it takes is a few mouse clicks. You can also set up your document library in such a way that only one person at a time can edit the document without blocking others from viewing a read-only copy of the file.

Your Employees are Facebook Friends

The world has become a giant network. Now more than ever, cloud technologies have enabled all of us to connect with friends, relatives, acquaintances, and even strangers without stepping outside of our homes. We're used to checking our smartphones for updates from our network, getting advice from Facebook friends on what movies to watch, and reading reviews from Yelp about a hotel or restaurant.

If you somehow find out that two or more of your employees are Facebook friends, then you know it's time to bring social networking to your organization. Empower your employees to use the social capabilities of Yammer in Office 365 to get information, share best practices, crowdsource ideas, have meaningful interactions, and stay connected with their colleagues — all within the confines of your company's secure virtual walls.

You are the IT Department

Enterprise-size companies spend a lot of money buying, installing, configuring, maintaining, and upgrading their IT infrastructure. In addition, there are soft costs associated with justifying these IT infrastructure purchases such as

» Writing the business case

» "Selling" the proposal to management

» Sending out the Requests for Proposal (RFP) to potential vendors

» Reviewing and vetting the bids received

» Selecting and contracting with the selected vendors

If you are running a small business, don't make the mistake of thinking that just because you don't do all the tasks that large companies do, your IT infrastructure cost will be negligible. You may not house a roomful of servers with technicians, but the time you spend maintaining even two servers — maintaining, patching, fixing, calling tech support, missing or forgetting an anniversary dinner in the process — all adds up to not just hard and soft costs but also productivity loss.

Office 365 saves you from all these troubles. Highly trained engineers are working and available 'round the clock to ensure your Exchange, SharePoint, and Skype for Business services are up and running so you don't have to worry about it.

So instead of doubling up as the IT guy, you can now relax and just focus on growing your business. And of course, have enough of a work/life balance so you won't forget your next anniversary.

Your Emails Got (Almost) Obliterated

Office 365 is the caretaker of your email data in Exchange Online. Regardless of whether your data is highly confidential or low priority, your data is stored, backed up, replicated, and protected in redundant remote data centers accessible anywhere there's an Internet connection. With a 99.9 percent uptime, financially backed service level agreement, you know that Microsoft is better positioned to help you avoid business disruptions due to a malfunctioning in-house email server than you or your IT team.

So don't wait until it happens again — move to Office 365 now before an email disaster causes work stoppage and customer dissatisfaction.

You Love Video On-Demand

Most of us have enjoyed the benefits of "on-demand" movies and TV shows from our cable companies. The model is simple. You sign up for a service and you get access to movies and TV shows at your leisure.

Office 365 is your "on-demand" cloud computing service provider. This means that you only pay for the capacity that you need at any given period. If you need 100 user accounts during the peak season of the business, then you pay for those 100 accounts. During the lean months when you only need 10 user accounts, you only need to pay for those 10. You don't have to own the infrastructure with capacity good for 100 users all the time. It's like paying for metered services just like you do for electricity and water.

So if you love "on-demand" video, we're sure you'll love Office 365.

You're a Tree Hugger (or Wannabe)

From recycling to composting to carpooling to driving hybrid cars, you've put in your share of effort to encourage a green workplace. Yet you still feel a yearning in your heart to do more. Listen to your heart because you're right; you can do more.

Logic dictates that shifting to the cloud will reduce IT carbon emissions footprint through data center efficiencies. And the good news? Microsoft's modular data centers consume 50 percent less energy than traditional data centers.

This means that if you subscribe to Office 365, you'll do the environment a favor through the reduction of your company's energy consumption from unneeded hardware, elimination of packaging peanuts and bubble wraps from packaged software, and doing away with paper printouts since your content can now be shared in full fidelity in the cloud.

You Don't Say "No" to Opportunities

We all want a work/life balance and would rather not do business while on vacation. But, if opportunity knocks in the form of a potential investor when you're on vacation and strolling on the beach, do you really want to ignore that knock?

Although it may be true that success is in large part due to luck, it's also true that the harder you work, the luckier you get. With Office 365, you don't have to work harder, just smarter!

For example, say that you're vacationing in a remote village in Asia when, to your surprise, you meet someone interested in investing in your start-up company. You intentionally left your laptop at home, so you begin to panic at the thought of a lost opportunity. Then you remember that all your demos and presentations are saved in your OneDrive for Business account. You relax and walk over with your potential investor to the nearest Internet café and conduct an impromptu presentation. The pitch works, and you now have a new partner!

You Want to Web Conference Like the Boss

Web conferencing is not new to the enterprise — the technology has proven to be a real timesaver and cost reducer. Most of us probably have seen movies of high-powered board meetings with good-looking CEOs and senior management hooked up by live video conferencing to their operations folks in multiple locations across the globe. As a small-business owner or a professional, you've probably secretly coveted the sophistication of the people and the meeting by virtue of the technology they used.

Well, covet no more. The very same technology the big guns are using is now available to non-enterprise companies at an affordable cost through Skype for Business in Office 365. You don't need to invest in expensive equipment or hire an IT staff to conduct effective, high quality, high-definition web conferencing. The service is built-in, it works, and it's great.

With Skype for Business, you can start out with an IM session with a co-worker, add voice to the session, invite more people to the conversation, convert the session into a web conference, share screen, whiteboard, conduct a poll, and for good measure, record the web conference. The web conferencing solution allows for high-definition video capability, using off-the-shelf webcams with a resolution display that adjusts to the waxing and waning of your Internet connection.

So put on a suit and a tie (or sweats), turn your webcam on, and start web conferencing like the boss from the comforts of your cubicle or your home office.

You Freaked Out Over a Lost Phone

Johnny, the tech-savvy new salesperson on the team, is leading the early adopters' pack by bringing in his own mobile devices to the workplace. He's got all his corporate email and other data synced to his smartphone and he's getting great results because he has access to information anytime, anywhere, and especially when he's with customers.

And then it happened. Somewhere between the huge industry conference with all your company's competitors and the big closing party, Johnny lost his phone. You freaked out, especially since you know Johnny's phone had all kinds of confidential, competitive data in it. Fortunately, some hotel personnel found the phone and Johnny got it back.

With mobile device management (MDM) in Office 365 and Intune, you never have to go through that stress again. With MDM, bring-your-own devices (BOYD) have security policies enforced to ensure compliance with corporate policies. Your IT department can remotely wipe all the data on the device, lock it, and reset the password in the event of loss or theft.

You Don't Want to Be the Next Hacking Victim

The last couple of years have been banner years for hacking. Just as you start thinking this isn't going to happen to your organization, you read about a ransomware attack on a Los Angeles hospital whose administrators had to cough up $17,000 to restore their computer network. So now, you start to panic.

You can relax. You can protect your data with Office 365 with built-in, integrated security and compliance services across applications and devices. Multi-factor authentication, Data Loss Prevention, Anti-Spam, Anti-Virus, Advanced Threat Protection, and Encryption are just the start of the story.

Encryption in Office 365 comes in two layers: from the service level (Microsoft manages this) and from the part where you, the customer, controls.

On the service level side, when your data is sitting or "at rest" in Office 365 data centers, they are encrypted so even in the unlikely event that a hacker gets access to the data, all the hacker sees will be garbled, unreadable text.

Microsoft also has a sophisticated data protection service referred to as "Fort Knox." Let's say, for example, you have a financial document. When you save that document in the cloud, that document is actually broken up into little parts (64 KB each). Each of those little parts is then encrypted with its own key and stored in separate locations, and, at each location, the parts get encrypted with yet another set of keys. Finally, all those different sets of keys are combined and yet again encrypted with another key. So in short, that's a lot of keys and broken up pieces of data a hacker has to hack.

From your end as a customer, there are a host of options available to prevent data loss. You can secure your SharePoint sites and OneDrive folders only to certain people, you can set your emails so they can't be forwarded, copied, or printed, and much more.

There are a lot of Microsoft partners who can help you move your business to the cloud, including this author's own company: Reed Technology Services. Don't hesitate to reach out to them — they'd be more than happy to assist you in your cloud journey.

Chapter 22

Ten Office 365 Value Propositions

I f you are relatively new to enterprise software, such as SharePoint, then moving to the Microsoft cloud is a straightforward decision. After all, you don't have an IT team in place and there is no chance of disrupting employees because they aren't currently using enterprise class software. In this situation, there is nothing but upside. If, on the other hand, you are a very technologically mature organization, then moving to the cloud can be a scary proposition. Anytime there is change at the enterprise level, there is a chance for things to go wrong. Even if the cloud assumes the risk of the technology causing problems, such as installation or patching, there is still the risk of user adoption, confusion, and push back for the new way of doing things.

In this chapter, you explore ten value propositions for Office 365. Although change can be scary, the cloud has a lot to offer regardless of the size of your organization. In particular, you explore some of the value that results from freeing up your technical folks and letting them focus on solving real-world business problems by using technology instead of keeping the lights blinking green. You also explore some of the productivity gains that come with moving to the cloud, such as the ability to connect anywhere you have Internet connectivity and the value added by using an integrated suite of products.

Offloaded Responsibility

You have probably heard the expression that "it takes an army" to do something. When it comes to Information Technology, this saying rings true. When you start thinking about all the people and resources responsible for enterprise class software, the results can be mind-boggling. You need networking people, operating system administrators, email administrators, server administrators, domain administrators, DNS people, web developers, programmers, provisioning experts, backup engineers, infrastructure, maintenance, patches, backup generators, and the list goes on and on. It is no wonder that it used to take a very large company to adopt software, such as SharePoint.

The cloud is changing the paradigm behind enterprise class software by offloading the responsibility for the infrastructure to someone else. In the case of Office 365, that someone else is none other than Microsoft. Microsoft has invested heavily in building out data centers, installing computers, operating systems, backup systems, and maintenance plans. Microsoft takes care of it all. When you use Office 365, you simply sign up and start using the products over the Internet. The result is that you don't have to worry about the heavy lifting. You are free to focus on using the software instead of worrying about keeping the software running.

Reduced Infrastructure

The infrastructure required to run software grows exponentially as the organization adopts enterprise applications. Even a relatively modest set of servers needs a redundant power supply, multiple Internet connections, a backup plan, and a secure and fireproof location in which to reside. As an organization grows, the amount of infrastructure required grows quickly until an entire team is dedicated to keeping the servers running 24 hours a day.

The costs involved in purchasing, managing, and maintaining the infrastructure involved for enterprise class software can be downright daunting. When you move to Office 365, you are removing the need for onsite infrastructure. That is all taken care of by Microsoft. Without the need for all the servers and software required to run the software, you can focus on the more important issues affecting your business. In a nutshell, you are removing the burden of having on-site infrastructure but still achieve the competitive advantage that comes with using software, such as SharePoint, Skype for Business, Office, and Exchange.

Flexible and Predictable Costs

If you talk to a chief financial officer, accountant, or project manager and ask them the type of project they prefer, they will tell you the one that comes in on budget. Unfortunately, in the technology industry, a predictable budget can be a difficult goal to achieve. Technology, by its very nature, has a lot of uncertainty and gray areas. An analogy people like to use for custom software or a difficult implementation has to do with painting. Great technologists are often more artist than engineer. As a result, you might get an absolutely phenomenal product, or you might get a complete disaster that is five or ten times over budget and completely unusable.

The result of uncertainty is difficulty in planning and conflict. A CFO or Project Manager would rather have an accurate figure than a low figure that could triple. When you move to the cloud, you are taking all the uncertainty out of the cost of the infrastructure and implementation. With Office 365, Microsoft has already undertaken all the risky implementation projects that come along with enterprise software. That is not to say that Microsoft teams did not come in over budget or that Microsoft did not spend three or four times what they thought it would take to get Office 365 up and running. But that doesn't matter to you. You know exactly how much Office 365 will cost you, and you won't have to worry about overruns. Microsoft won't tell you that it is actually going to cost four times more per month because the software is complicated. In fact, Microsoft has a service guarantee so that if the software is not up and running per the agreement, then they are on the hook for it.

To raise the value proposition even further, you can add and remove licensing as you need it. When you have a hiring spree, you may need more licensing; in slower times, you may need to reduce your licensing. Office 365 provides this ability to scale up or down your licensing, and costs, depending on your organization's situation.

Reduced Complexity

You would think that after being a SharePoint consultant for years and years and years, that Ken would know absolutely every possible thing you could or couldn't do with SharePoint. The secret that Ken will tell you that no other consultant will tell you is that consultants and experts still learn something new every single day. And just to clarify, Office 365 isn't just the SharePoint product. The Office 365 product includes Exchange, Skype for Business, Office, and SharePoint, plus such newcomers as Power BI and Sway. There are probably a few souls out there who are absolute experts on all these technologies, but the fact is that, to maintain such enterprise software, you need a fairly significant team.

Microsoft has made managing software systems easier by introducing products, such as Small Business Server, but the fact is that managing software is still a complicated endeavor. With Office 365, you remove that complexity by using a simple web interface to manage the various products. Need to create a new Share-Point site collection? You do it from within the Office 365 interface. Need to create retention rules for email? Again, the Office 365 management screens for Exchange are where you will find them. Microsoft engineers perform all the difficult responsibilities that go into keeping the lights blinking green on the servers. You just use the software in a way that best suits your business needs.

Anywhere Access

Office 365 lives in Microsoft's data centers and is accessed over the Internet. For this reason, you have connectivity to your enterprise software by using your desktop computer in your office, your laptop, or your mobile phone. In addition, all you need is an Internet connection rather than a special connection to your corporate network.

Having access to the software you use every day from anywhere provides a tremendous value and efficiency increase. When you have access, you can take advantage of unintended downtime. For example, you might be stuck waiting for someone and instead of just daydreaming away the time you could pull out your phone and respond to emails or tweak a Word or PowerPoint document. You will no longer feel that nagging urge that you need to get back to your desk to get work done. After all, other people might be waiting for you to respond so that they can do their job. In this way, you are not only maintaining your own efficiency during your downtime, but you are unblocking the people that require your input in order to maintain their efficiency and do their jobs. And, because Microsoft has embraced multiple operating systems, you can find your Office 365 apps on your iPhone, iPad, and Android device, in addition to Windows.

Synchronized Data

A real inefficiency booster is having different versions of documents scattered all over the place. You might have one version of a document at work and another version on your home computer and yet another version on your laptop. Documents have a bad habit of multiplying as well. When you send a document to people in an email, they save it to their computer and then make changes. Very quickly, there are multiple documents, and it becomes nearly impossible to determine which version contains the needed information.

With Office 365 and SharePoint Online, you have a centralized home for all documents. You can access those documents from multiple computers (or even your mobile phone) and by multiple people. Regardless of how many people or devices are accessing the document, only a single version of the document exists on SharePoint. Because SharePoint is in the cloud and accessed over the Internet, you only need an Internet connection or cell reception in order to access your enterprise data.

In addition to documents, Office 365 lets you synchronize all your email, calendar, and contacts onto multiple devices. If you use Outlook at home, at the office, on your phone, and on your tablet, you don't have to worry about being on the wrong device when trying to find a contact at work. You don't have to worry about missing an appointment because all the devices you use synchronize with Exchange Online. You don't have to worry about forgetting a Word, Excel, or PowerPoint document, because it is on your phone or tablet and can be opened with Office. The result is that your appointments, email, contacts, and documents live in the cloud and are synchronized with all of your devices.

TIP

You can sync nearly any smartphone and any email app with Exchange Online as well so that you are never far from your appointments, contacts, and email. This feature is one of the most valuable. Not to mention that Outlook is available for all types of devices now including iPhones and Androids.

Integrated Software

As we cover throughout the book, the Office 365 product is actually a suite of products that is hosted in the Microsoft data centers and accessed over the Internet. Microsoft has gone to great lengths to integrate the software as seamlessly as possible, which results in an increase in efficiency for users. For example, you might be performing a search for a document in your SharePoint portal. When you find the document, you can see the author and view his or her presence information based on the color of the icon next to their name in SharePoint. You can click the presence icon to launch Skype for Business for instant chat, voice, or video communications, or Outlook to send an email.

Office 365 even integrates with your phone system so you can even call the author directly from the SharePoint environment. The integration between SharePoint, Exchange, Skype for Business, and Office makes performing daily tasks as easy as possible. The end result is that the technology gets out of the way and lets you and those you work with do your jobs without fighting with technology.

Mobile Access to Enterprise Data

In the distant past (perhaps a few years ago in technology time), you most likely had to be at your desk in order to access your enterprise data. If you had an important Word document or needed a PowerPoint presentation, then you had to go into your office and copy it to a Flash drive or use a connection, such as Virtual Private Network (VPN) in order to connect remotely.

Being tied to your desk in this manner created a lot of frustration and inefficiency. Companies, such as Go To My PC, flourished by providing remote access to the computer in your office from a remote computer. And then, all of a sudden, smartphones appeared. Everyone quickly became accustomed to having a small computer with them in their pocket at all times. Need some information from the Internet? Need to check movie times? Need to browse a website or catch up on the latest news? All you need to do is pull out your smartphone.

The only problem was that the corporate environment did not move as quickly as the consumer market, so a gap emerged. Yes, you had the Internet in your pocket, but you still couldn't connect to your corporate network or access your enterprise data. With Office 365, you can finally access your data from anywhere by using your smartphone. Microsoft is taking anywhere access a step farther by building Office apps for Apple and Android devices that extend Office 365.

Now, for the first time, you can click a button on your phone and instantly browse your enterprise data in SharePoint, respond to corporate email, see your calendars, book appointments, and pretty much do almost everything you would do at your desk. Only now you can do it from anywhere you have cellphone reception and on almost any type of smartphone.

TIP

You don't need a Windows Phone in order to integrate with Office 365. Windows Phone provides the richest integration, but you can integrate with your enterprise email, calendar, contacts, and Office files from just about any smartphone device.

Increased IT Efficiency

Routine tasks have a way of creating snags that take hours or days to resolve. A small technical glitch has a way of cascading into an all-out war between the IT team and the software demons. What ends up happening is that the tech people spend all their time down in the weeds keeping the lights blinking green. The business folks become frustrated because they are not receiving the support they deserve, so the whole business and the culture suffer.

When you move to the cloud, you free up your IT resources to focus on working with your business users to solve problems that benefit the organization. Your business users receive the support they need, and the IT people receive the recognition they deserve.

Self-Service Enterprise Software

The most exciting aspect of Office 365 for many organizations is the inclusion of SharePoint Online in the mix. SharePoint provides a self-serve portal environment that can be developed to solve real-world business problems. The main premise behind SharePoint development is that you do not have to be a programmer to develop solutions on the SharePoint platform.

TIP

SharePoint is covered in Chapter 9, but if you really want to go deep into what is possible, check out *SharePoint 2016 For Dummies* (Wiley), which is dedicated entirely to the topic.

Chapter 23

Ten Tips for Increasing Productivity with Office 365

O ffice 365 as a cloud technology affords any organization the benefits of a sophisticated data center without the hassle and the cost of maintaining one. For as low as $5 per month per user, storing files in the cloud that are backed up to redundant servers relieves businesses of the burden of constantly backing up and archiving critical business data.

In this chapter, you find "ready-to-apply" tips and tricks for increasing productivity and efficiency in your organization or your practice. Think of this chapter as your shortcut to knowing how you can, as Bill Gates puts it, "magnify the efficiency" gains from a much-streamlined operation through the use of Office 365.

Self-Serve from the Service Health Dashboard

If you're the designated admin for your organization, you'll most likely receive inquiries about issues your users are experiencing in Office 365. Before you spend a lot of time troubleshooting an issue, check out the Service Health Dashboard in Office 365 first to determine whether the issue is from your end.

A new look and feel of the Office 365 portal is still in preview but scheduled to be rolled out soon, as of February 2016. In it, you can manage your Office 365 tenant: manage users, create groups, update subscription, review billing, contact support, configure settings, run reports, and view the health of the service (see Figure 23-1).

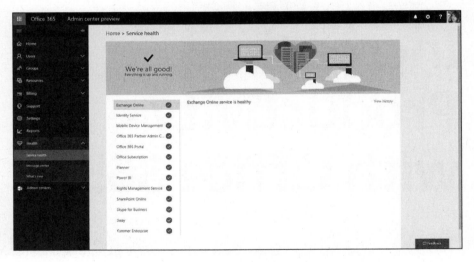

FIGURE 23-1:
Preview version of the new Office 365 admin Dashboard.

If any of the tracked services in the Service Health Dashboard isn't green, you see helpful information on the background of the issue, who is impacted, what Microsoft is doing about it, and what the next steps are.

Having insight into which service is up or down will save you a lot of time and even a phone call to support if you already know someone is working on it.

Act Like the IT Guy

At one point or another, we all secretly wish we had the awesome powers of the IT Guy. This is the person who can magically unlock your computer, reset your password, and give you access to privileged content in your organization.

So what happens if you lose your phone with confidential data info and the IT Guy isn't available? Well then, you can act as the IT Guy.

You can easily wipe data from your wireless device and even delete the device from your account to prevent a security and/or privacy breach.

Quickly wipe data or delete your device from your Exchange Online account by taking these steps:

1. **Log on to the Office 365 portal at** `http://portal.microsoft.com`.
2. **From the app launcher, click the Mail tile.**
3. **To the right of the Office 365 navigation bar, click the Settings icon.**
4. **Click Mail from the Settings pane on the right.**
5. **Click General from the left pane.**
6. **Click Mobile devices, then select the mobile device that's synced to your account.**
7. **Click the Wipe device icon (see Figure 23-2).**

   You may also want to remove the mobile device altogether from your account by clicking the Remove icon (looks like a minus sign).

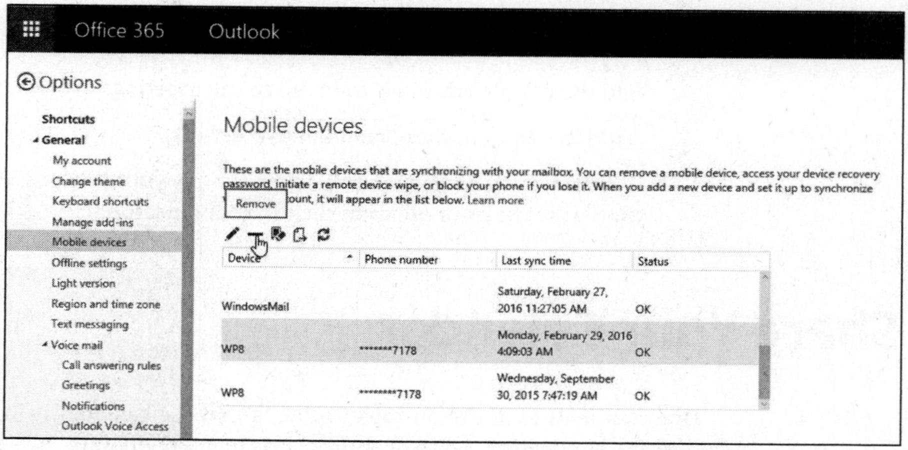

FIGURE 23-2:
Remotely wipe a device.

Share the Workload

It isn't uncommon for IT staff to end up spending a lot of time taking care of Help Desk types of tasks and not have a lot of time to be proactive and strategic.

In Office 365, IT staff can empower their users to manage SharePoint site permissions and even enable users to invite external users. Check the settings in the SharePoint admin center and choose one of the two external sharing options (see Figure 23-3) that meets your organization's needs to start sharing this workload with others in your organization.

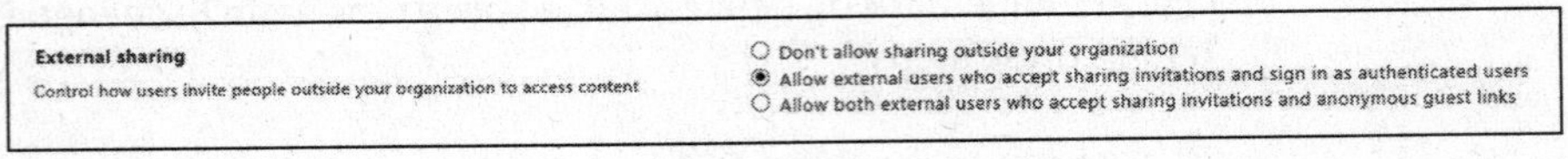

FIGURE 23-3:
External sharing
options in
SharePoint
Online.

Use the Scheduling Assistant

There's nothing more maddening than trying to set up a meeting with a bunch of people and not knowing their availability. In Office 365, the free/busy information in Exchange Online saves the day. This functionality lets you know whether the person is free, busy, working elsewhere, out of office, or has a tentative meeting on the calendar. It works not just for people but also for resources, such as conference rooms.

You see a person's free/busy information when you create a meeting and use the Scheduling Assistant. Here's how:

1. **Create a meeting invitation in Outlook.**

2. **Add the people you want to invite to the meeting.**

3. **From the Ribbon, click Scheduling Assistant.**

4. **If the time you picked looks blocked for any your invitees, find a time that works best for all, then click the Send button.**

Share Your Calendar

One cool feature of the Outlook Online is that the calendar is just as robust as the desktop application. You can apply colors to your appointments for an at-a-glance review of your day, week, or month, send a meeting request, set up alerts and notifications, and a whole lot more.

You can share your calendar to people outside your organization to make it easy for them know your availability. You can choose to give them full details for your calendar, limited, or just show your availability.

To share your calendar from the Outlook Online, follow these steps:

1. **Click the Calendar icon from app launcher.**

2. **Click Share from the top navigation, and then click Calendar.**

3. **Enter the email address or addresses of the people you want to share your calendar with, then choose the details you want to share.**

4. **Click Send.**

Do a Face Recall

If you work for a large organization, you may end up working with several people with the same name. If you search your inbox for an email from someone who shares the same name with other people you work with, you need to make sure you're picking the right person. You can quickly narrow your search results by looking at the picture that's displayed next to the contacts' name right from the search results. Neat, yeah?

Unclutter with Clutter

Filter low-priority emails from your mailbox using Clutter so you can focus on the messages that matter most. Office 365 keeps track of your email behavior and learns from it so it knows which emails matter or don't matter to you. The emails that end up in the Clutter folder still are there for review; they aren't deleted. You can also "teach" the system your preferences by moving an email back to the Inbox if it ended up in the Clutter folder.

The great part about this? You don't have to do anything! Clutter is on automatically so you can move right along to the next tip.

Sync Your Files

Regardless of how connected you are, you'll inevitably run into a situation where you don't have Internet access. Just because you're without access doesn't mean your efficiency has to go down.

You can continue to work on your OneDrive for Business or SharePoint Online documents offline and sync them back to the server when you have an Internet connection. The OneDrive for Business app should be installed as part of Office Pro Plus. If you don't see it, click on OneDrive from the app launcher in Office 365, click Sync from the top navigation, then follow the prompts. The same button is available in SharePoint Online document libraries.

Kill the Email Tree

Here's the situation: You have a report due in three days and you need input from John, Jane, Mary, and Peter. You email all of them asking for input. John and Jane reply with their input. Mary didn't see your email. Peter replies and copies Beth. Beth replies but bcc's David. David replies to all but forgets to include Beth. You finally have all the input and you're about to finalize the report but Mary, at the last minute, replies to all but doesn't look at the input from Beth and David. So now you have to add her feedback and resend the new version for everyone to review.

This story can go on and on until your hair turns gray out of frustration, but there's a better way to do this: Kill the email tree. Use Yammer instead.

With Yammer, everyone will see everyone's feedback. If someone new comes along, that person will see everyone's feedback. So there. No more email trees.

Get Modern with Your Attachments

In the old world, you would work on a document, save it in a document library, assign the right permissions to the library, grab the link for the document, fire up Outlook, start an email, then send the link to that document to your colleagues so they can coauthor with you.

In the new world, Modern Attachments is the thing. Here's how it works: You're on fire. You've got four documents you just finished and saved in SharePoint or OneDrive. You go to Outlook, create a new email, and add the recipients. When you click the Attach File button, you see a list of the most recent documents you were working on. From the list, you can pick the document you want to share. Then you remember one of the recipients doesn't have access to the library. No problem. You can grant access to the file right from Outlook to the recipient without going to OneDrive or SharePoint first. How's that for modern?

Glossary

Blog: A Blog is a web log or online journal. A blog provides a forum for people to write communications that can be viewed across the entire organization or Internet. After a blog entry is posted, the content can be commented on and discussed on the blog entry page. Blogs are prevalent throughout modern society and SharePoint provides the ability to get a blog up and running in a manner of minutes.

Cloud: A very broad marketing term and buzzword that refers to accessing software over the Internet.

Discussion Board: A discussion board allows for online discussion throughout the organization. A discussion board provides a forum for people to post questions and replies that can be viewed throughout the organization.

Excel Services: Excel Services is a feature of SharePoint that allows Excel documents to be accessed through a SharePoint site and thus through a web browser.

Exchange: Exchange is Microsoft's e-mail server designed to handle the heavy lifting of managing and routing e-mails. In addition, Exchange handles functionality, such as contacts, calendars, and tasks. Users generally use an e-mail client such as Outlook to connect to Exchange.

Exchange Online: Exchange Online is the term for Microsoft's cloud version of Exchange. The Online portion refers to the fact that you access your Exchange instance over the Internet while you are online. Microsoft installs Exchange on servers running in their data centers, and you connect to it and use it over the Internet.

Extranet: An extranet is a computer network that is accessible by people outside your organization's network but is not accessible by the public at large.

InfoPath: An application designed to create nifty and useful forms that are used to collect data from people. InfoPath is being deprecated and isn't part of Office 2016.

Intranet: An intranet is a computer network that is private and only meant for your organization.

JavaScript: JavaScript is a scripting language that is designed for the web. You can use JavaScript to interact with a web page programmatically. Since JavaScript is run from the client web browser, you can create a rich interactive experience without the web browser having to communicate with the server, resulting in the page flickering and reloading with each interaction.

Master Page: A master page is a template that is responsible for the layout of the components that are found on every content page. For example, you wouldn't want to have to add navigational components to every single new page you create. If you did, and ever needed to make a change, you must change every single page. Keeping everything in sync would be a nightmare. Using a master page, you would only create the navigational components once and then all the other pages would reference this master page for the common components.

Microsoft Business Intelligence: Business Intelligence means many different things to many different people. The generally agreed upon definition of Business Intelligence involves using computer software to get a handle on the mountains of data that flow from modern business. The data is turned into information that is used to run a business in an intelligent fashion. Microsoft Business Intelligence refers to the Microsoft tools and technologies that fall into the Business Intelligence space.

Microsoft .NET: The Microsoft .NET technology consists of programming languages and libraries designed to increase developer productivity and compatibility across Microsoft client and server computers.

Microsoft Office: Office is the nearly ubiquitous productivity suite used by information workers around the world. The Office product contains such applications as Word, Excel, PowerPoint, Outlook, OneNote, Publisher, Access, and Skype for Business.

Office 365: The Microsoft product that contains SharePoint, Exchange, and Skype for Business (among others; Microsoft is adding more services all the time); all installed and managed in Microsoft's data centers and accessed over the Internet (also called over the cloud or in the cloud).

Outlook with Business Contact Manager: An application used for e-mail, contacts, and calendaring, including scheduling meetings, meeting rooms, and other resources.

PowerShell: PowerShell is a shell interface similar to DOS. Products such as SharePoint have PowerShell instructions, called cmdlets, which let you build scripts to interact with the product. For example, you might develop a series of PowerShell cmdlets that increases the specific configuration information of your SharePoint site.

Report: A report is nothing more than information describing the status of some topic. A report can be developed by using a number of technologies, such as Report Builder, Dashboard Designer, Excel, or even SharePoint web parts.

SharePoint: SharePoint is a term used to describe a technology from Microsoft. SharePoint has become the leader in communication, collaboration, and content management. SharePoint continues to evolve as functionality is folded into the product and additional features are developed. SharePoint 2016 is the most current release of the SharePoint product.

SharePoint Designer: SharePoint designer is a software application that is used for SharePoint development. The content contained in a SharePoint application lives in a SQL Server database. SharePoint Designer provides a window into the SharePoint database that allows for customization and development. SharePoint Designer 2013 is the most recent version, and Microsoft doesn't seem to have plans to update it.

SharePoint Document Library: A Document Library is a mechanism to store content within SharePoint. A Document Library provides functionality for content management such as checkin and checkout, versioning, security, and workflow. An instance of a Document Library is called an app.

SharePoint List: A SharePoint List is simply a list of data. Much like you have a grocery list, a SharePoint List stores data in columns and rows. An instance of a SharePoint List is called an app.

SharePoint My Sites: The My Sites functionality of SharePoint offers every user her own SharePoint site.

SharePoint Online: SharePoint Online is the term for Microsoft's cloud version of SharePoint. The Online portion refers to the fact that you access your SharePoint instance over the Internet while you are online. Microsoft installs SharePoint on servers running in their data centers and you connect to it and use it over the Internet.

SharePoint Site: A SharePoint Site is nothing more than a website. At its root, SharePoint is a web site management system that provides a rich assortment of functionality that can be easily integrated into the SharePoint websites.

SharePoint Site Collection: A SharePoint Site Collection is a top-level site that contains other subsites. The difference between a Site Collection and a Site is that a Site Collection contains separate security and is isolated from other Site Collections. A Site, on the other hand, is contained by a top-level Site Collection and shares security and other aspects with other Sites within the same Site Collection.

SharePoint Workflow: A SharePoint workflow is a set of tasks and actions that can be associated with a list, library, or site. For example, you might have a workflow to request feedback on new documents. When a new document is submitted to a library the workflow might send an e-mail to a list of people for feedback. When each person has finished his task of reviewing the document, the workflow might send an e-mail back to the original author. SharePoint workflows are developed in a tool called SharePoint Designer.

SharePoint Workspace: SharePoint is great, but what happens when you aren't connected to the Internet and need to access and work with your website? SharePoint Workspace allows you to take SharePoint sites offline.

Silverlight: Silverlight is a technology designed to provide a rich user experience from within the web browser. The Web, in general, was not designed to provide the same rich user experience that an application running on your local computer provides. With a web application, the server is serving up pages that are viewed by the client computer by using a web browser. Each time the user interacts with the application, the web browser needs to send a message back to the server. This causes the web page to refresh and flicker. Silverlight runs on the web browser of the client computer and allows a rich interaction with the web application without the continual post-back of information to the server.

Skype: Skype is a consumer-based communications tool used by people all over the world. Microsoft acquired Skype and merged the development teams into the existing Lync teams, which later became known as Skype for Business.

Skype for Business: Skype for Business is a communications system designed to provide instant communication and ad hoc meetings. Skype for Business used to be Microsoft Lync. When Microsoft acquired Skype, it rebranded Lync into a business version of Skype called Skype for Business. Skype for Business lets you conduct online meetings by sharing your screen or presentations online with multiple users simultaneously, while communicating via voice, chat, and surveys. Skype for Business is integrated with the other products in Office 365 in order to provide instant ability to communicate regardless of what software you are using.

Skype for Business Online: Skype for Business Online is the term for Microsoft's cloud version of Skype for Business. The Online portion refers to the fact that you access your Skype for Business instance over the Internet while you are online. Microsoft installs Skype for Business on servers running in their data centers and you connect to it and use it over the Internet. If a company installs Skype for Business on their own in their local data server room, then it is called On Premises instead of Online.

Visio Services: Visio Services provides SharePoint with the ability to render Visio diagrams through the web browser. Visio Services diagrams can be embedded right inside a SharePoint page. Visio Services is also used to provide a diagram of SharePoint workflow in real time.

Visual Studio: Visual Studio is a software application that is designed for development of Microsoft technologies. Visual Studio is called an Integrated Development Environment (IDE) because many development features are integrated into the application, such as the ability to run and test code, color-coded keywords, and IntelliSense. IntelliSense allows developers the ability to type the beginning of a keyword and have the editor show a list of available words. The list of words narrows down as the developer continues to type additional letters of the word. This aids the developer in finding the correct keyword without having to type the entire word.

Web App: A web app is a software application that is accessed over the Web, using a web browser. For example, if you have used Facebook or LinkedIn, then you have used a web app. The Office 365 product includes a number of different web apps. In fact, even the administrative interface you use to configure Office 365 is a web app because you access it by using your web browser. In addition, web apps are available for Outlook, Word, Excel, PowerPoint, and OneNote.

Web Part: A web part is a component of a web page that can be added, removed, or edited right from the browser. A web part is contained in a web part zone. A web part can be dragged and dropped between web part zones, using only the browser.

Wiki: A Wiki is a specialized website that allows community members the ability to update the content of the website on the fly. A Wiki is not specific to SharePoint; however, SharePoint provides Wiki functionality as a feature.

Index

A

About Me page, Office 365, 215
About this community feature, community sites, 83
academic institutions, Office 365 plans for, 22
Access application, 30
Access list app, 145
accessibility, Office 365, 26–28, 288
account provisioning and licensing, 241
activating licensing, 253–254
Active Directory, 230, 244
Active Users screen, Office 365 admin center, 253
activity feeds, Skype for Business, 38
add-ins
  Excel Online, 174
  Outlook, 60–61
Admin section, Office 365 admin center, 263
administration. *See also* Office 365 admin center; *specific administrator roles*
  Exchange Online, 44–45
  Office 365, 121–122
  SharePoint Online, delegating, 125–126, 129–130
  SharePoint Online farms, 122–126
  SharePoint Online, overview of, 71, 121–122
administrators. *See also specific administrator roles*
  Office 365 control and efficiency for, 29
  training, in planning phase, 241–242
Advanced Threat Protection, 14
alerts, SharePoint document library, 95
alignment commands, PowerPoint Online, 189
Amazon Web Services, 13
Android devices
  Skype for Business app, 219, 220
  Word mobile app on, 115–118
Angry Birds, 12
Announcements app, 145
anywhere access

Exchange Online, 45–49
Office 365, 288
apps. *See also* SharePoint document libraries; *specific apps*
  Office 365, 230, 257–258
  Outlook add-ins, 60–61
  SharePoint, 140, 144–148, 273
  Skype for Business, 204, 219–221
  web, 123, 304
archiving, email, 33, 49–50
Asset Library template, 96
Assets Library app, 107, 146
at-mentions (@), in Yammer, 83
attachments, Outlook, 58, 298–299
audience, SharePoint, 272
audio
  in OneNote Online, 193
  in Skype for Business meetings, 211
availability, Exchange Online, 44
Azure, Microsoft, 13, 16–17
Azure Government, 17

B

backup, in SharePoint farm administration, 123
bandwidth, 232, 241
Basic Search Center template, 143
big data, 7–8, 13–14
Billing Administrator role, 125
Billing section, Office 365 admin center, 262
blog, defined, 301
Blog template, 143
boards
  Delve, 55
  Planner, 63
Boomerang Outlook add-in, 60–61
bridge, for conferencing, 269

Browse icon, team sites, 76
browser
  accessing Exchange Online from, 46
  Office 365 requirements, 231
  SharePoint Online development from, 140
  taking notes in, 198–199
bullet commands, PowerPoint Online, 189
Business Intelligence, 102, 302
Business Intelligence Center template, 143
business meetings, 213–214. *See also* online
    meetings
business plans. *See also* implementation; *specific*
    plans
  general discussion, 18–22
  getting started with, 249–250
  management page for, 260, 261
  overview, 235–237

C

Calendar app, 145
callout feature, SharePoint document library, 78
cards
  Delve, 55
  Planner, 63
cars, horseless carriage syndrome, 14–15
charts
  Excel Online, 174
  PowerPoint, 183
Charts view, Planner, 63, 64
cities, big data use by, 13
clients, Outlook email, 46, 47
cloud
  big data and machine learning, 13–14
  defined, 8–9, 301
  deployment models, 9–10
  as equalizer, 11
  horseless carriage syndrome, 14–15
  hybrid approach to, 228
  Microsoft solutions, 15–18
  moving to, experience of, 225–226
  Office Online compatible storage, 152–156
  offloading infrastructure to, 226–227

overview, 7–8
pros and cons of, 227–229
reasons to move to, 277–283
service models, 11–13
use with multiple devices, 227
value propositions for, 285–291
Clutter feature, Outlook, 47, 58–59, 297
co-authoring
  with Excel Online, 179
  OneNote Online, 196, 197
  PowerPoint presentations, 182
  role of cloud in, 278
  SharePoint Online, 78–79
  from within Word, 109–110
collaboration tools
  Exchange Online, 48
  Groups, 61–62
  Office and SharePoint integration, 106–113
  overview, 61
  Planner, 63–64
  role of cloud in, 278
  SharePoint Online, 74–81
  social, 81–87
comments, Excel Online, 174
communication planning, 242
communities, online, 34
Community Portal template, 142
community sites, 83–85, 142, 143
Company Profile section, Office 365 admin center,
    262
Compliance Policy Center template, 142
computer, syncing OneDrive for Business to,
    112–113
conferencing. *See also* online meetings
  dial-in, 269
  web, 281
consumer plans, 234–235, 248–249, 260. *See also*
    specific plans
contacts, Skype for Business
  checking presence of, 217
  tagging for status change alerts, 217–218
Contacts app, 145

documents
  accessibility of, 27
  as attachments, 58
  Excel Online, 172, 176, 179
  Office Online, 151, 152
  SharePoint, sharing and co-authoring, 78–79
  SharePoint, version control, 80–81
  SharePoint content types, 134–136
  syncing, 298
  underscoring in link names, 77
  viewing in Delve, 55
  Word Online, working with, 165–167
Documents area, team sites, 76
Documents library, SharePoint, 97–98
Domain Name System (DNS), 243, 257
domains, configuring, 268
Domains section, Office 365 admin center, 262
Dropbox, integrating Office Online with, 155–156
Dynamics CRM, Microsoft, 17

E

Edge, Microsoft, 198–199
eDiscovery (Electronic Discovery), 50
eDiscovery Center template, 142
EDIT command, SharePoint document library, 79
EDIT LINKS icon, team sites, 76
Edit Presentation command, PowerPoint Online, 183
Editing View, Word Online, 164, 166
education, Office 365 plans for, 22
efficiency. See productivity
email. See also Exchange; Exchange Online; Outlook
  archiving, 33, 49–50
  attachments, 58, 298–299
  Group, 62
  grouping conversations, 32–33
  managing in Exchange admin center, 265, 268
  migrating data, 254–255
  Outlook Online, 32
  overload, handling, 47–48, 58–59
  overview, 31–32
  in planning phase, 240–241
  in preparing phase, 243
  as reason to move to Office 365, 279
  replacing with Yammer, 298
  web, 32
email clients, Outlook, 46, 47
Email Etiquette section, Delve Analytics, 56, 57
encryption, 282–283
end users
  SharePoint Online, 70
  training, in planning phase, 241–242
enterprise class software. See value propositions for Office 365
enterprise plans, 20–21. See also business plans; specific plans
Enterprise Search Center template, 143
Enterprise Wiki template, 143
envelope icon, Yammer, 65
environmental friendliness, of Office 365, 280
equipment mailbox, 266
exabytes, 7
Excel application
  versus Excel Online, 171–172
  overview, 30, 102
  SharePoint content types, 136
  Skype for Business integration, 219
Excel mobile app, 114
Excel Online
  advanced features, 177–179
  Editing Mode and Reading View, 176–177
  versus Excel, 171–172
  functions, 177–178
  interface, 172–175
  manipulating data, 179
  overview, 102–103, 171
  workbooks, 176
Excel Services, 301
Exchange, 32, 41–42, 301
Exchange admin center
  additional options, 267–268
  managing permissions, 266–267
  managing recipients, 265–266
  overview, 264–265
  simplicity of, 44–45

HELP IMPROVE OFFICE link, Office Online, 158

Help Viewer, Outlook, 59

high-speed Internet, 230

Home feed, Yammer, 64

Home link, team sites, 76

Home tab

  Excel Online, 173

  PowerPoint Online, 183–184

  Word app on Android devices, 116

  Word Online, 161, 162

horseless carriage syndrome, 14–15

Hub, Planner, 63

human-based resources, for implementation, 239

hybrid cloud, 9–10, 228

hyperlinks. *See* links

I

IaaS (infrastructure-as-a-service) service model, 12, 13

icons, explained, 2

IDE (Integrated Development Environment), 304

images, in OneNote Online, 193. *See also* photos

implementation

  For Business plans, 249–250

  getting users ready for, 250–252

  For Home plans, 248–249

  as iterative cycle, 238, 243, 245

  migration phase, 252–258

  Office Support site, 244–245

  overview, 247–248

  partner, choosing, 245–246

  phases of, 237–238

  plan, choosing, 234–237

  planning phase, 238–242

  preparing phase, 242–244

Import section, Office 365 admin center, 262

Import Spreadsheet app, 145

importing custom taxonomy, 131–133

inbox, Yammer, 65. *See also* email

InfoPath, 301

information protection, Exchange Online, 49–50

Information Technology. *See* IT

infrastructure

  offloading to cloud, 226–227

  reduced, with Office 365, 286

infrastructure-as-a-service (IaaS) service model, 12, 13

inking feature, Office, 110–111

Insert tab

  Excel Online, 174, 175

  PowerPoint Online, 184

  Word app on Android devices, 116, 117

  Word Online, 161, 162

installing Office mobile apps, 115

Integrated Development Environment (IDE), 304

integration

  Groups with Planner, 87

  Office 365 software, 46, 91, 92, 289

  Office and SharePoint, 96, 106–113

  Office Online with Dropbox, 155–156

  Office Online with OneDrive, 152–154

  SharePoint Online with PowerPoint Online, 94–96

  SharePoint with Outlook, 46

  Skype for Business, 48, 91, 204, 218–221

IntelliSense, 304

Internet

  accessing Office 365 software on, 26–27

  bandwidth, 232, 241

  cons of cloud solutions, 228

  in implementation planning phase, 241

  Office 365 requirements, 230

  Skype for Business requirements, 231

Internet Explorer, 231

Internet Protocol (IP) addresses, 243, 257

Intranet, 30, 301

introducing yourself, on Yammer, 82

inventories, software and hardware, 241

invitations, Skype for Business meeting, 270

iPad Skype for Business app, 219, 221. *See also* mobile devices

Issue Tracking app, 145

issue tracking, in planning phase, 240

Publishing Portal template, 142–143

Publishing Site template, 142

Publishing Site with Workflow template, 142

Purchase Services section, Office 365 admin center, 262

Q

Quick Access Toolbar, 118

R

Rackspace, 13

ratings, SharePoint document libraries, 107–108, 109

Reading View

  Excel Online, 174, 176–177

  PowerPoint Online, 182, 183, 186

  Word Online, 166–167

Recent Sites, Sites page, 72

recipients, in Exchange admin center, 265–266

Recommended Sites, Sites page, 72

Record Library app, 147

recording Skype for Business meetings, 211–212

records, DNS, 257

Records Center template, 143

recovery, in SharePoint farm administration, 123

refiners, SharePoint search, 101

reliability

  of Exchange Online, 42–45

  Office 365, 28–29

Remember icon, explained, 2

report, defined, 302

Report Document Library app, 147

Report Library app, 147

Reports section, Office 365 admin center, 262

requirements, Office 365, 229–231

Resource Usage Quota, 129

Resources section, Exchange admin center, 266

Review tab

  Excel Online, 174

  Word app on Android devices, 117

  Word Online, 163

reward system, community sites, 83, 84

Ribbon

  Document Set tab, 98–99

  Excel Online, 173–174

  OneNote Online, 195

  PowerPoint Online, 183–184

  team sites, 76

  Word Online, 161–164

room mailbox, 266

S

SaaS (software-as-a-service) service model, 11–12, 42, 43–44

SAP Workflow Site template, 142

Scheduling Assistant, 296

scheduling Skype meetings, 209–210

SCRUM methodology, 240

search features

  OneNote, 193

  SharePoint Online, 100–102

  Sites page, 72

  team sites, 76

security

  cloud computing, 14

  Exchange Online, 49–50

  Microsoft Azure, 16–17

  Office 365, 28–29, 282–283

  in SharePoint farm administration, 123

security group, 266

self-service enterprise software, 291

servers. *See also* Exchange; Exchange Online

  DNS, 257

  SharePoint farm, 122

Service Administrator role, 126

service applications, 123

Service Health dashboard, 262, 294

service models, cloud

  compared, 12

  infrastructure-as-a-service, 12, 13

  overview, 11

  platform-as-a-service, 12

  software-as-a-service, 11–12, 42, 43–44

versioning
  OneNote Online, 197–198
  role of cloud in, 278
  SharePoint document libraries, 93
  SharePoint Online, 80–81
video, in OneNote Online, 193
video conferencing. *See* online meetings
View tab
  Excel Online, 174
  Word app on Android, 118
  Word Online, 164
Visio Process Repository template, 143
Visio Services, 304
Visual Studio, 304
voicemail, Exchange Online, 49
VoIP Connections, 206–207

W

waffle menu, 34–35, 261
Warning icon, explained, 2
web apps. *See also* Office Online; *specific apps*
  defined, 304
  in SharePoint farm administration, 123
web browser
  accessing Exchange Online from, 46
  Office 365 requirements, 231
  SharePoint Online development from, 140
  taking notes in, 198–199
web conferencing, 281. *See also* online meetings
web designer galleries, 137–138
web email, 32. *See also* email
web page, taking notes on, 198–199
web parts, 148, 304
web portals
  migrating data, 255–257
  in preparing phase, 243
Who can see this? icon, Delve, 55
Wiki, defined, 304
wiki page (content page), SharePoint, 147

Wiki Page Library app, 147
Windows Azure. *See* Microsoft Azure
Windows phone, 219, 220
wiping mobile device data, 295
Word application
  overview, 30
  SharePoint integration, 108–111
  sharing documents, 79
  Skype for Business integration, 218–219
  versus Word Online, 159–161
Word mobile app
  on Android tablet, 115–118
  premium features, 114
Word Online
  advanced functions, 167–169
  behind the scenes look at, 160
  Editing View, 164, 166
  interface, 161–164
  overview, 103, 159
  Reading View, 166–167
  sharing documents, 79
  styles, 167–168
  tables, 168–169
  versus Word, 159–161
  working with documents, 165–167
WordArt, PowerPoint, 183
workbooks, Excel Online, 176, 179
workflow, SharePoint, 303

Y

Yammer
  best practice tips, 81–83
  versus Groups, 87
  productivity with, 64–65, 298
Your Apps page, SharePoint Online, 96

Z

zoom, in OneNote Online, 193

About the Authors

Rosemarie Withee is President of Portal Integrators LLC (www.portalintegrators.com) and Founder of Scrum Now (www.scrumnow.org), the first Philippine-based Scrum organization with locations in Seattle, Washington and Laguna, Philippines. Portal Integrators is a Scrum-based software and services firm. She is the lead author of *Office 365 For Dummies* (Wiley, 2016), *SharePoint 2016 For Dummies* (Wiley, 2016), and *Office 365 Apps For Dummies* (Wiley, 2016).

Rosemarie earned a Master of Science degree in Economics at San Francisco State University. In addition, Rosemarie also studied Marketing at UC Berkeley-Extension and holds a Bachelor of Arts degree in Economics and a Bachelor of Science degree in Marketing from De La Salle University, Philippines.

Ken Withee is Founder of Portal Integrators LLC (www.portalintegrators.com), a Scrum-based software and services firm. He lives with his wife Rosemarie in Seattle, Washington. He is the author and co-author of a number of books on Microsoft technologies and currently writes TechNet articles on Office Server products for Microsoft.

Ken earned a Master of Science degree in Computer Science at San Francisco State University. He has more than 14 years of professional computer and management experience working with a vast range of technologies. He is a Microsoft Certified Technology Specialist and is certified in SharePoint, SQL Server, and .NET.

Jennifer Reed is founder and president of Cloud611 (www.cloud611.com), a Seattle area-based consulting and strategy implementation firm focused on helping small- and medium-sized businesses, nonprofit organizations, and local governments achieve their goals through the use of Office 365. The firm's core service offerings are grounded on increasing productivity, enhancing collaboration, simplifying communication, and enabling data-driven decisions using Microsoft cloud technologies.

Jenn holds a bachelor's degree in Economics and has for many years provided consulting services to a wide range of clients including a Fortune 500 company. She is a frequent speaker in business forums on the subject of Office 365 productivity and provides trainings geared toward user adoption of Office 365. She is a Microsoft Certified Professional in Office 365 Administration, a certified project management professional (PMP), and a certified Scrum Master.

Jenn lives with her husband Rick, a former All-Coast defensive back at Washington State University and a retired Hawaii state senator, and son Siddha in the lush, farming valley of Snohomish through which run not just one but two rivers 45 miles northeast of Seattle. When not working on a cloud technology-related book, Jenn spends her spare time growing an organic garden, skiing, and running. She frequently signs up for more half-marathons than she has time for but she always finds time to blog about the latest on Office 365 and cloud technologies at www.reedtechnologyservices.com.

Dedication

We would like to dedicate this book to Vestina (Tiny) Withee, Ken's grandma, who passed away this year (2016). She was born in 1913 and lived a very full and fruitful life. We are amazed thinking about how the world changed just in her lifetime. — Ken Withee — Rosemarie Withee

My work on this book would not have been possible without the love and support of my husband and best friend Rick and my wonderful son Siddha. I dedicate this book to both of you for understanding my late nights and busy weekends, forgiving my absence at sports practices and basketball games, stepping up and learning to cook and bake when I became too busy, and encouraging, supporting, and loving me. I love you both and you inspire me. — Jennifer Reed

Authors' Acknowledgments

Rosemarie Withee and Ken Withee: We would like to acknowledge our families in both the United States and Philippines. An extraordinary amount of special thanks to Katie Mohr, Pat O'Brien, Elaine Marmel, Antony Sami, and the rest of the *For Dummies* team for providing more support than I ever thought possible. It is truly amazing how much work goes into a single book.

We would also like to thank the Portal Integrators team in Laguna, Philippines for their hard work, dedication, and late nights. They are truly an extraordinary team and we are very lucky to work with them. A little about them below, in alphabetical order:

Ace Cyrille Gatcion earned a degree of Bachelor of Science in Computer Science from Laguna College, and has been a Web developer in Portal Integrators for two years. He specializes in programming with JavaScript and PHP and has also been a Microsoft Certified Professional and Specialist in HTML5 with JavaScript and CSS3 since May 2014. Ace has also just recently finished leading a SharePoint-based project which has been one of the biggest challenges he has faced and conquered. When he's not working, he de-stresses by playing with his beloved Siamese cat, and working on his photo editing skills.

Genelyn "Gen" Ancheta is a graduate of Bachelor of Science in Computer Engineering from Colegio de San Juan de Letran. She is a tireless seeker of knowledge, a thinker, and incidentally, also a Web developer with Portal Integrators. Gen has more than ten years of Web, Mobile, and Database development experience. She is a Microsoft Certified Solutions Developer specializing in SharePoint Applications. She loves listening to music, and when she is not busy debugging codes, she indulges in watching movies and TV series.

Jeff Michael De Las Alas is a developer with Portal Integrators who has finished his bachelor's degree in Computer Science from Laguna College. Before being with Portal Integrators, he has also worked as an intern in a Cable TV company from his hometown. Jeff's passion in his chosen field was shown when he received several awards from his college including Best in Thesis, Excellence in Programming, and a Leadership award. Achievements aside, Jeff is just a regular guy who likes watching anime in his free time.

Mariel Pamulaklakin is a developer at Portal Integrators. She graduated from the University of the Philippines – Los Baños with a Bachelor's degree in Computer Science. She has been with Portal Integrators for over 2 years, continuously honing her skills in Web and mobile development in the company. She is also a Microsoft Certified Professional and a Specialist in Programming in HTML5 with JavaScript and CSS3. Outside of work, Mariel is a church choir member, a dog-lover, and a self-confessed nerd who dreams of traveling the world in the near future.

Marriel Bondad is a Bachelor of Science in Information Technology graduate from Laguna College. She is a developer with Portal Integrators, and has worked as an intern in a local government office. She can be described as a responsible and diligent person when it comes to her career, which was proven by her achievements as a Best in Programming and Leadership awardee, and a scholarship grantee. Marriel has also served as president of the Junior Philippine Computer Society – Laguna College Chapter. Outside her professional life, she is a semi-introvert person and an aspiring photographer who often enjoys the adventurous side of life, discovering new places, and working on achieving her dreams.

Jennifer Reed: I owe my deepest gratitude to my husband Rick Reed for providing valuable feedback as my non-technical, test "dummy" reader and for helping me find my "voice."

I am indebted to my clients, employers, co-workers, and friends for the opportunities to learn and enrich my life, and grateful that I can share those positive, relevant experiences in this book. I want to call out a colleague, Trevor Olson, for his support and advocacy of my efforts to move small businesses to the cloud.

It's been an honor and a pleasure to have the support and guidance of Katie Mohr, Pat O'Brien, and the rest of the *For Dummies* team. They are truly a dream team to work with.

Publisher's Acknowledgments

Project Manager: Pat O'Brien

Technical Editor: Elaine Marmel

Sr. Editorial Assistant: Cherie Case

Production Editor: Antony Sami